MARIANNE MOORE AND THE ARCHIVES
FROM MATERIAL CULTURE TO THE DIGITAL HUMANITIES

MARIANNE MOORE AND THE ARCHIVES

FROM MATERIAL CULTURE TO THE DIGITAL HUMANITIES

EDITED BY
JEFF W. WESTOVER

CLEMSON
UNIVERSITY
PRESS

© 2024 Clemson University
All rights reserved

First Edition, 2024

ISBN: 978-1-63804-097-2 (print)
eISBN: 978-1-63804-098-9 (e-book)

Published by Clemson University Press
in association with Liverpool University Press

For information about Clemson University Press,
please visit our website at www.clemson.edu/press.

Library of Congress Cataloging-in-Publication Data
CIP Data available on request

Typeset in Minion Pro by Carnegie Book Production.

Contents

List of Illustrations   ix

Acknowledgments   xi

Introduction   1
    Jeff Westover

Primary Sources and Resources

1. Postmarks and Watermarks: Reading through Marianne Moore's Letters   11
    Aurore Clavier

2. The *Literary Digest*, Moore's Scrapbooks, and the Archive of Mass Print   27
    Bartholomew Brinkman

3. The Poet's Room as Archive   43
    Robert Volpicelli

Sex, Race, and Economics in the Archive

4. Out-Casts and Stay-at-Homes: Marianne Moore, Arthur Mitchell, and LGBTQ Migration in NYC   61
    Elizabeth Gregory

5	"His Shield": Prester John, Amphibiousness, and Black Fugitivity in Marianne Moore's Haile Selassie Poems *Ryan Tracy*	79
6	Archives of Excess and "power over the poor": Marianne Moore's "The Jerboa" *Linda Kinnahan*	107

Archives and Meanings

7	"Possible Meaning": Marianne Moore's Anagogical Reading of Rilke, Herbert, La Fontaine, and Hölderlin *Luke Carson*	131
8	Questioning Categories to Revitalize Words: Meaning and Mottoes in the Poetry of Marianne Moore *Jeff Westover*	153

Archive as Product and Process

9	"This is how the mind works": Marianne Moore and the Aesthetics of Notebooks *Roger Gilbert*	175
10	Robert Duncan, "On Reading Marianne Moore": An Introduction *James Maynard*	189

Teaching and Learning in the Digital Archive

11	The Marianne Moore Digital Archive: Teaching and Research *Claire Nashar*	197

Origins of the Archive

12	An Interview with Patricia C. Willis *Karin Roffman*	209

Notes	237
Contributors	283
Index	289

Illustrations

2.1 Cat's Paw Rubber Heel Ad from the *Literary Digest*. Thank you to the Moore Estate for permission to print this image   35

2.2 Bernhardt, Wilson, and Hardy (scrapbook). Thank you to the Moore Estate for permission to print this image   40

3.1 Moore's mantlepiece. Image courtesy of Rosenbach Museum and Library   45

3.2 Moore's bookshelf with elephant figurines. Image courtesy of Rosenbach Museum and Library   45

4.1 Arthur Mitchell and Diana Adams in *Agon* (1957). Photo by Martha Swope © The New York Public Library for the Performing Arts   70

4.2 Arthur Mitchell as Puck (1962). Photo by Martha Swope © The New York Public Library for the Performing Arts   72

5.1 Moore's transcription of Haile Selassie's "3 Priorities." Thank you to the Moore Estate for permission to print this image   85

5.2 Photograph of Haile Selassie from item in *The Christian Science Monitor*. Moore's clipping of this article is held at the Rosenbach Museum and Library   88

8.1 Moore's drawings of butterflyfish and batfish from her Reading Notebook 1930–1943 (www.moorearchive.org. Notebook 7.02.02). Thank you to the Moore Estate for permission to print this image   156

9.1 "I am not 'quiet.' I am morose—" www.moorearchive.org. Notebook 7.04.07, page 31-recto. Thank you to the Moore Estate for permission to print this image   185

Acknowledgments

The editor is grateful to the anonymous reviewers for recommendations about how to improve this book. Thank you to David M. Moore, Esquire, for permission to quote from Moore's archives and published writing and for permission to print images from her archives. Thank you to the Jess Trust for permission to print the unpublished poem by Robert Duncan. The editor and contributors acknowledge the Rosenbach Museum and Library, which curates the largest collection of Marianne Moore's archives, as well as the Poetry Collection at the library of the University at Buffalo, which houses other archival materials relevant to her life and writing. The editor is especially grateful to Alison Fraser, Stacy Carson Hubbard, and Cristanne Miller for their valuable advice, and to Cristanne Miller for permission to use digital images available from the Marianne Moore Digital Archive. It is not possible to thank Alison Fraser adequately for her expert advice and her editorial contributions to this volume.

Thank you to the New York Public Library for the Performing Arts for permission to publish the photographs of Arthur Mitchell in the essay by Elizabeth Gregory. Thank you to Tom Hillard for feedback on a draft of the introduction.

Thanks to the Interlibrary Loan Department of the library at Boise State University.

Introduction

Jeff Westover

The essays that comprise *Marianne Moore and the Archives: From Material Culture to the Digital Humanities* use new archival research to explore the work of a major American modernist poet, providing innovative critical approaches to Moore's career as it is documented in the archives. The volume showcases recent discoveries and new interpretations of archival materials found at the Rosenbach Museum and Library in Philadelphia, where Moore's archives are held. This volume also draws upon the Marianne Moore Digital Archive (MMDA), a project founded and directed by Cristanne Miller that is digitizing, transcribing, and annotating Moore's notebooks for use by scholars, students, and others, making these materials widely accessible for the first time. Moore's habit of quoting other sources in her poems makes her work archival by its very nature. As Wei Liu writes, her quotations "constitute a distinctive archival form, and critics often compare her to a collector, an editor, a curator, and a compiler."[1]

Scholars in this collection draw on a range of archival material, demonstrating the different ways in which the archive might be conceived. Essays explore letters, notebooks, and the recreated Greenwich Village apartment room that has been carefully curated by the Rosenbach Museum and Library. This focus on archival material sheds light on Moore's poetry and in doing so raises questions about the new methodologies that emerge with digitization. These questions are particularly resonant at a moment when humanities disciplines are under increasing pressure to demonstrate the contribution they are making beyond the academy.

Moore has one of the most extensive archives of the modernists, making her collection important not only for the study of her work but also for the study of modernism, and Moore scholarship has benefited from sustained scrutiny of many of these documents. *Marianne Moore and the Archives* brings together established Moore scholars with new voices. The essays in this volume take a wide-ranging view of Moore's career, poetics, and material life, considering both archival materials familiar to researchers—such as manuscripts and correspondence—as well as new approaches to archival research that take in realia and ephemera, peripheral or miscellaneous materials, and even furniture. They also reflect on Moore as an archivist of her own work and on the work of archivists, curators, and digital archivists in Moore's collection.

While the foundational methodology of this book is archival, the twelve chapters provide a diverse approach to Moore's work and archives, covering the length of her fifty-plus-year career. This book asks what are new ways we can approach the archive, what are new materials we can discover, and how can they inform and complicate readings of Moore and of modernism. As recent scholarship attests, attention to archives has made it possible to see Moore's career in engaging ways. Two recent articles model such engagement, providing important points of departure for this volume. In the first, Peter Howarth ("Marianne Moore's Performances") characterizes Moore's poems as both texts and events, and he bases his argument for events on lecture notes and recordings of Moore's performances of her poems in public venues later in her life.[2] In his view, Moore's willingness to adapt her poems in response to her immediate audience shows the importance of context to her adaptations of the poems as she performed them. It also suggests that her poems can be regarded as processes as much as products.[3] Instead of regarding composition and completed text as incommensurate, a text can be seen in terms of a continuum, as Sally Bushnell has suggested.[4] Like the animals to which Moore devoted so much of her attention, Moore's poems evolve (both before and after publication). In the second article that informs this volume, Alison Fraser ("Mass Print, Clipping Bureaus, and the Pre-Digital Database: Reexamining Marianne Moore's Collage Poetics through the

Archives") argues that a book should be reconceived as an open-ended form.[5] Both approaches also situate Moore in historical contexts that are relevant to the study of modernism.

Recent Moore scholarship is at the forefront of rethinking archival practices as well as the strengths and possibilities of digitizing archival manuscripts. In Cristanne Miller's words, "The *Marianne Moore Digital Archive*, or MMDA, was designed to make unpublished materials in Moore's archive easily accessible to the public in ways that both enhance the study of Moore and make Moore more obviously important to scholars and teachers across a range of fields where she previously has not figured largely."[6] Contributions to this volume by Roger Gilbert, Claire Nashar, Ryan Tracy, and Jeff Westover draw on material made available through the digital archive, demonstrating the way it "extends and enriches Moore studies primarily by making the poet's numerous, previously unpublished, working notebooks readily available."[7]

The development of the MMDA (www.moorearchive.org) parallels other digital projects and websites devoted to the scholarship and teaching of modernism, such as the Modernist Journals Project (https://modjourn.org/), the Modernist Archives Publishing Project (www.modernistarchives.com), and Mina Loy: Navigating the Avant-Garde (mina-loy.com).[8] Like other digitized archives, MMDA seeks to increase access to information about Moore's thinking and writing for scholars, students, and the general public.[9] As large-scale digitization of modernism's archives continues, Moore's archives serve as a case study for a consideration of the future of modernist studies.

Stephen J. Mexal has argued that "Democracy … means digitalization."[10] In particular, he argues that democracy depends on open access to information embodied in archives. Instead of restricting material archives to a class of accredited professionals who mediate the information in them, he claims, archives should be directly available to the general public. At the same time, Mexal acknowledges the special kind of experiential knowledge made available by physical contact with material objects, and he points out the drawbacks of technological change when it comes to building and sustaining virtual archives over time.[11] While digital archives can provide wider access they cannot substitute for the rich sensuous experience of interacting directly with material artifacts or documents, and they cannot supply the kind of knowledge such direct interaction engenders. Digital archives are also vulnerable to being eclipsed by new forms of technology that might threaten their stability over time and require new means of preserving access in digital form. Such issues are important factors for the growth of the MMDA as well as its use and future. On the other hand, digital archives can provide tools for interacting with texts not available in physical archives. This includes the transcription and annotation of archival texts, the ability to search terms across multiple texts, and the capacity to collaborate on research with equal access to primary materials. The MMDA provides such transcription and annotation as well as other resources to contextualize documents for scholars and promote their use in the classroom, including plans for introducing keyword searches.[12]

This book includes research that situates Moore's work in various material contexts. These include her letters, her active engagement with magazines, the preservation and display of her living room, her appreciation of dance, her response to the Depression, her interest in Haile Selassie and racial justice, her reading and notetaking, and her complex syntheses of such phenomena in her publications. It also addresses the development of Moore's archive and the teaching possibilities made available by the MMDA. In the first section of this volume, "Primary Sources and Resources," contributors focus on Moore's physical archive and theorize about it. Writers address Moore's letters, the archive of a magazine, and the object-archive of Moore's living room preserved at the Rosenbach. Aurore Clavier analyzes the relationship between letters and poetry in Moore's career. She focuses on the figure of the letter in "Walking-Sticks and Paperweights and Watermarks." Clavier makes a case for a triadic view of the poem by focusing on the analogy between poems and letters. While the dual relationship between letter and addressee is primary, a third position emerges in view of the archive, when letters and other texts win new readerships. Her reading of the poem allows for an "increased reversibility between public and private expressions."

Building on the arguments of his book *Poetic Modernism in the Culture of Mass Print*, Bartholomew Brinkman evaluates Moore's archive of mass print by focusing on the excerpts she culled from the *Literary Digest*.[13] Through word vectorization, he considers these scrapbooked excerpts as collage-indices in order to assess Moore's intervention in "the nexus of art and politics" they embody. By harnessing computing tools for interpretive ends, his approach bridges a divide in digital humanities between the identification of data through computing and the interpreting of texts through critical analysis.[14] In a related approach, Robert Volpicelli considers the poet's reconstructed living room in the Rosenbach Museum in Philadelphia as a form of archive. More specifically, he considers the significance of the objects in the living room in relation to the papers in the archives held by the Rosenbach, making the case for theorizing the living room as a para-archive.

Other contributions to this volume address such critically important matters as race, sexual orientation, and economics in Moore's work and life—reflecting an integration of cultural critique with the more data-driven or computational aspects of digital humanities, something Alan Liu called for explicitly in 2012 and which commentators have subsequently addressed.[15] As Lisa Stead has pointed out, "The archive ... turns us towards the archivist and the institution as well as the discourses of power, knowledge and memory that surround the impulse towards archivization as much as it does towards the author."[16] Elizabeth Gregory attests quite strongly to the latter in her investigation of the archival traces of Black dancer Arthur Mitchell and "LGBTQ migration" in relation to him and Moore's poems about him. Her essay compares the lives of the two artists, breaking new ground. By focusing on their migrations, she extends the idea to sexuality through the idea of coming out of the closet or staying in it. For his part, Ryan Tracy addresses Moore's representations of Haile Selassie in relation to Prester John and Black fugitivity, a critical concept developed by Fred Moten. Tracy reviews a range of news clippings about the ruler and other archival resources at the Rosenbach to analyze Moore's poems referring to Selassie, situating them in various historical contexts. Linda Kinnahan explores the economic contexts of "The Jerboa" in terms of "object archives" and the "shadow archive." For Moore, the dignity and freedom of the jerboa provided an antidote to what she perceived as the dependency on government aid during the administration of Franklin D. Roosevelt. Kinnahan concludes that "Thinking through objects becomes a way of thinking through history, of interpreting a material archive to narrate our past while remaining aware of the non-neutral pressures shaping the act of interpretation."

In the "Archives and Meanings" section, which spotlights hermeneutics, Luke Carson draws on Moore's Reading Notebook 1938–1942 (RML VII:02:03) to explore her concept of "possible meaning" in relation to anagogical meaning and the visionary poetic tradition. To flesh out his concept, he analyzes Moore's translation of Jean de La Fontaine and her engagement with Friedrich Hölderlin's evocations of the divine. Drawing on Moore's Reading Notebook 1930–1943 (MMDA 7.02.02), Jeff Westover analyzes the poet's critical analysis of categories by focusing on her adaptation of mottoes in many of her poems.[17] Because they organize knowledge, categories are an important conceptual tool of archives, libraries, and museums, but they can also constrain, distort, or obscure knowledge at times. Reframing categories can have eye-opening effects, leading to useful new ways of thinking.

Considering the archive as both product and process, Roger Gilbert focuses on the aesthetic features of Moore's notebooks. As Linda Anderson, Mark Byers, and Ahren Warner point out, archival material allows longitudinal close reading, in which scholars can track "the changing shape of the poem and its evolving tropes and textures."[18] Though Gilbert prefers the "finished" versions of her poems, his approach echoes that of Howarth, who theorizes Moore's poetry in the contexts of her public readings and conceptualizes them as both texts and events. In Howarth's line of argument, her poems become mutable, taking on new forms in response to the public context of particular performances. Gilbert's appreciation of the aesthetic pleasures of Moore's notebooks, which include remarkable phrases she never included in published poems, also brings to mind Alison Fraser's argument that, in light of Moore's multiple revisions of her poems, the book should be regarded as an open-ended form instead of a perfectly stable, fixed object.[19] For his part, James Maynard provides an introduction to Robert Duncan's unpublished poem, "On Reading Marianne Moore," which appears in print here for the first time. The draft of the poem comes from a notebook of Duncan's in the Poetry Collection of the University at Buffalo Libraries, which Maynard curates.

Claire Nashar discusses her experience in contributing to the development of Moore's digital archive and of using archival materials in the classroom. Her contribution provides an exemplary model of the pedagogical opportunities afforded by the Marianne Moore Digital Archive. (So do various teaching materials posted on the MMDA.) Although Stephen Brier lamented the paucity of pedagogical emphasis in the digital humanities over a decade ago, he also reported some positive accomplishments in the use of digital resources and teaching.[20] Even before Brier's essay appeared, Mary Chapman reported on her students' research assignments using archival resources and the web,[21] and more recently Madeline B. Gangnes has explained how "Drawing on archival materials helps students engage with the historical, cultural, and material contexts of the time periods in which works of literature were published."[22] The MMDA exemplifies such endeavors, given that it has been integrating educational resources into its design in an ongoing way. Finally, Karin Roffman documents Patricia Willis's pioneering work with Moore's archival materials. In their interview, Willis looks back on the challenges and achievements of making Moore's archives available for scholars.

In several of the essays collected here, the emphasis is on the poet's later work, reflecting a shift in critical perspective and counteracting the tendency in Moore scholarship to prefer the aesthetics of her early career. By concentrating on the later phase of Moore's long career, contributions in this volume offer some hints at her influence on post-war American poetry and culture. In "Archive Fever," Jacques Derrida writes, "the question of the archive is … a question of the future, … the question of a response, of a promise and a responsibility for tomorrow."[23] I hope this volume offers responses to the Moore archives that will inspire others to realize their promise for the future in their own ways.

Primary Sources and Resources

CHAPTER ONE

Postmarks and Watermarks
Reading through Marianne Moore's Letters

Aurore Clavier

> *Utilizey la poste aerienne*, trade will follow the telephone.[1]

When an earlier version of this chapter was presented at the 2021 "Moore and the Archives" Conference, the pandemic left us no choice but to use airmail and the telephone indeed—or rather their modern-day counterparts, a PowerPoint and a hopefully good Zoom connection. However frustrating it may have been not to meet and discuss in person, long-distance communication provided an efficient reminder of the power traditionally attributed to letters: "For what is a letter," Mary Ruefle asks, "but to speak one's thoughts at a distance? Which is why poems and prayers are letters. [...] They each originate in the pressing need to make a message directed at something unnear, that the absence of the unnear be made to appear present—that the presence of absence be palpably felt."[2]

In addition to writing poems, Moore was herself a firm advocate of prayer, and a prolific, if not at times compulsive, letter writer. For Jonathan Ellis, her unique epistolary voice, along with a few of her contemporaries', suffices to prove that the great age of letter writing did not end after 1918, as the *Oxford Book of Letters* would have it.[3] In her introduction to the *Selected Letters of Marianne Moore*, Bonnie Costello

11

reminds us that Moore wrote daily for most of her life, "long, intense letters to friends and family," or "shorter, but always distinctive letters to an ever-widening circle of acquaintances and fans."[4] That Moore wrote out of a sense of urgency seems evident in both cases, whether the drafting of her letters was compelled by duty or by a more genuine desire to respond to a specific occasion, a generous gift, an inspiring or irritating comment. But equally visible now is the longer temporality letters also partake of when willingly submitted to the memorial work of the archive. As the urgency evaporates, or gets fossilized, layer after layer of correspondence file, the "telepathy of archives"[5] replaces that of letters, which it imperfectly replicates by transferring it to other readers. "For what is a letter?" then finds its necessary complement in that other question, which I wish to address here: "For whom is a letter?" If Moore, as Cristanne Miller explains, seems from very early on to have brought her poetry and its quotational method of composition to "resembl[e] letter writing,"[6] how much did she anticipate the way multiple readers and scholars would approach her letters, and for that matter, her own accession to "stampdom"?[7] Though of course I do not pretend to guess at Moore's most intimate motives, my contention is that her use of the epistolary form, both in her published texts and private correspondence, made room for a third party—reader, scholar, librarian—in a way that both illuminates and interrogates the porous partition between private and public reception, intended and added layers of reading, and individual expression and communal sharing.

"Walking-Sticks and Paperweights and Watermarks," rests on such a paper-thin division. First published in the November 1936 issue of *Poetry*, before featuring in a rather heavily revised form in *What Are Years*, it was never to appear again in Moore's subsequent collections, a decision Heather Cass White and Luke Carson attribute to the transitional status of this and other poems of the 1930s. One of Moore's most intricate and densely allusive texts, "Walking-Sticks and Paperweights and Watermarks" is best understood, they suggest, in light of the tensions the author was trying to negotiate between personal vision, material production, and social relations. In this perspective, the "act of renunciation" evinced by its publication history is to be read "not solely in psychological, moral, or biographical terms," but as evidence "that there was a reasoned philosophical motivation for the transformation in and of her work" toward a more shareable form of poetic "fabric."[8]

The poem's disappearance from publishing circuits until its recent restoration into Moore's corpus seems both ironical and revelatory considering the emphasis it lays on the circulation of writing. Circuitous as it may itself appear, the original version progresses from physical to textual routes, from an embodied perambulation, under the filigree of tree branches, to a catalogue of items all involved in the production, diffusion, and reception of writing, and of correspondence in particular. Seals, rag paper, watermarks, stamps, printing types, and paperweights provide various stations in one of those "anthologies in transit" that William Carlos Williams so admired in Moore.[9] While preventing the kind of stasis their solidification might entail,[10] these stationery articles all retain the trace of their own artisanal making, when not reenacting it in the poem itself:

> as when a seal
> without haste, slowly is impressed,
> and forms a nest
> on which the raised device reversed,
> shows round.

A few lines further down, the globe-shaped glass paperweight, while scrutinized for the minute details of artistry it contains, also seems to act as a magnifying glass to the next stanza:

> The paper-mould's similarly
>
> once unsolid waspnest-blue, snow-
> white, or seashell-gray rags, seen through, show
> sheepcotes, turkey-
> mills, acorns, and anvils.

In turn, these marks become part of a larger communication system, which, although largely aerial, continues to leave visible marks:

> The post's jerky
>
> cancellings ink the stamp, relet-
> tering stiltedly,
> […]
> an alphabet
>   of words and animals where the
>   wire-embedded watermark's more integral
> expressiveness had first set
>   its alabaster effigy.[11]

Just as the matrix of the first stanza molds the following, in its finely drawn alternation of long and short lines, accented and unaccented rhymes, each new marking shapes the next one, through a growingly intricate system of correspondences that also seems to draw on the Renaissance model of *signatura rerum*.[12] If circulation entails dispersion, the material origin of these objects is here to guarantee the authenticity of their correspondence. Even the print face should bear the "visible evidence" of its maker's "sincerity," Moore wrote among the abundant notes she took on book- and paper-making while preparing the poem. A few pages further up, a meditative remark discreetly anticipates the poem's later connection between personal expression, translation, and transatlantic correspondence:

> French Illustrations
> La lettre attendue   The welcome letter
> Faut-il l'envoyer?   Shall I mail it[13]

In this vast network of motifs, impression only appears as the reverse side of expression, print, as another form of signature, an equation James Jiang also identifies in Moore's enduring fascination for graphology and techniques of mechanical reproduction. Despite their apparent opposition, he argues, these interests equally evince the poet's concern for affective transmission and shape the most central tenets of her criticism. As his essay demonstrates, such elusive concepts as style, feeling, or gusto are illuminated by the various scriptural, stamping, printing, or embossing images Moore recurrently associates with them, thus manifesting her hope to preserve expressivity throughout the chain of composition and reception.[14] By bringing together similar images, "Walking-Sticks and Paperweights and Watermarks" does not only extend and complicate this line of (re)production, it seems to me, but also dramatizes its stakes through the added layer of letter writing and the entailed duality of presence and absence. Paradoxically, the poem suggests, the integrity of the message is at once guaranteed and threatened by dissociation. Because they fit with each other, missive and answer—just like print and imprint—can be reunited as parts of a single exchange, and yet only their separation can truly motivate the correspondence, at the risk of failed delivery. The same tension sustains the interpretive ambivalence of the text, whose correct transmission depends on the reader's ability to treat the listed items as both actual objects and metaphorical vehicles, as poetic symbols whose material and ritual origins are simultaneously revived by etymology: "thrown together" they seem to form the halves of a broken token that only the two rightful sharers can bring together.[15]

The poem's complex dialectics would therefore seem to confirm the dominant view that epistolary communication primarily relies on a one-to-one, and often intimate exchange. As Jonathan Ellis puts it, in his introduction to *Letter Writing Among Poets*:

> Most of the stereotypes about letter writing revolve around the number two. One person writes a letter; a second person reads it. They then swap roles. There are crossed letters, lost letters, unread and unsent letters, but the idea of two people writing and reading persists. Daily life, disagreement, the vagaries of the postal service and, most obviously, death are some of the events that intervene to break up this game of exchanging roles, but most of us continue to see letter writing as an identifiable "I" writing to an identifiable "you."[16]

That the complex references of the poem are best understood in light of a private exchange of gifts between Moore and various friends and family members, only tends to confirm this binary conception. Only by "reprivatizing"[17] the poem, as it were, can we hope to make complete sense of the "special language" Warner once recognized in his sister's "postscript" to the *Selected Poems*.[18] In this case, not holding the other half of the symbol would indeed mean treading on "difficult ground," standing at a crossroads forsaken by Hermes of the Ways and being left with a mere dead letter, an irremediably sealed, hermetic message, however open it— quite uneasily—professes to be:

> Part Pelican, I,
> doubting the high-
>   way's wide giant trivia where
>   three roads meet in artificial openness,
> am obliged to justify
> outspoken cordiality.[19]

The "act of renunciation" Heather White and Luke Carson identify in the poem's fate,[20] I believe, implicitly presupposes such a *dual* paradigm. Despite its efforts to negotiate between the contradictory poles of visionary impulse and material production, the poem was revised and then later abandoned because the author's "I" failed to address a collective "you" beyond the circle of its intimate addressees, at a time when political unrest made successful delivery more urgent than ever. While I actually side with this reading, I suspect the poem bespeaks a less tragic plight if read as an attempt to formulate or even formalize a *tripartite* system of epistolary exchange, one that admits of a *third*, and potentially disrupting or distorting element. The poem's relegation to archival status and the changed inflections of Moore's later poetry could, in this perspective, rather propose a conversion of the system, based on a refined swapping of roles, and on the increased reversibility between public and private expressions that the poem explores.

That according to Moore's queer mathematics two equals three[21] appears even more visibly in the revised 1941 version of "Walking-Sticks and Watermarks and Paperweights." As has been noted, most of the changes bear the stamp of the author's response to the tragically altered context of the 1940s, and of her effort to make the subtle "watermarks" approach the clarity of "postmark behests."[22] Simultaneously, however, the reworked pattern of the poem reinforces the threefold equilibrium of the piece: while it initially took a roundabout walk in the woods to establish a link between "walking-sticks" (the supporting third—or first—term of the title), and the more tightly related "paperweights" and "watermarks," the later version displaces the more explicit image of the "triskelion" from the fourth to the first stanza of the poem:

> Jointed against indecision,
> the three legs of the triskelion
>   meeting in the
> middle between triangles, run
> in unison,
>   self-assisted.[23]

In the process, the opening lines get more firmly connected with the final succession of tripartite structures: the pelican and its "nest's three-in-one upturned tri- / form face," "the high- / way's trivia or crow's-foot where / three roads meet," "the awl-leafed juniper's / whorls of three," the "fugue's three times three / reiterat- / ed chain of interactingly / linked harmony" and the Christian Trinity that those symbols collectively celebrate, whether in the cheerful spirit of a Christmas carol,[24] or through their deeper connections to self-sacrifice and charity.[25] In that sense, the final sequence of images represents no more of a closure than the poem's disappearance from Moore's late corpus, but rather leaves a space open for a continuation of its ternary associations. The intricate economy of gift that underlies "Walking-Sticks," and that motivates so many of Moore's epistolary and poetic responses, is itself based on such a form of conversion. Thanking Bryher for a gift of money that had been astutely arranged for her to accept, Moore wrote to her, in a way that echoes both the seal's reversible imprint and the *ad libitum* progression of the fugue: "The addition you speak of makes me realize more than ever, that one's debts of gratitude must needs be paid to someone other than the one from whom one receives it."[26] Calling it even could only result in another odd number.

As Moore's private correspondence reveals, letter writing, if often motivated by love, was always more of a *ménage à trois* than an affair of pairs, let alone of amorous coupling. In her analysis of "Moore's Numbers," Fiona Green identifies the "three legs of the triskelion" as "the threesome (Moore, her mother, and brother) whose familial bonds were so tight as to keep others away,"[27] an image of familial unity also evinced by the motherly pelican's nest of three. Equally evocative in the poem is Moore's play with letters: in the spinning circle of "*W*alking-Sticks and Paper*w*eights and *W*ater*m*arks" (emphasis mine) the three-legged W and M appear as strangely reversible initials—in addition to being typefaces, which, Moore's notebook indicates, require the utmost patience to cast[28]—letters whose evocative power was certainly not lost on a poet so sensitive to the delights of monograms and acrostics.[29] While these initials may bring to mind Moore's provocative twist on Ezra Pound's quotation of John Cournos in "Marriage" ("turn to the letter M / and you will find / that 'a wife is a coffin'"[30]), they also conjure up the Mary–Warner–Marianne triad—or trilogy—and the many ways in which their correspondence could not only evince union, but also "objectify welded divisiveness," from the early round-robin mail they circulated among themselves to the more-sophisticated hide-and-seek of the adult letters.[31] Quite strikingly, many of Moore's most intimate friendships came to rely on similar epistolary patterns, as Bryher and H.D., James Sibley and Hildegarde Watson, Elizabeth Bishop and Louise Crane, and Kathrine Jones and Marcia Chamberlain were invited to join the household's postal fugue, "repaying gifts with a few verbal pineapples,"[32] trading books for reviews, or answering to flowers with bouquets of descriptive prose that could just as well feature in a published poem. In this sense, Moore's epistolary threesomes could be said to rely on a "code" not unlike the "amorous Topic" described by Roland Barthes in *A Lover's Discourse: Fragments*:

> Each of us can fill in this code according to his own history; rich or poor, the figure must be there, the site (the compartment) must be reserved for it. It is as if there were an amorous Topic, whose figure was a site (topos). Now the property of a Topic is to be somewhat empty: a Topic is statutorily half coded, half projective (or projective because coded). What we have been able to say below about waiting, anxiety, memory is no more than a modest supplement offered the reader to be made free with, to be added to, subtracted from, and passed on to others: around the figure,

the players pass the handkerchief which sometimes, by a final parenthesis, is held a second longer before handing it on. (Ideally, the book would be a cooperative: "To the United Readers and Lovers.")[33]

Just as lovers and readers are made to change parts in the projective game of love, each participant in Moore's epistolary exchange is invited to align with successive points of the triangle and to play, in turn, the roles of addresser, addressee and external reader, thus complicating the traditionally binary terms of the correspondence and blurring the line between private and published texts.

As is well known, such interactions could be tied to more difficult kinds of triangulation. Even uncalled for, gifts such as Bryher and H.D.'s 1921 edition of *Poems* needed to be acknowledged, driving Moore to many epistolary contortions to accept the new terms of the exchange. In the famous response she addressed to Bryher upon receiving a copy of her poems in the mail, the exposed pterodactyl—one of her epistolary personae—tropes her uneasy navigation between the confidential space of the letter and the open scene of public appearance, the private refusals addressed to would-be impresarios and the professed appreciation of the published product:

> I received a copy of my poems this morning with your letter and a letter from Miss Weaver. Now that I am a pterodactyl, it is perhaps well that you even with your hardened gaze, cannot see what it is to be *a pterodactyl with no rock in which to hide*. In *Variations of Animals and Plants under Domestication*, Darwin speaks of a variety of pigeon that is born *naked* without any down whatever. I feel like that Darwinian gosling. [...] I had considered the matter from every point and was sure of my decision—that *to publish anything now would not be to my literary advantage; I wouldn't have the poems appear now if I could help it and would not have some of them ever appear and would make certain changes*. [...] Despite my consternation, the product is remarkably innocuous. I should have used *Observations* I think, as a title but I like *Poems*. *I am very much touched by the beauty*

> *of all the printing details. I like the paper, type, title-label, the fact that the printing was done at the Pelican Press*, there is not a single misprint and nothing could exceed my appreciation of the unstinted care and other outlay bestowed on the book. But *what shall I say of your activities as press-agent!* [...] *I wrote Ezra not long ago that I "was not at pains to investigate small books of verse" and told T. S. Eliot that I did not wish to reprint work of mine that has been published unless it were supplementary to something substantial!*[34]

As various critics have underlined, the breach in epistolary trust was probably as disturbing as the interference in Moore's own choices on how to address her readers.[35] However disruptive the experience of *Poems*, it somehow reflected a pattern Moore had already begun to establish herself within her poetry. For instance, the note appended to "Injudicious Gardening" in *Observations* traces the poem back to its epistolary origin, the *Letters of Robert Browning and Elizabeth Barrett*, and reaffirms its initial response "To Browning," the title under which it was first published in the *Egoist*. Robin Schulze provides a useful reminder about Moore's reference: reacting to her love's gift of a sprig of hawthorn, Elizabeth Barrett had reminded him of his early mistake: "The first [flower] you ever gave me was a yellow rose sent in a letter, and shall I tell you what that means—the yellow rose? 'Infidelity' says the dictionary!" To which reproach Browning had responded by "plant[ing] a full dozen more rose-trees, all white—to take away the yellow-rose reproach!"[36] Quite ironically, while Moore's second stanza celebrates "the sense of privacy" that can "deflect [...] offending eyes" from the poet's estate, the opening lines bluntly profess the speaker's own intrusion into the domain of his private correspondence and propose to inflect the coded language of flowers by an explicit act of reinterpretation:

> If yellow betokens infidelity,
>   I am an infidel.
>   I could not bear a yellow rose ill will
>   Because books said that yellow boded ill,
>   White promised well;

> However, your particular possession—
>   The sense of privacy
>   In what you did—deflects from your estate
>   Offending eyes, and will not tolerate
>   Effrontery.³⁷

Not unfrequently, Moore thus endorsed the reader's right to turn personal exchanges into public property, all the while valuing their authors' "sense of privacy." While some of her poems continue to use letters as occasional sources for quotations or ambiguous models of falsely personal address, significant passages of her critical prose explicitly envisage literary issues through the prism of correspondence. Poring over a variety of items—articles about epistolary salutations, letters by Keats, Shelley, or Diderot, correspondence handbooks and an autograph collection on display at the Anderson Galleries, among others—an editorial comment for the *Dial* proposes to compare the respective merits of English and American letters and to question the delicate equilibrium between formality and naturalness, before concluding that "one can safely affirm at any rate that a writer of letters is not one of those who know much and understand little,"³⁸ words that strikingly conjure up the closing maxim of "Bowls": "he who gives quickly gives twice / in nothing so much as in a letter."³⁹ In a later reminiscence of her *Dial* years, she writes: "Rivaling manuscript in significance were the letters; indivisible as art in some instances from their authors' published work," and then quotes various pieces of professional exchanges involving D. H. Lawrence, Paul Valéry, or Kenneth Burke.⁴⁰ But nowhere does she elicit the inherent paradoxes of letter writing more than in the long review she dedicates to the 1931 edition of Dickinson's *Selected Letters*, by Mabel Loomis Todd.⁴¹ After conjuring the rather traditional portrait of Dickinson's "seclusive, wholly non-notorious personality," Moore rapidly comes to the more fine-grained admission that "if Emily Dickinson's notable secret has not perfectly the aspect of a secret, it is revealed by herself rather than by 'so enabled a man' as the twentieth-century critic" and that "[s]he was not a recluse, nor was her work, in her thought of it, something eternally sealed."⁴² One can hardly resist the temptation shared by many "twentieth-century critics," for sometimes wrong reasons, to read Moore's comments as self-reflexive.[43] Through a careful choice of quotations voicing Dickinson's uncertainties about life after death and the spirit's ability to outlive bodily existence (a dozen lines are cited from "The spirit lasts, but in what mode—"), Moore's review reaffirms the posthumous reader's inclusion within her predecessor's epistolary poetry: "The frankness with which in a letter—as above—she speaks verse as if it were prose, to the one to whom she writes, is strange. In these days of composite intellect and mock-modest impersonalism, this nakedness is striking."[44] In their more open way of conversing with print and publishing circuits, Moore's letters did not exactly reach the degree of sophistication displayed by Dickinson's own system of private publication,[45] but the review does acknowledge the possibility that one letter writer might replace another under the eyes of a third reader.

It would not take long after Moore's review for this awareness to become more pressing. By the mid-1930s, Moore's status had begun to change, as made clear in her response to a gift sent by Louise Crane, along with a magazine clipping (also forwarded by Bishop in a separate letter), and listing the poet among "the girls to ask in to dinner at your own house":[46]

Dear Miss Crane,

It is well I did not know when I received the mysterious box, that a nautilus was inside, or my hand might have shaken so as to injure it. A nautilus has always seemed to me something supernatural. The more I look at it the less I can credit it,—this large yet weightless thing, with a glaze like ivory on the entrance and even on the sides. How curious the sudden change of direction in the corrugations, and the transparent oyster white dullness of the "paper." The wings are so symmetrical I should not know any part had been broken if you had not said so.

The clipping you enclose makes me need a house by no means transparent. But I protect myself by a ruse. There is another Marianne Moore, I have heard,—the daughter of a professor in the west; and there are two other Marianne Moores in Brooklyn. Nevertheless I am dismayed.[47]

Although not "for writers entrapped by teatime fame," "the paper nautilus" would soon be seen to "construct her thin glass shell" in the 1940 poem Moore first published as "A Glass-Ribbed Nest," publicly "giving her perishable / souvenir of hope," all the while holding to its "fortress" of love.[48] If "the germ" of Moore's paean to protective love thus "glows in the phrases of her letter" and provides one more example of the refined economy of exchange Moore participated in, its images of transparency and protection also need to be read in the context of Moore's growing vulnerability to public "unboxing," and her need for more "Moores" to serve as homonymic decoys.[49]

The following decades, of course, brought much worse than "teatime fame" to Moore, the self-described "Coney Island fun fair victim."[50] As her private sphere was increasingly assailed by "tons of irrelevant mail," and "obliterat[ing] trespassers,"[51] her intimate letters continued to provide a welcome shelter of course. Yet she was also growing more and more conscious that these would one day be made accessible to a wider circle. As Linda Leavell notes, "[r]eviewing Emily Dickinson's letters ... had brought her to the realization that her own letters might one day be published, and she thus began shaping her life and persona for public consumption," sifting her own papers and privately editing her letters as early as 1934.[52] A now well-known section of her mail even made it through the press during her lifetime, when she allowed her correspondence with the Ford Motor Company to be published in the *New Yorker*, reprinted in a Pierpont Morgan Library limited edition, and later included in *A Marianne Moore Reader*, marking the shift from "her younger, armored self" to a more "unprotective" persona.[53]

While deploring increasing intrusions into her personal sphere, Moore therefore adopted a most paradoxical line of defense, by somehow flipping round or thinning down the partition between private and public writing. Many of her intimate letters of the time revolve almost entirely around her public life and show the same blend of playful and serious styles as that of her published verse.[54] Conversely, a lot of her late poems approach the tonal and thematic features of letters, when they are not simply phrased as such. Various occasional poems of the late 1950s and early 1960s take the guise of conventional greetings sent for such popular celebrations as Valentine's Day ("For February 14th,"

"Saint Valentine,"). As Elizabeth Gregory keenly demonstrates, by publicly embracing romance through a mode of communication traditionally construed as sentimental and feminine, the older single poet was actively "featuring her own alternative life and love plot," at the intersection of affective, spiritual, and intellectual planes. As sites of "libidinized literary connection, animated across time and space by shared interest,"[55] these poems certainly enrich Moore's democratic performance by positing a revaluation of affect, but I submit they also play up the revised epistolary plot she was engaging in, blurring the line between the domestic and the public scenes of writing. Building on Elizabeth Wilson's and Elizabeth Gregory's thorough reconstructions,[56] readers may thus retrace the threads with which Moore fastened her Valentine poems to the various letters that spurred or followed them, virtually gesturing toward future archival research. While a note attributes the first quotation in "For February 14th" to "a poem to M. Moore by Marguerite Harris," doubling the address and potential gifts to Saint Valentine with a response to Moore's own admirer, Harris's original "overture"[57] remains untitled and unreferenced, and therefore partly kept within the domain of personal correspondence. In turn, "Saint Valentine," gets woven into the chain of exchange, its title, structure, and images directly echoing "For February 14th." As Elizabeth Gregory notes, such similitudes were partly inspired by a letter in which editor Katharine White had invited Moore to submit a poem to the *New Yorker* in the manner of the former text. The message, it should be added, politely reminded the poet of a suggestion, once inscribed in a copy of *O To Be a Dragon*, that her gift should be expandable at will, and solicited in response to a list of valentine presents whose poetic shaping would in itself constitute the offering.[58] Although much shorter and apparently simpler than "Walking-Sticks and Watermarks and Paperweights," Moore's sequel to "For February 14th" is certainly no less sophisticated in its epistolary play. Not only does the poem explicitly address "Saint Valentine," (the comma highlighting the written nature of the greeting) and complicate the circulation of gifts to and from its tutelary figure, but the intricate oscillation of its pronouns simultaneously opens the exchange to endless role-shifts, involving White, Harris, Moore's readers, and others as potential addressees or recipients:

> **Saint Valentine,**
> permitted to assist you, let me see ...
>   If those remembered by you
> are to think of you and not me,
>   it seems to me that the memento
>   or compliment you bestow
> should have a name beginning with "V"[59]

Moore's readers certainly know better than to enjoy the listed "mementoes or compliments" as mere conventional gifts or clever linguistic play. Just as, according to Elizabeth Gregory, Vera's falsely true effigy opens the way to Moore's "triangulated self-portrait," and gestures toward other potential lives for the poet, the "violet," the "vignette" and its "vinelet" border, "verse," and the "vine"-like "valentine" invite us to activate infinite combinations, rotating initials, or turning the poem over in search of an unacknowledged letter. Is the saint whose name begins with a V to be identified as Vera-Moore? What secret Valentine may the lines be speaking to, beyond the circle of its recognizable addressees?[60] Is the all-pervasive monogram but a false lead, meant to prove how versatile verse can be, when composed as the flip side of a letter? Moore's non-hierarchical mode of response is here given full sway. As the "most careful writer's '8,'" it should not be conceived as a horizontal, linear exchange between two but rather made to follow the unexpected twists and turns of round-robin correspondence. Verse, like the written valentine, is as the *vendange* to the vine, waiting for the decanting of the unpredictable "wine." Granting us access to the vast continent of her letters—the ones, at least, she was willing to include in her papers—was giving us permission to prolong the game of correspondences and engage in the kind of guess with which Elizabeth Bishop concludes "Efforts of Affection," her posthumous tribute to Moore:

> I find it impossible to draw conclusions or even to summarize. When I try to, I become foolishly bemused: I have a sort of subliminal glimpse of the capital letter *M* multiplying. I am turning the pages of an illuminated manuscript and seeing that initial letter again and again: Marianne's monogram; mother;

manners; morals; and I catch myself murmuring, "Manners and morals; manners *as* morals? Or is it morals *as* manners?" Since like Alice, "in a dreamy sort of way", I can't answer either question, it doesn't much matter which way I put it; it *seems* to be making sense.[61]

Pulled out of Bishop's own archive, the puzzle inevitably exerts its telepathic pull: could anyone resist the temptation to step through the looking-glass of Moore's letters, add to the spinning round of monograms, and join the ever-expanding circle of "her United Readers and Lovers"?[62]

CHAPTER TWO

The *Literary Digest*, Moore's Scrapbooks, and the Archive of Mass Print

Bartholomew Brinkman

If omissions are not accidents, as Marianne Moore has famously pointed out, it stands to reason that inclusions are deliberate. Such logic applies not only to Moore's published work, but also to what is available in her archive—by which I mean the institutionalized collections at such places as the Rosenbach Museum and Library and the University at Buffalo, which give tangible insights into Moore's life and work through a wealth of papers, books, and other material objects, as well as to more recent online archival manifestations, such as the Marianne Moore Digital Archive.[1] While others in this volume have elaborated on the practice of archiving Moore, I will focus here on how Moore's archive lends insight into her own preservation practices as I recount how Moore was herself an archivist of mass print.

As Alison Fraser has observed, Moore's archival impulses can be seen in the extensive clipping files she kept throughout her career, which would serve as both poetic inspiration and "an alternative method for long-term media management and retrieval."[2] Rather than attempt to address Moore's career as a whole, however, I restrict my focus here to the formative years just before Moore first published her poems in the little magazines and before she became a central hub of New York City's artistic circles. During this time, Moore was employed as a teacher at the Indian School in Carlisle, Pennsylvania, and while Lesley Wheeler and Chris Gavaler have focused on Moore's experience at Carlisle itself as instrumental, her development can also be attributed to her exposure to a world beyond Carlisle that was often mediated through mass print.[3] As Linda Leavell explains, during this time Moore "subscribed to *The Atlantic Monthly*, *International Studio*, and *Life*, and brought home more periodicals from the Indian School library over the weekend. Friends gave or loaned her other magazines, and after she no longer worked for the Indian School, she went to Dickinson College and sometimes Harrisburg in search of periodicals."[4]

One magazine notably missing from this list—and that generally has been overlooked by Moore scholars and scholars of modernism at large—is the *Literary Digest* (1890–1938). The importance of the magazine for Moore is evident in a pair of scrapbooks that she kept between 1909 and 1914 that I have discussed elsewhere.[5] Through their constellation of mass-printed clippings and other ephemera, these scrapbooks exhibit a "scrappy poetics" that can be seen as a particular manifestation of "writing with scissors" but also a direct challenge to high modernist notions of collage and literary tradition.[6] As such, they might be taken as preliminary markers of what Nikolaus Wasmoen has identified as Moore's "serial imagination" that carries through her manuscript notebooks and into her publishing practices, in which an "author–editor" arranges texts into larger structures so that "conflicting points of view and ideas could be synthesized into unison or counterpoint without the need to authorize."[7] Such an "author–editor" function can be seen not only in Moore's own poems and poetic arrangements, but also in her more public editorial work in venues such as the *Dial*. As Victoria Bazin explains, for Moore, "the process of revision through excision and substitution is bound up with editorial practice and is itself a creative one," on display in such places as the deliberate clustering of women writers and artists in the *Dial*'s pages.[8] Such practices, I suggest, can be traced back, at least in part, to these early scrapbooks.

Given the importance of these scrapbooks for Moore's development, I aim in this essay to more fully explore the *Digest* clippings that make up so much of their source material, focusing on the relatively short time period of July 1912 to June 1914.[9] I will first consider the magazine itself and offer an initial overview of its contents through word vectorization clustering. I will then turn to scrapbook pages focused on current poetry, political cartoons, and the nexus of art and politics, reading them as meaningful constructions in their own right and as a means of indexing the *Digest*'s own periodical contexts as I further make a case for Moore's archiving practices.

Digesting the *Literary Digest*

While Moore is typically understood in relation to the little magazines in which she first published, or to the *Dial* that she would later edit, the influence of the *Literary Digest* and other periodicals on Moore's developing sensibilities should not be underestimated.[10] Such influence might best be seen in one of Moore's early poems, "Leaves of a Magazine," which I have taken up elsewhere.[11] It can also be seen in "To See It Is to Know That Mendelssohn Would Never Do:" with the epigraph, "*The* Times, *commenting on Norman Wilkinson's settings in the Granville Barker production of* A Midsummer Night's Dream."[12] The poem opens with "Newspaper comment, that stiff-jawed, / Black bodied puppet show" (lines 1–2) so that "stiff-jawed" modifies both the production and the newspaper comment itself. The second quatrain continues with "Its gestures print conviction on / My mind" (lines 5–6), where the gestures would seem to be those of the production, but with the reference to print also pointing to the newspaper comment itself. The poem takes as its subject matter not only a new production of Shakespeare's play, but the mass-print-mediated criticism of it as well, suggesting the extent to which Moore was contemplating such issues in her early poetry.

And Moore could do worse than focus her attention on the *Literary Digest*. Started in 1890, the *Literary Digest* was a popular weekly magazine published by Funk & Wagnalls, reaching a circulation of more than one million issues by the 1920s.[13] Even by the time Moore was clipping from the magazine, though, its title was a bit of a misnomer. It had merged with *Public Opinion* of New York to become a general-purpose magazine, with (often reprinted) material on politics, literature, culture, and the arts. It included such sections as "Topics of the Day," "Foreign Comment," "Science and Invention," "Letters and Art," "Religion and Social Service," "Motor-Trucks and Motor-Cars," and "Reviews of New Books," as well as photographs, editorial cartoons, and a variety of back matter interspersed with advertisements—including a column of "Personal Glimpses," one on

"Current Events," a humor column on "The Spice of Life," one from "The Lexicographer's Easy Chair," and one on "Current Poetry."

All told, the issues for the two-year span I am examining here amount to approximately 5.6 million words.[14] While this corpus is too large to consider exclusively through traditional reading methods (and it is doubtful Moore herself read every word), we can gain an overall sense of the magazine's subject matter through digital humanities methods, such as the use of a word embedding model.[15] Clustered terms from such a model reveal that government and politics are dominant themes, with attention to national and state-level politics, concerns over imperialism (particularly in an Asian and American hemispheric context), Mexican revolution, and a brewing world war.[16] Relatedly, geographical terms are common, with references to U.S. cities and states (as well as former "Indian" Territory), Canadian cities and provinces, and other countries and cities of the world.[17] This geography is often experienced through travel, as evidenced through invocations of historical England and through various methods of transportation, including ship, railroad, and automobile.[18] Economics is another area of focus, with references to trade and investment as well as construction, factories, and farm production.[19] There is likewise a focus on professions and on a variety of social activities, highlighting law, medicine, science, religion, higher education, baseball, horticulture, food and cooking, art, photography, and stage performance.[20] Advertising, although relegated to the back pages, is evident in clusters centered on such items as jewelry, razors, clothing, tires, cigars, cereals and other foods, medicines, floor cleaning products, and offers of mail-order catalogs.[21] Of particular note are advertisements for books and writing implements, complementing attention to writing and literature (including poetry) elsewhere in the magazine.[22] In short, the magazine was wide-ranging in its content, matching Moore's own capacious interests.

Although the magazine remains largely unstudied, Isabelle Parkinson has recently considered the *Digest* in relation to modernist literary production, arguing for how issues published in the immediate aftermath of World War I informed Gertrude Stein's nationalism and aided in the production of "A League" (1919) and "Woodrow Wilson" (1920).[23] Focusing on the invocation of "My literary digest" from "Woodrow Wilson" (a figure who would differently intrigue Moore as well), Parkinson notes that "there are the dreamlike scraps of half-remembered details gathered from the excess of information and there is the *Digest*'s staging of events and instances of dialogue, its juxtapositions of alternative stances that make up the drama of news."[24] While Parkinson uses these "scraps of detail" figuratively, such details are literalized in Moore's scrapbooks.

Current Poetry

It is hardly surprising that Moore would include poem clippings in her scrapbooks, as these give glimpses into the current state of poetry and offer possible (good and bad) models for her own writing. One page in particular exhibits an anthologizing impulse that brings together four *Digest* poems from across multiple issues, displaying them in a three-column format. In the top left corner, the title "CURRENT POETRY" in bold also serves as a title for the scrapbook page itself.[25] The column focuses on John Masefield's poem "The Wanderer," a narrative poem in rhymed quatrains, the first twenty-four of which are reprinted from the September 1913 *Harper's Magazine* (where it is printed over six pages within an ornate floral border). The poem begins:

> All day they loitered by the resting ships.
> Telling their beauties over, taking stock:
> At night the verdict left my messmate's lips,
> "The *Wanderer* is the finest ship in dock."

Moore includes the comment prefacing the poem, declaring that this is Masefield's greatest poem, free of the bathos and sordidness that mars some of his other poems so it all is "clear and direct and full of the sea's own strength." While Moore does not go on to write narrative poetry in the sense that Masefield does, the praise for a poem as clear and direct, eschewing bathos, is instructive. Even the subject of the sea itself would be of enduring interest for Moore, a choice setting for many of her poems.

It is also worth noting the extent to which the poem echoes other content in the *Digest*, so that poetry can be recognized as part of a larger periodical discourse and not simply a departure from it. For example, "ship" appears 707 times in the issues I am examining here and "sea" appears 965 times.[26] While these terms are often invoked in a political context, as in references to the Sea of Marmora in the Balkans, they also hold more tragically Romantic connotations (with "widower" being one of the most closely associated terms with "sea") that resonate with Masefield's poem more directly.

By contrast, the inclusion of a Celtic poem by Alfred Perceval Graves, "O Drimin Dhu Deelish," would seem to caution what not to do. Taken from the previous week and reprinted from "Miss Harriet Monroe's excellent *Poetry: A Magazine of Verse*," Graves's poem follows Masefield's in Moore's scrapbook and begins:

> O Drimin Dhu Deelish, my kind Kerry cow.
> As black as the night with one star on her brow,
> For Drimin Dhu Deelish, the silk of the kine,
> For Drimin Dhu Deelish I mourn and I pine.
>> *As O ru Drimin Dhu, och oru agraw,*
>> *As O ru Drimin Dhu, go dhu tu slaun!*[27]

The poem is X-ed out in pencil. This might suggest a kind of checking off of the poem, but is more likely a case of Moore discounting the text. This could have been done some time after the initial pasting (the X is in pencil while the date is in ink), or it could have been done at the time of the pasting as a form of disapproval that is more evident (both for Moore and for future scholars) than if she had simply not pasted the poem in the first place. In either case, it appears that Moore was not happy with the poem. It is doubtful Moore would have objected to the subject matter; some of her best-known poems, including "Spenser's Ireland" and "Sojourn in the Whale," are about Ireland ("Ireland" was common throughout the *Digest* as well, appearing 273 times across these issues).[28] Rather, it could be what the *Digest* identifies as a "tendency away from mythology toward the simple beauties of common life" and a "romanticism of the commonplace" that contrasts with the harder edge of Masefield's poem.

Moore punctuates her critique of the poem with a joke taken from "The Spice of Life" (reprinted from *Puck*), placed immediately following the poem:

Proof of Intelligence.—Cholly—"Is this horse intelligent, me good fellah?"
Groom—"Very! Look out he don't kick you, sir!"²⁹

The joke suggests that the smart horse (roughly corresponding to Graves's cow) might outwit "Cholly" (a high-class pronunciation of "Charlie," suggesting the journalistic pseudonym "Cholly Knickerbocker")—perhaps not unlike Ireland kicking back at the poet's attempts to prettify her.

Likewise, Moore would seem to disagree with the "Current Poetry" editors through her inclusion of Maurice Hewlett's "Night-Errantry."³⁰ The poem is introduced with the commentary that the "first three stanzas are excellent. ... But the rest of the poem is a little too fantastic, a little too intense, to be effective." Immediately following this statement is a retort, handwritten in pencil, "not at all." Hewlett's poem concludes:

> O wild white face that's none of mine.
>   O eager eyes unknown.
> What will you do with Proserpine,
>   And what shall I, alone?
>
> O fleeting feet. O naked sides,
>   O tresses flying free,
> And are you his that all day bides
>   So soberly in me?
>
> The sun streams up behind the hill
>   And strikes the window-pane;
> The empty land lies hot and still—
>   And I am I again.

The final stanzas (particularly with the apostrophizing Os) might seem a bit over the top, but it is important to note here that Moore, whose own poetry is typically more restrained, doesn't object to fantastic and intense verse as long as it seems authentic.

To round out the page, in the top right corner are remnants of a newspaper article poem (materially marked by the cheaper, discolored paper) depicting the top of a head that was presumably "hinged" over a poem—a common practice in Moore's scrapbooks—and that has now been unhinged from its original scrapbook context. In the bottom right corner is another newspaper clipping (possibly related to the first) on "Miss Herne" as a Shaw heroine (resonating with other pages I will soon consider).

In addition to highlighting engagement with individual poems, this poetry page suggests Moore's evolving editorial and anthological practices. First, since there were multiple poems to choose from, it is reasonable to assume that there are principles of selection at work.[31] The pasted poems are all in traditional verse forms (mostly quatrains) and are not by the figures we have come to most closely identify with modern poetry (if we identify them at all), but this likely says more about the mainstream poetry landscape in the first decades of the twentieth century than it does about Moore's poetic temperament—and serves as a reminder of just how radical Moore's own poems were. Even given such aesthetic constraints, however, Moore exercises clear critical judgment in selecting some poems over others and demonstrates a willingness to push back against editorial opinions with commentary that suggests her own maturing sensibilities.

Second, the ordering of the scrapbook page suggests some degree of premeditation. Since the clippings do not appear chronologically, Moore had presumably clipped and retained the poems until she was ready to use them, or clipped from multiple issues in one setting. In either case, rather than choosing to arrange them by publication date, she relies on a different principle of organization (possibly in accordance with the material constraints of the scrapbook page itself—some configurations may have more easily fit on the page than others).

Finally, this page should be recognized as an act of radical decontextualization. Turning to the pages of the *Digest* itself, it becomes obvious that "Current Poetry" has been relegated to the magazine's back pages (a not uncommon occurrence in such magazines, suggesting its lesser, feminized status and ties to consumerism), typically occupying one column of the magazine, with the other two columns taken up by advertisements. For example, in its original periodical context, Masefield's "The Wanderer" is nearly stomped on by an advertisement for "Cat's Paw" rubber heels, and is accompanied by smaller ads for letterhead stationery, a vacuum

438 THE LITERARY DIGEST September 13, 1913

THAT FOSTER PLUG PREVENTS SLIPPING

The Heel With Nine Lives

CAT'S PAW

CUSHION

RUBBER HEELS

The moment you have a pair of **Cat's Paw Heels** attached to your shoes you feel a greater degree of safety.

Your shoes will be more comfortable—they will wear longer.

And, best of all, you will walk safely, with a sure-footed tread. The Foster Friction Plug won't let you slip—prevents your footsteps from sounding like a "gum-shoe" artist.

There are no holes in the heels to track mud and dirt. They cost no more than the ordinary kind.

The name is easy to remember. Get a pair today.

50c. attached

All dealers

FOSTER PATENT NON SLIP CAT'S PAW CUSHION HEEL 7 8 FOSTER RUBBER CO.

FOSTER RUBBER CO.
105 Federal Street, Boston, Mass.
Originators and patentees of the Foster Friction Plug, which prevents slipping.

HAVE YOU A DOG?

POLK MILLER DRUG COMPANY

AGENTS A BRAND NEW LIGHTER

D. Brandt Lighter Co., 148 Duane St., N. Y.

8½ Pound Electric Suction Cleaner

The Morrow

10 Days Free Trial

The Morrow Company, Dept. 2276, Waukegan, Ill.

5,000 Letter Heads

"Be Judged by Your Stationery"

$10 for 5,000 Good Bond Letter Heads in substantial dust proof boxes delivered anywhere east of the Mississippi.

ARTISTICALLY PRINTED

J. J. CONNORS

CONNORS, GOOD PRINTING, Saranac Lake, N. Y.

CURRENT POETRY

"JOHN MASEFIELD'S GREATEST Poem" is the confident characterization of "The Wanderer" printed on the cover of the September number of *Harper's Magazine*. Sometimes the contents of a magazine fail to live up to the cover. But in this case, the publishers' announcement is not too enthusiastic. It is dangerous to use the word "great" in writing of contemporary verse. But certainly "The Wanderer" approaches greatness more closely than any other poem that Mr. Masefield has written, with the possible exception of "Ships," which appeared in *The New York Times Review of Books* during Mr. Wetmore's editorship. In "The Wanderer" are no instances of the bathos which mars "The Widow in the Bye Street" nor of the deliberate sordidness which mars "The Everlasting Mercy." All is clear and direct and full of the sea's own strength. Few poets of this generation could equal the description of the ship returning after the storm with "her masts like trees in winter, frosty bright." We have not room to reprint more than half the poem.

The Wanderer

By John Masefield

All day they loitered by the resting ships,
Telling their beauties over, taking stock;
At night the verdict left my messmate's lips,
"The *Wanderer* is the finest ship in dock."

I had not seen her, but a friend, since drowned,
Drew her, with painted ports, low, lovely, lean,
Saying, "The *Wanderer*, clipper, outward bound,
The loveliest ship mine eyes have ever seen—

"Perhaps to-morrow you will see her sail,
She sails at sunrise"; but the morrow showed
No *Wanderer* setting forth for me to hail;
Far down the stream men pointed where she rode,

Rode the great trackway to the sea, dim, dim,
Already gone before the stars were gone,
I saw her at the sea-line's smoky rim
Grow swiftly vaguer as they towed her on.

Soon even her masts were hidden in the haze
Beyond the city; she was on her course
To trample billows for a hundred days;
That afternoon the norther gathered force;

Blowing a small snow from a point of east;
"Oh, fair for her," we said, "to take her south."
And in our spirits as the wind increased,
We saw her there, beyond the river-mouth,

Setting her side-lights in the wildering dark,
To glint upon mad water, while the gale
Roared like a battle, snapping like a shark,
And drunken seamen struggled with the sail.

While with sick hearts her mates put out of mind
Their little children left astern, ashore,
And the gale's gathering made the darkness blind,
Water and air one intermingled roar.

Then we forgot her, for the fiddlers played,
Dancing and singing held our merry crew,
The old ship moaned a little as she swayed,
It blew all night, oh, bitter hard it blew.

So that at midnight I was called on deck
To keep an anchor-watch: I heard the sea
Roar past in white procession filled with wreck;
Intense bright frosty stars burned over me,

And the Greek brig beside us dipt and dipt,
White to the muzzle like a half-tide rock,
Drowned to her mainmast with the seas she shipped
Her cable-swivels clanged at every shock.

And like a never-dying force, the wind
Roared till we shouted with it, roared until

Figure 2.1: Cat's Paw Rubber Heel Ad from the *Literary Digest*

cleaner, a watch-shaped lighter, and a dog elixir (Figure 2.1). Similarly, Graves's "O Drimin Dhe Deelish" is dominated by an advertisement for Quaker Oats puffed wheat and puffed rice. Hewlett's "Night-Errantry" is printed in three columns across the page, although each of these columns is truncated by an advertisement for "The Travelers Insurance Company" that occupies the bottom third of the page. The format is clearly such that poems are made to fit around advertising and not the other way around.

On Moore's reconstructed page, however, poems are removed from their more obviously commercial contexts and juxtaposed with one another in ways that are not available in the *Digest*, likening their presentation to that of a book collection, anthology, or some of the little magazines that were starting to make their way onto the literary scene. In their movement from periodical to (scrap)book, poetry is prioritized, poems more readily resonate with one another, and more space is made available for their contemplation. Such recontextualization extends to other magazine genres as well, including the political cartoon.

Political, Cartoons

Rachel Trousdale has recently argued that in Moore's poetry, humor enables intimacy and bridges public and private discourse, because for Moore, "humor's essential feature is its multivalence: her use of the comic encapsulates the way that self and other interpenetrate and enrich each other, showing that humanity's flexibility, sympathy, and inventiveness are all linked to our ability to laugh."[32] Such interpenetration is materially evident in Moore's scrapbooks as well, conveyed through the humorous clippings she chooses to include and through their strategic arrangement. These clippings generally take the form of jokes and political cartoons—the latter of which, as Victor S. Navasky has argued, have had an enduring force in periodicals and other venues owing to their content, form, and elicited neural responses.[33]

Moore's engagement with political cartoons is particularly evident in a two-page spread that takes as its basis an article, "He Makes Germany Laugh," about the German illustrator Gerhard Oberländer, which Moore augments with other political cartoons in various artistic styles.[34] In the top right corner of the page, Moore leaves intact Oberländer's illustration of "The Business Man" stuck in a tree, who is attempting to peddle his wares while trapped by a ferocious bull. In the bottom left corner, however, the original illustration, "In the Sentry-Box," in which Oberländer "betrays two unconscious actors in an intimate scene," their shadows caught in an embrace on the façade of a nearby building, has been pasted over with the "Latest Photo of William II," taken from the previous week's issue.[35] The added image, printed alongside an article on "Spanish Fears of Armageddon," is a surreal illustration depicting Kaiser Wilhelm II in military garb with two revolvers for eyes, a canon for a nose, six swords for a mustache, and a brick tower for a collar. It indicts a bellicose emperor who was largely responsible for the onset of World War I. Moore's inclusion of the image here echoes the attention given to the Kaiser in the *Digest* more generally as it figuratively places him in the sentry box, pointing to how he is standing sentry but also to how others need to remain on their guard.[36]

Above this image is a cartoon depicting "A Presidential Visit" of Woodrow Wilson, carrying a "Jersey Politician" and making the steep climb from New Jersey to the U.S. Capitol building.[37] The caption declares, "That's where you belong, Mr. President." The cartoon is printed alongside the article "Mr. Wilson's Stormy Home-Coming" and is one of two opposing views on the presidential visit, the other entitled "Old Home Week," reproduced from Macauley in the New York *World*, and depicting Wilson with an "Anti-Boss Rule" ruler, chasing corrupt politicians.[38] As these political cartoons suggest, Wilson was another oft-considered figure in the *Digest*, and one that Moore was following closely.[39]

On the next page, Moore retains the cartoon of a Renaissance figure writing on a semi-automated scroll with the caption "Don Smearus of the Papyrus" and the further explanation that "in this drawing by Oberländer the critic calls attention to 'the admirable composition' and 'the humorous Gothic unity of the style.'" The commentary on style and humor (topics taken up in such later poems as "To a Snail") would have appealed to Moore, persuading her to keep this cartoon visible. By contrast, Moore pastes over an image of a woman at her dressing table being squeezed into her dress, with the caption, "Pride Must Suffer Under Pressure." It is reasonable to assume Moore is signaling her disapproval of the notion and the gender implications of suffering under pressure (it is also worth noting that earlier in this same issue appears an article, "The March of Suffrage," accompanied by a photograph of women marching down Fifth Avenue with the caption, "Ten Thousand Reasons for Woman-Suffrage").[40] Moore overlays this image with one that resonates more clearly with the Wilhelm portrait and concerns over world war: one of smokestacks belching out shadowy figures fighting on the ground and on horseback, wielding daggers, swords, and scimitars, with the accompanying caption, "The Gun Foundries Are Busy!" As noted in pencil, the image is clipped from the May 17 issue, juxtaposed with a "Foreign Comment" on "The 'Real Cause' of the Balkan War" and "Seeds of More Balkan Troubles."[41]

Moore also covers up the adjacent article, "Is there any Test of Good English," in which a "Miss Learned" maintains that "we do not show a proper respect for 'the priceless heritage' which is our native tongue, but have drifted into 'a prevailing slovenly use of language which is really abuse.'" As if to pointedly counter this contention, Moore pastes a cartoon of a GOP elephant with the caption "Putting a lamp in the window for her stray son," with a dialogue bubble lamenting, "Mebby he'll see this and come home." While Moore may have selected this clipping in part for the political commentary that would resonate with the page's other clippings, it also points to a slovenly use of language, with "mebby" being substituted for "maybe," that she would relish.

At the bottom of the page is a related cartoon on "Delaying the Prodigal's Return," with a "prodigal son progressive" asking "who gets the fatted calf" of "party control" that stands tethered to a stake on a suburban front lawn. In the center of the page, Moore has pasted the question, "Where is the wandering boy to-night?" which becomes an overwhelming question for the page as a whole. Notably, however, these last two cartoons and the pasted question were all included together at the bottom of an article on "Sifting West Virginia Wrongs," taken from a June 7 issue, with the two cartoons in counterpoint and the question at the bottom.[42] Rather than simply clip the bottom third of the page and paste it into the scrapbook, Moore finds it necessary to atomize the composition so that its individual components are more directly juxtaposed with other clippings. Such atomization suggests the extent to which Moore is deliberate in her arrangement of clippings, which is similarly evident in pages that rest at the nexus of art and politics.

Of Art and Politics

In another instance, George Bernard Shaw, who is briefly referenced on Moore's "Current Poetry" page, takes center stage on a page that triangulates art, literature, and politics through portraits of three prominent men. The page leads off with an article, "How Shaw Saw Rodin at Work," taken from the November 30, 1912, issue of the *Literary Digest*, sandwiched between articles on Mark Twain's profanity and sacred subjects in the movies.[43] Shaw recounts sitting for a portrait-bust by Auguste Rodin, describing how Rodin "plodded along exactly as if he were a river god doing a job of wall-building in a garden for three or four francs a day." The contrast between Rodin's god-like artistic abilities and his workaday attitude is striking and instructive for how art is actually created, and an interest in Rodin can be seen in such early poems as "Rodin's *Penseur*."[44] Such interest is shared by the *Digest* more generally (in which both Shaw and Rodin frequently appear) and suggests a more general commitment to the literary and visual arts.[45]

The accompanying image of the bust has been pasted over with a newspaper photograph of "The President-Elect," printed two weeks earlier.[46] The original caption for the image of the Shaw bust is "Shaw for all Eternity," and one is tempted to attribute such "eternal" status to Wilson as well. The sub-caption potentially undercuts such a reading, however, noting that "Shaw secured Rodin for the job of making his bust in order that he might not go down to posterity 'as a stupendous nincompoop.'" One wonders if Wilson's reputation is in similar jeopardy.

Pasted on top of this article is a photograph of a soldier leaning against a tree, depicting a leisured masculinity that might also describe these three great men.[47] Below this photograph is a definition of "Earthly Punishment" reproduced from the *Kansas City Journal* and included in the "The Spice of Life" column: "The way of the transgressor is well written up."[48] The term "transgressor" might similarly serve as condemnation of the photograph and of these men as it underscores the power of writing to expose such transgressors.

If this page is centered on issues of masculinity in relation to artistic and political legacy, another page more clearly foregrounds the feminine, with the top third of the page consisting of a photo of the actor Sarah Bernhardt in a lush white dress with cuff and collar taken from a "Letters and Art" article on "The Legend of Sarah Bernhardt" (Figure 2.2).[49] The caption notes that Bernhardt is the first actress to receive the Cross of the Legion of Honor, and is called the "greatest missionary whom France or any other nation has sent abroad." The image's geopolitical dimension is echoed by an editorial cartoon taken from the following week, depicting Woodrow Wilson prying up a boardwalk plank labeled "Canal Tolls Exemption for U.S. Ships" that had abutted a plank labeled "One Presidential Term" and a man taunting Wilson to "Spare That

Figure 2.2: Bernhardt, Wilson, and Hardy (scrapbook)

Plank Woodrow."⁵⁰ Beneath this image is a clipping from a newspaper that presents an Art Deco sketch of a woman with cropped hair and a garishly patterned dress posing with one hand caressing a curtain and the other at the base of a vase.⁵¹ The image balances visually against that of Bernhardt's and emphasizes the French–international style that was in vogue.

The rest of the page is devoted to poems and a joke. Both of the clipped poems are by Thomas Hardy: "My Spirit Will Not Haunt the Mound," taken from the "Current Poetry" column, with the accompanying remark: "This bit of cynicism is from *Poetry and Drama*."[52] Also from "Current Poetry" is Hardy's "The Plaint of Specters," reprinted from the London *Saturday Review*.[53] The *Literary Digest* notes that "Mr. Hardy's verse has a small but enthusiastic company of admirers. ... But it is not for his poetry that Mr. Hardy is to receive the Nobel Prize." Hardy is mentioned eleven times in the issues I have been examining, including bylines for poems, and was of course a world-famous novelist at this point (although, despite twice being nominated, never did receive the Nobel Prize), but it isn't clear that Moore shares this criticism of the poems. The fact that Moore includes multiple Hardy poems in her scrapbooks suggests the extent to which he was a formative influence on her work in ways that critics have not fully accounted for.[54] Hardy's presence, and that of other figures included in the scrapbooks, is evident in "To a Cantankerous Poet Ignoring His Compeers—Thomas Hardy, Bernard Shaw, Joseph Conrad, Henry James."[55] The final text on the page is a joke, reproduced from *Tit-Bits*, that compares being in charge of "the front of a cinema show" to falling at Waterloo.[56] The joke itself concisely brings together French history, geopolitics, cinema, and the emergence of the modern that is suggested by the scrapbook page as a whole.

While there is a danger in reading too much into this constellation of clippings or, indeed, into any of Moore's scrapbook pages, I have attempted to show here the extent to which they demonstrate her engagement with a wide variety of subjects, genres, and discourses gathered from the realms of art, politics, humor, and poetry. Coming at a formative period in her intellectual and literary development, the material reading practices demonstrated through her cutting and pasting of clippings and through their arrangement into elaborate archival structures informed Moore's later poetic and editorial practices. At the same time, they illuminate the importance of the *Literary Digest* itself as they foreground Moore's identity as an archivist of mass print.

CHAPTER THREE

The Poet's Room as Archive

Robert Volpicelli

On November 15, 1972—Marianne Moore's first posthumous birthday—the Rosenbach Museum and Library in Philadelphia opened "The Marianne Moore Room" on the third floor of the institution's nineteenth-century townhome.[1] Featuring items Moore bequeathed to the Rosenbach just prior to her death in the same year, the Moore Room recreates the living room from the poet's apartment at 35 West Ninth Street in Greenwich Village: mismatched couches and chairs, as if still readying themselves for conversation, huddle together around a modern coffee table; just behind them, several of the poet's favorite animal figurines, a clock with a painted landscape on its face, and two brass and crystal candelabra look out from atop the fireplace mantelpiece (Figure 3.1); and, on either side of that, looming sets of shelves showcase the books from Moore's personal library, many of them volumes gifted to her by other esteemed modernist poets (Figure 3.2).[2] Aside from installing the bookshelves, the Rosenbach didn't have to make any major alterations to its original room in order to pull off what, by all accounts, is a stunningly accurate assembly. (Elizabeth Bishop, who was there on the night of the

---

I would like to thank Alison Fraser and Jeff Westover for their thoughtful feedback on this essay. I am also grateful to the staff at the Rosenbach Museum and Library for answering my questions about the Moore Room. Special thanks are due, finally, to Cris Miller and Patricia Willis for their insights into the origins of the Moore Collection.

exhibit's opening, apparently found it eerily so.[3]) Indeed, the summary note for the Moore Collection still even touts the room as "a remarkably close recreation of the poet's *environment*"—a phrasing that suggests through its brief yet notable appeal to the language of natural history that we should read the exhibit in the vein of exacting scientific observation, as a kind of full-scale diorama of Moore's poetic habitat.[4]

In so carefully preserving the dimensions of Moore's domestic life, the Moore Room participates in a tradition of transforming writers' spaces— and, in particular, their homes—into museum displays. The Rosenbach's exhibit therefore sits alongside other curated literary sites like the Emily Dickinson Homestead—the birthplace of the American poet, which was opened to public visitors after Amherst College purchased it in 1965.[5] The Ralph Waldo Emerson Study perhaps offers an even better corollary: the contents of the study in which Emerson famously entertained other writers and thinkers were relocated to the Concord Museum in 1930 so as to better accommodate "the year-long demand for visitation by pilgrims to Emerson's doorstep."[6] And "pilgrims" is the right word here since these displays are typically constructed around literary relics—the sort of objects that emanate a certain aura because of their close association with a particular author. As Nicola J. Watson argues in her study of the "writer's house museum" as a specific cultural form, such museums are in fact "designed to 'effect' the figure of the author ... through the preservation and display of his or her belongings, or 'effects,' within quasi-domestic space."[7] In other words, the writer's house museum promises an intimate sort of "encounter with the author's absent body."[8] Thus, the Moore Room is filled with objects that conjure the poet at different phases of her writing career: there is the desk from Bryn Mawr, at which Moore was likely to have written some of her first published poems (for undergraduate publications like *Tipyn O'Bob* and *The Lantern*); the footstool she received from T. S. Eliot, which speaks to the rather domestic intimacy she achieved with many of her modernist peers; and the signed baseball from Yankee legend Mickey Mantle, a symbol of how, later in her life, she was thoroughly embraced by her city as a New York icon.[9]

Yet the Moore Room also stands apart from many other curated literary spaces because of its close connection to the poet's archival collection of manuscripts and papers, which is also located at the Rosenbach. As

THE POET'S ROOM AS ARCHIVE 45

Figure 3.1: Moore's mantlepiece. Image courtesy of Rosenbach Museum and Library

Figure 3.2: Moore's bookshelf with elephant figurines. Image courtesy of Rosenbach Museum and Library

I will explain in greater detail below, Moore first decided upon Rosenbach as the destination for her papers and then later supplemented this collection with the bequest of the contents of her living room.[10] So while it is clear that the objects in the Moore Room are *valuable*—as collector's items, museum pieces, or even consecrated literary relics—their close proximity to Moore's papers also raises the question of their value as objects available to serious literary research. The answer to this question is far from clear: obviously, the footstool passed from Eliot to Moore gestures at aspects of the poet's personal history, but what further observations could we make about it? And what about the autographed baseball? How about the chairs, desk, and other furniture? What, specifically, do these belongings lend to the practice of archival *research*? In this essay, I approach such questions by examining how Moore's living-room objects at the Rosenbach do, and do not, augment the "literary archive" as it is commonly understood. Such an investigation ultimately leads me to create a new category, that of the *para-archive*, in an effort to describe the way these domestic items appear to exist both within the archive proper and alongside it, in tension with it. Said differently, I find that the items in the Moore Room embody a curious archival ambiguity or *adjacentness*—one that I take here as an opportunity to explore how such objects intervene in the history of modernist poetry archive as well as in our conception of the literary archive more generally.

Collecting Moore

In pursuing the meaning of the poet's room as archive, it is worth first considering how Moore's career intersects, at several points, with the larger history of modernist poetry archives in America. In many ways, Moore is emblematic of the progression—call it an "archive drive"— that led to the founding of these archives, mostly at university libraries, during the second half of the twentieth century.[11] And yet, the poet's early responses to the idea of collecting her papers at an academic institution reflect a certain degree of ambivalence about this project. Moore received her first requests about archival materials from the University of Buffalo librarian Charles D. Abbott in 1936.[12] In his effort to build the first comprehensive modernist poetry archive, Abbott began writing letters to prominent living poets in the mid-1930s to ask whether they would donate draft materials, what he was then referring to as "worksheets," that illustrated the evolution of their writing process.[13] As Jeremy Braddock argues, Abbott's decision to focus on drafts, although at least partly borne of the need to economize, demonstrates how he viewed "ephemeral poetic materials" as "objects of speculation and investment."[14] This was a view that Moore apparently didn't always share. As late as the 1950s, the poet still questioned whether her drafts—or the drafts of any author short of Shakespeare's stature, for that matter—were even worth saving.[15] And what's more, her correspondence with Abbott, which stretches out over an impressive twenty years, only ever resulted in a small handful of donations to Buffalo's Poetry Collection.[16]

Any reluctance Moore displayed about archiving during this period, however, was far from an indication of the attitude she would adopt later in life. In 1968, Moore in fact became one of the first modern poets to establish a major archival collection at a single location when she sold all of her remaining papers to the Rosenbach Museum and Library.[17] Here, it is important to note that this seeming shift in thinking took place at the end of a decade that saw a substantial increase in the institutional collecting of literary papers—an increase that, in turn, greatly raised the monetary value of manuscripts and other related papers.[18] Moore's case is exemplary in this respect. The University of Texas at Austin, whose Harry Ransom Center had already become a premier destination for modernist literary manuscripts by the end of the 1960s, was willing to pay Moore the (at that time) relatively large sum of $100,000 for her collection.[19] Unfortunately, there is little existing documentation that speaks to why Moore chose to sell her papers to the Rosenbach instead of an institution like the University of Texas; but considering that she settled on a deal with Rosenbach director Clive Driver for the same amount that the Ransom Center was willing to offer, it stands to reason that her choice had to do with the Rosenbach's specific attributes as a place and its difference from the other, more academic, sites known for collecting modernist papers.[20]

Founded in 1954, the Rosenbach Museum and Library was formed around the personal collection of the brothers A. S. W. and Philip Rosenbach, two of America's most successful and influential dealers in rare books, manuscripts, and other collectibles.[21] A.S.W. Rosenbach, in particular, was an example of what Walter Benjamin called a "genuine collector."[22] In his memoir, *Books and Bidders: The Adventures of a Bibliophile* (1927), he describes how he became "spellbound" by the "mystery and intangible beauty" of fine books while working in his uncle's bookshop as a young boy.[23] Rosenbach was in fact so enchanted by this work that he later gave up a fellowship in English at the University of Pennsylvania—and thus also a career in academia—to pursue what he considered the more adventurous "sport" of book collecting.[24] The move provides an early suggestion of how the Rosenbach Museum and Library would stand apart from academic archives like Buffalo's Poetry Collection or Austin's Ransom Center. Although it is fairly common for university libraries to absorb personal collections, the Rosenbach, as a personal-collection-turned-public-institution, inevitably retained more of the personal stamp of its namesake. From the vantage point of the rapidly specializing university, its collection appears rather idiosyncratic and eclectic.[25] For instance, while Abbott concentrated most of his energy on acquiring the drafts of modernist poets, Rosenbach's collection—at the time it was transferred over to the foundation—encompassed a wide variety of materials, including early Americana, children's books, incunabula, important early Bibles, and the manuscript of James Joyce's *Ulysses*.[26]

Yet the Rosenbach departed even more significantly from these other institutions in its location. In setting up their foundation, the Rosenbach brothers dictated that their collection continue to be housed in their Philadelphia residence on Delancey Place, in effect transforming their private home into a library and museum.[27] With many of their pieces of furniture, paintings, and entire rare book library inhabiting their original spaces, the home subsequently served not only as a place to display these items but also as a shrine to the brothers' love of collecting. Such a sentiment surely resonated with Moore, herself a fastidious collector. In her recent biography of the poet, Linda Leavell describes how Moore, when she was making the decision of where to send her collection, thought back to her earlier visit to the Rosenbach's rare book shop in New York, at which point she fondly recalled "'the electrically-lighted, suspended magnifying glass,' various examples of the art of bookbinding, and a first folio of *Othello*."[28] As other critics have already pointed out, the memory highlights how the Rosenbach's shop "spoke to Moore's own passion for interiors and for collecting—encapsulated in her own densely personalised and old-fashioned living space."[29] The Rosenbach Museum and Library announced similar passions. It conjured up a *homey* atmosphere that contrasted greatly with the other (one might say, more institutional) places that served as potential sites for Moore's papers. So while Moore may have greeted the earlier appeals of librarians like Abbott with some hesitation, she was quite decisive in making the Rosenbach a permanent home for her papers—so decisive, in fact, that shortly before her death in 1972 she also chose to archive the entire contents of her living room at the same site, thereby creating a permanent home for her home.

If Moore's bequest of her living room to the Rosenbach shows how she had become fully committed to the idea of the archive, then it also speaks to how she was invested in extending that archive far beyond its usual limits. Relevant here is Bartholomew Brinkman's argument that "the rise of the modern poetry archive" was predicated on the concomitant expansion of the archive itself—or, more specifically, on the expansion of what counts as archivable content from the rare books sought by collectors and librarians to a much wider array of ephemeral materials that includes drafts, correspondences, and periodicals.[30] It follows, then, that this expanded set of materials, these various scraps of literary history, acquire their value, not so much through a sense of rarity or prestige, but as fragments of potential evidence that could be used by scholars in piecing together the contexts of modern poetry. At first glance, Moore's Rosenbach collection seems to be a representative example of this archival development in that it contains a substantial amount of the poet's ephemera (such as the periodicals she saved, the notebooks she worked in, and even the print clippings she collected).[31] However, I would hasten to add here that Moore's inclusion of her living room in her Rosenbach collection takes this idea of archival expansion to a new, as yet unaccounted for, level.[32] This is to say that Moore's decision to save the contents of her room alongside her papers pushes back the boundaries of the literary archive even further: if the purpose of adding ephemera to this archive is to give scholars a look into the broader ecology of modern poetry, then one way we could understand the Marianne Moore Room is as a radical extension of this (as the Rosenbach's summary note puts it) "environment," a widening out of the literary archivist's purview from the (printed) spaces in which modernist poetry appeared to the (physical) spaces in which it was written.

The *Arkheion* of Modernist Poetry

That the space being archived here is a domestic one is especially noteworthy, for, as Jacques Derrida theorizes in *Archive Fever* (1995), the "domicile" is at the very root of the archive.[33] More specifically, in his analysis of the archive as a place that structures both memory and knowledge, Derrida begins by tracing the etymological foundation of the term "archive" back to a "taking place": the Greek root "*arkhē*" carries the primary sense of commencement, beginning, or source, providing it with the double meaning of a happening, the occurrence of an event, and a place, the making of a space or shelter.[34] These dual meanings then come together in the more complex "*arkheion*," which Derrida glosses as follows: "initially a house, a domicile, an address, the residence of the superior magistrates, the *archons*, those who commanded."[35] As Derrida goes on to detail, the *arkheion* is the home in which these superior magistrates filed their important documents—the documents, in this sense, also require a place to dwell. And it is this function of filing and storing that makes the home a seat of authority from which official events can be recorded and laws or commandments pronounced. Derrida writes: "It is thus, in this *domiciliation*, in this house arrest, that the archives take place."[36] Most essentially, then, the archive is a private home that has taken on an authoritative, public function, and, in the process of doing so, has transformed from one type of place (the home) into another (the museum).

And, for an example of this process, Derrida didn't have to look any further than the site in which he was delivering the lectures that were later collectively published as *Archive Fever*: the Freud Museum, London, which prior to becoming a museum had served as Sigmund Freud's final home. Freud moved into this house at 39 Elsworthy Road after fleeing the Nazi annexation of Austria in March 1938; he would die the next year, but his family, including his daughter Anna Freud, continued living in the home until it was turned into a museum in 1982 (which was then opened to the public in 1986).[37] Derrida at one point addresses this site directly: "This brings us to the question, which is always open, of what the title 'Freud's house' means, the Freud Museum as a 'House of Freud,' the *arkheion* of which we are the guests, in which we speak, from which we speak."[38] The very formulation of this "question" underscores the dual nature of the *arkheion* as both museum and house: the Freud Museum was of course born of "Freud's house"; but it also remains, as Derrida puts it, a "House of Freud" because this is the place where "Freud" continues to be housed or archived after his death, as a body of knowledge. This duality then explains the way the museum functions for Derrida as the site of hospitality "in which we speak" as well as the site of archival authority "from which we speak."

As anyone who has visited this museum can attest, the specter of Freud's domicile is most palpable in the exhibit of his study, kept intact with its original oriental rugs, various totems, and iconic patient couch. Derrida isn't particularly attentive in his analysis to domestic belongings like these. However, what he says while pursuing Freud's thoughts on the "*mystic pad*" (an erasable tablet that Freud likens to the psyche) is relevant to the archival nature of such objects: the "*domestic outside*" helps to register a "psychic archive" in the way that it serves as a "*prosthetic of the inside*."[39] In other words, since we express ourselves through the objects around us (the "domestic outside"), these things bear the mark of our psyches (like writing on the surface of an erasable tablet). In this sense, the personal belongings found in Freud's study offer their own *impressions*— to use a Derridean word—of Freud's mind. Take, for example, the antique bas-relief of a woman named "Gradiva" that hangs upon the study's wall. This object relates to one of Freud's most important studies, *Delusion and Dream* (1907), in which he analyzes Wilhelm Jenson's 1902 novel *Gradiva* in order to reveal how the protagonist's archaeological obsession with the same bas-relief originates with his unconscious memories. The relief thus indexes a significant moment in Freud's professional and intellectual development. What's more, though, as a casting, a *relief*, the object is itself a (prosthetic) figure of Freud's thinking more generally—his psychoanalytic endeavor to find the mark or imprint left by (psychic) material that is no longer available to us.[40]

As a space devoted to such objects, the Freud study highlights the way rooms of this sort can themselves function as archives (and thus reverses something of the usual practice of erasing or covering over the domestic foundation of archival space). In this way, it also serves as one of the better analogues to the Rosenbach's Moore Room. Just as the Freud

Museum preserves the doctor's study as the primal scene of psychoanalysis, the Rosenbach Museum archives the poet's room as the true *arkheion* of Moore's modernist poetry—the place from which it commences, its source. Accordingly, the many objects in Moore Room are not just mementos or collectibles; they are archival materials that reflect the interior life of the poet, her aesthetic preferences as well as the terms and conditions of her creativity. As such, they hold the same promise as any other material commonly found within the literary archival collection, which scholars consult in the hope of gleaning more information about the processes of poetry—processes that, in Moore's case, inevitably point back to the idea of domesticity itself.

Poetry Rooms

It is entirely fitting that one of Moore's final acts was to make a museum of her living room. Moore was a notable homebody.[41] But, even more importantly, the emphasis she placed on this domestic scene by directly incorporating it into the archive resonates with aesthetic principles that she had developed across her whole career. As critics have noted previously, Moore departed from the company of many of her male contemporaries— poets who had pitched their aesthetic projects against the household and all of its feminine connotations—by cultivating a poetics that arises directly from the domestic sphere.[42] Trading on a famous line from "When I Buy Pictures," Leavell even goes so far as to suggest that "each of Moore's poems is a room that contains the things she *sees*, the things of which she is 'the imaginary possessor.'"[43] This idea—that Moore's poems function analogously to domestic spaces—was earlier affirmed by an exhibit that accompanied the opening of the Rosenbach's Moore Room, in which various possessions from Moore's living room were displayed alongside their corresponding poems.[44] For example, one display placed a toy horn Moore's brother Warner once received for Christmas next to a short lyric Moore wrote when she was only eight years old (a card with the poem written on it was distributed to the exhibit's visitors as a keepsake): "Dear St. Nicklus; / this Christmas morn / you do adorn / bring Warner a horn, / and me a doll / that is all."[45] In drawing a line between material object and poetic material in this way, the exhibit that launched the Moore Room emphasizes—indeed, *materializes*—Moore's idiosyncratic ethic of using her poems to present everyday objects in a sense of space.

The exhibit also offers an exceedingly materialist mode of interpretation that encourages us to read Moore's poems *through* the Moore Room, as ekphrastic representations of domestic objects that the poet either owned or encountered.[46] Such an approach is applicable to a wide variety of poems in Moore's oeuvre. In particular, the many poems in which Moore touches upon decorative arts objects immediately come to mind here. As Sarah Berry notes in a recent article about how Moore's poetry engages the aesthetic history of curiosity cabinets, Moore "lavishes precise attention and observational wit" on a broad range of decorative items ("jewelry, furs, a cane, Chinese porcelain, jeweled goblets, a ceramic pitcher, Florentine goldwork, Chippendale furniture, ornate candelabra," to name just some of the ornamental objects that appear in her verse).[47] According to Berry, these objects generally serve in the imaginative context of Moore's poetry as springboards for artistic "digression[s]" about the relationship between subject and object.[48] Consider the aforementioned "When I Buy Pictures," which centers on a series of decorative, if also somewhat mundane, domestic objects—"pictures," a "hat-box," and even "a square of parquetry."[49] In the larger scope of the poem, these objects are what spark the speaker's meditations on the things that give "pleasure in [her] average moments" as well as on the forms of artistic looking that are needed to illuminate them—that is, the kind of "piercing glances into the life of things" that can turn household items into high art.[50]

In some instances, this materialist mode of reading can even be applied to poems that, upon first inspection, appear to have little to do with the domestic scene. A provocative example here is Moore's 1918 "Black Earth."[51] Critics universally classify "Black Earth" as one of Moore's many animal poems. In her analysis of the poem, for instance, Cristanne Miller focuses on how the poem's elephant, as an animal-speaker, delineates the "difference between human and elephantine limitation," principally through an exploration of its own physical features.[52] Miller also examines how the elephant—in probing the relationship between its soul and skin, interior and exterior—arrives at important philosophical questions about the nature of subjective experience more generally.[53] This is a compelling reading of the poem. And yet, an entirely different reading comes out of the 1919 letter Moore sent to Ezra Pound, in which she—while attempting to address Pound's notoriously racist suggestion that the poem's title was an indication that Moore herself must have been "Ethiopian"—reveals that "Black Earth" was about one of her figurines, "an elephant that I have, named Melanchthon."[54] This 1919 letter is regularly cited by scholars who find that the poem does in fact engage with matters of racial identity.[55] However, the implication that the poem's speaker is an object instead of an animal (it should be noted that the former scenario is not any *more* implausible than the latter) has gone completely unexamined.

Indeed, once this poem's material origins are highlighted, it is hard to miss the many ways in which the speaker's description of itself repeatedly comes back to its physical properties as an inanimate object. For example, in commenting upon the "sediment of the river" that clings to its body and "makes [it] very grey," the speaker asserts that "the / patina of circumstance can but enrich what was / there to begin / with"—"patina" being a word normally used to describe the tarnished appearance of metal or wood antiques.[56] Or slightly later, when returning to "This elephant skin," the speaker calls its "skin" a "piece of black glass through which no light / can filter."[57] A statement like this last one may initially seem like a metaphor (in which the speaker compares its skin to "black glass"). But within the context of Moore's poetry rooms, it actually functions as a *collapse* of metaphor in which the material substrate undergirding this exercise (where the poet is imagining what life is like from the point of view of one of her beloved glass figurines) filters through to the surface of the poem. In this sense, Moore's domestic aesthetic hinges upon the objectification of poetic *figures* into literal *figurines*. And this material turn enhances the poem's larger theme, which suggests that what lies on the outside—river mud, for instance—is not separate from the inside but rather helps to lend it clarity and definition. In other words, subjectivity, which is frequently seen as some pristine and rarified core of experience, only finds expression in the matter external to it, in the outside world. This, finally, is the radical idea at the core of "Black Earth" as an object poem: the poet's subjectivity, her imagination, speaks through the everyday items that surround her—in this case, one of her favorite elephant figurines.

Rather surprisingly, then, "Black Earth" returns us to the archival value of the belongings found in the Moore Room. This is a value neatly summed up in the first lines of another one of Moore's poems: "People's Surroundings / They answer one's questions."[58] The material artifacts that make up an individual's environment provide us with additional insights into that person: "insights" because such a notion relies on the shift from the exteriority of physical things to the interior richness of human experience. This is precisely the dynamic that Moore hints at in the rest of the first stanza of "People's Surroundings," where she describes how, even in the "dried bone of arrangement," an individual's surroundings—like a "deal table compact with a wall"—still bespeak something of "one's style," a highly subjective part of their psychology or personality.[59] These objects thus make good on what is one of the archive's fundamental promises, which is an access to interiority: we *enter* the archive because the materials contained there permit us a (voyeuristic) glimpse *into* the life of this or that author. Or, to put this in slightly different terms, the archive takes the private into the public—which explains why there is so often a concern that something in the archive will reveal a private fact that an author or their family wishes not to publicize. The ethics of such access put aside for the moment, Moore's contention in archiving her living room is that an author's domestic objects contain the same sort of secrets as, say, their correspondence. In fact, as a private room made public, an interior made exterior, Moore's living room puts on display something of the very essence of the archive.

The Para-Archive

Yet the Moore Room's relationship to the archive is still more complicated than this. As I've argued in the preceding sections, the Moore Room, located in the same repository as the rest of Moore's collection, takes on its own archival function in the way it offers the poet's domestic objects as part of the context of her poetry. At the same time, though, I want to recognize the ways in which this room also stands apart from the "literary archive" as it is usually construed, as a site of scholarly study and inspection. Something of this deviation is signaled by the Moore Room's physical position *within* the Rosenbach, where it exists as a space distinct from the institution's other literary holdings as well as the reading room to which those holdings are delivered. It is also present in the different social practices and procedures that accompany these spaces: the Moore Room is a cordoned-off display that invites all of the museum's visitor to briefly peer into Moore's life but generally prohibits the sort of intimate handling and sustained close reading that we typically associate with archival research. It is for such reasons, then, that I name the Moore Room a *para-archive*: a space that exists within the overall place we designate as the archive and in some ways functions very similarly to it, but that also distinguishes itself from this same archive and many of the assumptions we hold about it in a variety of important ways.

Such a distinction can be immediately discerned in the Moore Room's overall sense of organization. As Michel Foucault puts forward in *The Archeology of Knowledge* (1969), the archive is perhaps best defined by its strict adherence to organizational law: the archive does not allow things to "accumulate endlessly in an amorphous mass"; rather, it sees they are "grouped together in distinct figures, composed together in accordance with multiple relations, maintained or blurred in accordance with specific regularities."[60] Indeed, from this perspective, the archive epitomizes the systemization of knowledge. The collection of Moore's papers at the Rosenbach comprises exactly this sort of system. The contents of this collection have been grouped into a number of "series" that organize Moore's papers according to their type: "Poetry," "Prose," "Book manuscripts," "Translations," "General correspondence," "Family correspondence," "Notebooks," "Datebooks and calendars," etc.[61] And then, the items in each of these series have been further broken down according to an internal system of organization, such as chronological or alphabetical order. Of course, all of this systematizing suits the purposes of scholars who are looking to examine specific items within such a vast array of material. But it also throws into relief an important difference between the Moore Room and the rest of the poet's archival collection: while Moore's papers have been stored and filed in a way that accords with what we have come to expect from the literary archive, the Moore Room abides by no such system of organization—or, perhaps more accurately, no such system of *scholarly* organization. The objects in the Moore Room have not been re-organized for the purposes of classification (the room's contents are not even fully itemized in the Collection Summary); instead, they abide by Moore's own arrangements, her deeply personal order of things.[62]

In maintaining the latter method of organization, the Moore Room on some level resists its full incorporation into the archive. The resulting position—the room's situation both inside and outside of the archive—again speaks to its status as a para-archive. It is also what allows it to operate as a critique of what Shane Vogel has termed the "official archive."[63] In this sense, the para-archive, by abandoning certain archival rules and regulations, is capable of highlighting the less desirable aspects of the archive, including the "acquisitive violence" upon which the archival collection's discursive formations are necessarily based.[64] This is the way the archival process commonly involves disassembling and redistributing a poet's body of work, which of course also represents the body of the poet herself: the archive not only makes the private body into a public one, it asserts a new institutional logic over that body and reconstructs it according to its own (frequently more orderly) terms. The personal violations that attend this kind of removal and reconstruction are perhaps what at first made Moore—a poet known for her keen attention to the specifics of place—hesitant to sign on to the project of archiving her materials. In this light, then, the Moore Room constitutes both the poet's statement on the larger ethics of the archive and her attempt to gesture at an alternative, perhaps less invasive form of collecting through her domestic aesthetic.

Finally, this rejection of archival logic is useful for underscoring the limitations of the literary archive as we most often encounter it. As I suggested earlier, the Moore Room—by amassing so many domestic objects from Moore's personal life—puts a kind of critical pressure on the typical shape of the archival literary collection. More specifically, the room's presentation of these objects as potential source material for Moore's poetry calls into question what should even count as "literary" material in the first place. All of the books in Moore's personal library seem easy enough to consider part of the poet's literary archival materials.[65] The many pictures and photographs scattered about the room also seem relatively at home here. But what of the miscellaneous "unsorted material"—financial records, notes, scraps, empty envelopes—that Rosenbach archivists found stashed away in pieces of Moore's furniture?[66] What of the furniture itself? What of the exercise bar that hangs in the doorway? The piece of cake that librarians found years after the materials had been transferred to the Rosenbach? Are these, too, literary materials? In prompting a cascade of questions as to what does and does not count as part of the literary archive, the Moore Room plunges the very idea of this archive into crisis through its expansive re-imagining of the contents contained there. Indeed, the radical inclusivity gestured at here (Moore's archive needs to contain not only all of her papers but also many of the *things* represented by those papers) seems to stretch this collection to the point where we begin to wonder whether it defeats the notion of selectivity that remains essential to any collection. Even though the archive may reach toward a sense of completeness, in practical terms it gathers its meaning through what it leaves out.[67] Moore's archival collection at the Rosenbach troubles this notion with all of the untraditional materials it leaves *in*.

"Omissions," Moore knew well, "are not accidents," so neither we might suppose are these inclusions.[68] As I've discussed in this essay, Moore's inclusion of her living room among her other archival literary materials at the Rosenbach presents very intentional challenges to the way we think about the archive in general and the literary archive in particular. First, the Moore Room underscores the potential archival value of rather mundane domestic objects; then, it reveals how these objects threaten to undo the boundaries of the literary archive. Both of these provocations arise from the Moore Room's status as a para-archive, a room situated both within and without the traditional archive. If this ambiguous position is what has kept such a space on the outside of the critical discourse about modern poetry, then it is also what constitutes it as a space from which to view and critique the institutional practices that have consolidated around the literary archive. The Moore Room offers such a space, but I'd like to suggest that it isn't the only one: the para-archive has many more rooms for us to explore.

Sex, Race, and Economics
in the Archive

CHAPTER FOUR

Out-Casts and Stay-at-Homes
Marianne Moore, Arthur Mitchell, and LGBTQ Migration in NYC

Elizabeth Gregory

> New York
> the savage's romance
> accreted where we need the space for commerce—
> ...
> it is not the atmosphere of ingenuity,
> the otter, the beaver, the puma skins
> ...
> it is not the plunder,
> it is the "accessibility to experience."
> Marianne Moore (1921)

Often when we think migration, we think long distances. Everyone in the United States has a backstory of family emigration from other continents, even Native peoples, often followed by movement around this continent, once arrived. Prior to that, all humans build on long histories of ancestral travels around and from Africa and into all reaches of the planet, seeking resources and opportunities. Migration is us. But even short distances can be meaningful: nowadays, traveling a mile or two to a different neighborhood, or just a few blocks, can make a difference in the way one lives one's life.

This essay will plot the trajectories of two artists' local travels—around New York City, against a background of nineteenth- and twentieth-century family travel across the United States, to reflect on how such travel has signified and connected to another kind of travel: in and out of the closet. In particular, I'll begin to explore the interactive dynamics of place with bias—around race, sexuality, and gender—and the attempt to escape or transform bias, in the lives of two queer New York artistic leaders whose archives do not represent them as gay but who have been variously perceived as queer: poet Marianne Moore (1887–1972) and dancer Arthur Mitchell (1934–2018), about whom Moore wrote two poems.

The project will draw on my own travels through Moore's extensive archives—including a lifetime of letters, poetry, and conversation notebooks and decades of detailed appointment books, and much more. Arthur Mitchell's family's backstory is much less well documented than Moore's, but while the personal details in his archive are sparse, he did record oral histories, and other documents and related histories exist.[1] His biographer in progress, Lynn Garafola, has kindly shared some details from her research as well.[2]

Moore

Moore's complex family history went public in Linda Leavell's biography, which drew on their extensive family archive (now housed in the Rosenbach Museum and Library in Philadelphia) to reveal that before her birth the poet's father became a mentally unstable bibliomane, to the point that her mother left him, with their young son Warner in tow and Marianne still in the womb—a migrant from the start. Since divorce was then frowned on, Mary Warner Moore never officially split from John Milton Moore, who was soon committed to an asylum. Marianne never met him, her family barely spoke about him, and she only became acquainted with some of her paternal relatives after her mother's death, sixty years later.

The young Mary Warner Moore (MWM) and her son returned from Newton, Massachusetts, to the home of her Presbyterian minister father, John Riddle Warner, in Kirkwood, Missouri (with a stop along the way at J. H. Kellogg's Battle Creek Sanitarium to improve her health through fresh air and exercise). The Reverend had himself become a single parent upon the death of his wife Jennie—of typhoid she contracted while assisting in the aftermath of the battle of Gettysburg, where he led a church. During the battle, Jennie and little Mary had hidden in the basement of the church manse while John Warner watched the fighting from the roof. Once widowed, unable to care for his one-year-old daughter alone, he sent her to live first with her mother's sister and then with his parents, until they died when she was fourteen.[3] Father and daughter kept in touch through detailed weekly letters, and when she rejoined him as a young teen at his new ministry outside St. Louis, he enrolled her in the Mary School, a progressive academy for girls focused on academic excellence (as most girls' schools were not at the time), founded by another minister in the area, William Greenleaf Eliot—T. S. Eliot's grandfather.

The poet's mother clearly experienced her own early isolation from *her* father as a negative; the break-up of her marriage suggests an unwillingness to settle for undesirable circumstances as an adult. As counter, she emphasized family closeness thereafter to a level that most would view as excessive—effectively shaping her daughter to eschew other bonds and remain as her companion for the next sixty years. After her father's death, MWM moved her two children to be near relatives in Pennsylvania, and then to the small town of Carlisle in that state—home, among other things, to Dickinson College, a progressive Presbyterian church headed by the Rev. George Norcross that the family soon joined, and the Carlisle Indian Industrial School, the first such Native reprogramming academy in the nation. In this very particular version of small-town America, MWM fell in love—with the minister's daughter, also named Mary, and for eleven years they were romantically bonded. Thus, the young poet and her brother grew up in a household led by a very Christian lesbian single mom. And in this particular place and moment, the couple seems to have been effectively out to their families and immediate community. MWM responded to the difficulties thrown at her by organizing her life on her own terms,[4] and the likelihood that the children she raised would also be unusual people was fulfilled.

Moore was apparently a happy and self-confident child: she bonded with her brother from the start, preferred adventure stories to romances, and insisted on being addressed with male pronouns from an early age, a requirement with which her family willingly complied throughout her life.[5]

She left home for Bryn Mawr College in 1905, then returned upon graduation to Carlisle where she studied business for one year, then left briefly to work for Melvil Dewey at his Lake Placid resort dedicated to health and spelling reform. Upon returning home, she took a job teaching business and commercial law for three years (1911–14) at the Indian School, participating in its dismantling, and learning much about the blurriness of race categories.[6] Advocacy for racial equity became an ongoing concern of her work from there on (see *Apparition of Splendor*).

Moore wrote more than fifty poems during her post-Bryn Mawr Carlisle period and was beginning to be published in international modernist journals when she and her mother moved in 1916 to live with Warner at his first ministerial post, in Chatham, New Jersey. Two years later, when he married and then joined the Navy as a chaplain, Moore decided their next move: to 14 St. Luke's Place in Greenwich Village. Arriving in 1918, smack in the midst of the modernist scene, Moore was already a rising star, and within a few years she ruled there, as editor of the preeminent *Dial* magazine (1925–29). In those days she could walk to work at their offices on West 13th Street between 6th and 7th Avenues.

In *Gay New York*, George Chauncey describes the attraction of the Village to bohemians and modernists in the nineteen-teens as lying first in the cheap rents and then in the openness to eccentric lifestyles, including unmarried female and male "artists, free-lovers, and anti-materialists," whose unconventional behavior and art work often overlapped with unconventional sexual behavior, sometimes including homosexuality.[7] Moore felt very at home in the space. She displayed no romantic interests in people of any sex or gender. Nevertheless, her *Dial* colleague Kenneth Burke described her as a very "sexual woman," for whom intimacy consisted of intellectual play: "Every damn thing was turned into little twists and turns."[8] Moore's mother felt at home there too. As Leavell notes, "Contrary to what any of Moore's Village acquaintances might have imagined, Mary actually preferred the company of homosexuals to heterosexuals. Marriage was a continual subject of scorn for her."[9] Moore's 1922 poem "Marriage" reflects a similar view. Although apparently not "out" in the way she'd been in Carlisle, and there are no evidences of MWM's having further romantic liaisons, both mother and daughter were at home in the queer community in the Village.

Moore's editorial work at the *Dial* stopped her poetic production for those five years. After the magazine closed in 1929 just before the crash, Moore's brother seems to have pressured Moore and her mother to move to the Fort Greene neighborhood in Brooklyn, close to the Navy yard where he was a chaplain at the time. There, although removed from the *Dial* arts community, Moore was soon making poetry of her new place. For instance, her 1932 poem "The Steeple-Jack" was inspired initially by work done to take down the steeple of the nearby Lafayette Avenue Presbyterian Church that Moore and her mother attended. The steeple had been destabilized by the drilling of the subway—which catalyzed interborough travel and undid the isolation that a move to Brooklyn could have created in years prior. The poem explores the complexities of small town morality, drawing on Moore's combined experience of Carlisle, Chatham, the Village, and now Brooklyn, as well as their favored summer resort, Monhegan Island, Maine.

In *When Brooklyn Was Queer: A History*, Hugh Ryan tracks buried stories of the precarious gay and lesbian communities present and often flourishing there in the 114 years between the publication of Whitman's *Leaves of Grass* in Brooklyn in 1855 and the emergence of the Gay Rights movement at Stonewall (in Manhattan) in 1969. He includes Moore as a queer Brooklynite, perhaps best described in current terms as "asexual" or "a-romantic," and suggests that she, her mother, and their many visitors, many of them gay and lesbian, were part of what made Brooklyn a generative queer nexus.[10] In her years in Brooklyn Moore wrote roughly one hundred poems and published fourteen books of poetry and prose, becoming celebrated in her latter phase as "the poet of Brooklyn," in particular due to her status as a Dodgers fan, as documented in her world series poem, "Hometown Piece for Messrs. Alston and Reese" (1956).

Though for her whole life she'd favored ties, suits, and clothing with a masculine cast, Moore kept at least one foot on the feminine side of the gender sumptuary line through the 1940s. But in the early 1950s, after the success of her *Collected Poems* made her a celebrity, she became a public crossdresser, adopting her signature look as "Washington crossing the Delaware," as she put it,[11] wearing a tricorne hat and dark cape around town regularly. The outfit was part of a comedic self-characterization that allowed her as an elderly woman to wield poetic authority on the public stage, without seeming to threaten the rigid social orders of the day.[12] The revolutionary garb, as I argue in *Apparition of Splendor*, served to raise questions about gender, authority and who had voice in the clamped-down 1950s version of American democracy, every time she entered a room or a subway car. It was as this evolved public figure that Moore published two poems involving Arthur Mitchell, in 1962.

Mitchell

Arthur Mitchell's parents, Willie Mae Hearns Mitchell and Arthur Mitchell, Sr., were born in or around Savannah, Georgia. They moved in the 1920s to Philadelphia, joining the Great Migration of African Americans from south to north. In Philadelphia, Mitchell's sister Frances was born in 1922, and, according to family lore, Arthur Sr. supported the family as a bootlegger. The three later moved to Harlem, likely in the early 1930s, where their second surviving child Arthur was delivered in 1934, on West 112th Street and Lenox Avenue.[13] The family then moved several more times, to West 148th Street, then West 151st, and, when he was ten, he, his parents, and three younger siblings settled on West 143rd Street, where his dad worked as the superintendent for two adjacent apartment buildings. Arthur assisted his father in his work and helped the family further, per his account, by taking on what jobs he found: running errands for the bordello across the way, working in a butcher shop, and dancing for spare change at Lucky's bar nearby.[14]

The elementary and middle schools Mitchell attended were largely but not exclusively Black, since Harlem in the 1930s and 40s had more of a white, largely Irish, population than it did thereafter. Mitchell studied tap early on, and in 1948, at the recommendation of a counselor, he auditioned for and was accepted into the new High School for the Performing Arts, which took him out of Harlem to West 46th Street, between 6th and 7th Avenues, where the student body was largely white. Mitchell's first chosen migration was both into a new neighborhood and into a very different cultural environment in a barely integrated arts high school.

There he throve, studying with skilled teachers, polishing his entrepreneurial skills, and evolving his goals.

It was mostly Caucasian and a few minorities. ... I being a very enterprising young man, I became like an agent and I said "Okay, we need money." I got a pianist, I got [actress] Diana Sands, and I got a couple of dancers and we put on a show and I would advertise it ... people could book us. ... I always had this look and I've always loved clothing. ... Tom Nip was the name of the old vaudevillian who taught me tap dance. He'd say, "Kid, you got style." ... All the teachers kept saying to me, "You've got talent, but you're very elegant, you're very classy." And I said, "Okay." I was really tap dance and I didn't have any formal training like ballet and modern, but I studied with some of the great dance artists today. Bob Joffrey was at the school, Alwin Nikolais, and I would go and take classes with them. And that is where my whole horizon began to open up, 'cause I was finding another world other than where I came from.

In his senior year, in 1952, he appeared in a new production of Gertrude Stein and Virgil Thomson's *Four Saints in Three Acts* on Broadway, with a young Leontyne Price, and in June of that year they traveled to perform it in Paris. Mitchell traveled far in those years, in many realms at once: of education, racial context, cultural dynamics, personal success, and literal geography.

For his graduation piece, he performed what he describes as an intense ballet, called "Wail," set to Bartók.[15] Lincoln Kirstein, co-founder of the New York City Ballet with George Balanchine (and a friend of Moore's) saw the performance and offered him a scholarship to their School of American Ballet.

I got a scholarship to the School of American Ballet and I was like seventeen ... I decided ... if I wanted to be a performer I should get the technique. And I went to my first ballet and I fell madly in love with it, which was New York City Ballet. And I said, "Mitchell ... what could you do that would make you so good that people would hire you regardless of your skin color." And I said, "You can do jazz, you can do tap," sort of faking all of that, but I said "if I got the classical ballet training, that would make me unique." ... I realized I was starting everything very late. ... I started studying singing, voice and diction, anything to make myself better to be able to compete. And I'd had that little taste of going to Paris with "Four Saints in Three Acts." And something in my mind connected that, "Arthur, you've got to catch up to what other people have been studying since they were five, six, seven, eight, nine, ten."

He also studied not far from the High School for the Performing Arts at African American dance innovator Katherine Dunham's School of Dance on West 43rd Street, with Karel Shook (1920–85). Shook, a white dancer turned dance educator, was one of the few teachers to work extensively with Black dancers: Alvin Ailey, Mary Hinkson, Geoffrey Holder, and Carmen de Lavallade were among his students as well.

Mitchell was working extremely hard, but his immense dedication to catching up was interrupted early in 1953 by catastrophe. Although in later oral histories Mitchell obscured what happened, it is now clear that Mitchell Sr. was incarcerated after admitting to manslaughter related to an attempt to place a bet without paying up front, followed by a struggle and a fall, and to then decapitating and dismembering the body of the deceased bookie to hide the crime.[16] While Mitchell says in oral histories that his dad's jailing occurred in the mid-1940s, when he was ten or twelve, and that rather than being the killer, his dad took responsibility for someone else's crime in hopes of monetary gain, Mitchell Sr.'s file in New York City's Municipal Archives indicates it occurred in 1953, and that he was clearly responsible.[17] This event would have brought immense psychic and monetary stress to his whole family, just at the time a nineteen-year-old Mitchell was breaking into the world of ballet. Garafola suggests that Kirstein likely found a lawyer for Mitchell's dad, who convinced him to withdraw his initial Not Guilty plea to a charge of Murder and negotiate a Guilty plea to the lesser Manslaughter charge. A father's involvement in that combination of death and dismemberment would be traumatic and something anyone might want to try to hide—from oneself as well as others, and especially when embarking on a public career, as Mitchell was. The story was not widely covered in the press, and the details effectively disappeared for decades. From early days, Mitchell's transition to the celebrity phase of his life involved suppressing elements of his story. Moore too strategically omitted aspects of her and her family's history from her public presentation. In both cases, some documentation remains in the archives and can now be explored by scholars.

In 1954, Mitchell returned to Broadway in Harold Arlen's *House of Flowers*, with Diahann Carroll, Geoffrey Holder, Alvin Ailey, and Pearl Bailey. In 1955, at twenty-one, he joined the corps de ballet of the New York City Ballet as the first African American permanent member of the company.[18] Kirstein and Balanchine soon became role models and what he described as "surrogate fathers,"[19] making up for the one he'd effectively lost. He debuted as a soloist in 1956 in *Western Symphony* with Tanaquil le Clercq and became a principal dancer in 1962. For most of his tenure (he left in 1966, but returned for occasional roles through 1971), he was the only Black dancer in the company.

Moore described being impressed by Mitchell's performance in *Western Symphony*, when she saw it in 1957, in a letter to her friend Hildegarde Watson:

> The real feature of the evening was Arthur Mitchell, a Negro dancer (in dungarees & cowboy hat), in the Western Symphony. His resilience, his ease, his pleasant face, his joyous boundings and sudden dignity, as light [as] a bouncing ball; (besides the little things he did, backing away and fighting the air, winding it all up with a snappy stamp)—are formula, I know, but done with a grace and sense of timing that no old time cakewalker could surpass. (Jan. 25, 1957)

In her cakewalk reference, Moore connects Mitchell's work with the history of African American dance, valuing the addition that history brings to ballet in that moment—a view contrary to the fallacy that Mitchell regularly encountered, which held that Blacks were not physically or culturally suited to ballet. In a letter to Kirstein about the same performance of Western Symphony, she noted, "So very genuine; he has genius."

Also in 1957, Balanchine choreographed *Agon*, a twenty-two-minute modernist ballet, with startling twelve-tone music by Igor Stravinsky, exploring many tensions—as its name suggests. The dancers were

Figure 4.1: Arthur Mitchell and Diana Adams in *Agon* (1957).
Photo by Martha Swope © The New York Public Library for
the Performing Arts

costumed in offset black and white—the men in black tights and white t-shirts and the women in white tights and black leotards, like modern dancers, but *en pointe*. The dances manifest strains between the seventeenth-century ballet traditions the piece builds on and twentieth-century realities—of dance and also of post-World War II society (Figure 4.1).

While the piece has no specifically articulated plot, Mitchell's presence on the stage framed by the black and white costumes creates a race focus. Balanchine choreographed the *pas de deux*, the first pointedly interracial duet in American ballet, for Mitchell and southern ballerina Diana Adams, highlighting tensions around race and sexuality in every move, and paying careful attention to the juxtapositions of skin color.[20] Recognition of Mitchell's sexuality might have mitigated their duet's challenge to heterosexual taboos for some, but in so doing would only have introduced new complexities and challenges. Due to its intimate partnering of a Black man and a white woman, *Agon* was viewed as provocative.[21] All of this fraught history remains part of the core of this ballet, even when the dancers in later productions are all of one color. It is not clear whether Moore saw *Agon*. But she may well have, and she certainly would have known of it three years later.

Moore and Mitchell

In 1961, Moore was invited by Kirstein to write a poem about Mitchell to be included in the program for the *Midsummer Night's Dream* premiere in January 1962. Balanchine had choreographed the role of Puck specifically for Mitchell (Figure 4.2). All the principal dancers in that show were honored in separate poems by well-known poets, including W. H. Auden, James Merrill, Leroi Jones, Robert Lowell, and Kenneth Koch. Kirstein asked his friend Moore to write on Mitchell because he knew she was a fan. Here is her poem:

> **Arthur Mitchell**
> Slim dragonfly
> too rapid for the eye
>   to cage—
> contagious gem of virtuosity—
> make visible, mentality.
> Your jewels of mobility
>
>   reveal
>   and veil
>   a peacock-tail.

The last three lines suggest a peacock tail, trailing behind the body of the bird.

But images of Mitchell as Puck hint that the "reveal and veil" of the peacock tail may describe an active part of his costume: fabric hangs from

Figure 4.2: Arthur Mitchell as Puck (1962). Photo by Martha Swope
© The New York Public Library for the Performing Arts

his right shoulder, which he could *reveal* by pulling it out like a fan. If the "peacock-tail" was at Puck's shoulder, not behind him, it does nonetheless look like a sideways tail, as well as a dragonfly's wing, and clearly is made of a kind of veiling.[22] But Moore wrote and submitted the poem to Kirstein in November 1961, well in advance of the first performance, so unless she saw the costume sketches at that time, she would not have known of this veil. On the other hand, it is also possible that the costumer, the exotic Barbara Karinska, may have read the poem while designing and the costume may reflect its influence.

Soon after the premiere, Moore included mention of Mitchell in a second poem, "Blue Bug" (1962), in which she compares him to the eponymous polo pony and also to a dragonfly:

> bug brother to an Arthur
> Mitchell dragonfly,
>   speeding to left,
>   speeding to right; reversible

Where in the first poem Mitchell's continuous movement across space is implied, here it is named specifically (again in connection with Puck as choreographed by Balanchine)—and of course dancing operates as a form of ongoing migration, across a stage and through the world.[23]

Returning to migration of the biographical kind, I'll note that Mitchell's move into the ballet scene after high school was matched by a change of residential neighborhood—he left Harlem and moved downtown to 23rd Street in the 1950s to live with Karel Shook, his teacher, mentor, and later codirector of the Dance Theatre of Harlem, and they seem to have been romantically involved for some time.[24] By the 1960s Mitchell was living in an apartment on the Upper West Side, in the upper 70s, and eventually he bought a co-op at West 78th and Riverside Drive, where he lived until his death in 2018.

A number of Black theater people lived in the West 70s in the 1950s and 1960s, including Mitchell's friends Cicely Tyson, Harry Belafonte, and Diahann Carroll. The neighborhood was convenient to Lincoln Center and the theater district, welcomed Blacks, and, perhaps less overtly, was not unfriendly to gay people. A migration into a life as a gay adult man was also part of Mitchell's experience in the 1950s.

In a letter, Moore indicates that she is also aware of and perfectly comfortable with Mitchell's status as a gay man. Writing to Albert Gelpi in 1964, she described her poem for Mitchell as "just fanmail" about "the least affected and most graceful 'outright' fellow in the troupe."[25] "Outright" is in quotes in the letter and makes a specific statement about his sexuality—unusual for Moore, but she seems to expect Gelpi (a straight man) to recognize the term.

While Moore's biographers have to some degree noted that she had gay friends, the depth of the queerness of her community has yet to be explored. While she seems not to have had romantic relationships after some girl crushes in college, Moore herself had been gender fluid from childhood. And she had many gay friends from her earliest days in New York and thereafter, including long-term couples like Bryher and H.D.; Elizabeth Bishop and her various partners (beginning with Louise Crane); later, Crane and Victoria Kent; Kathrine [sic] Jones and Marcia Chamberlain; W. H. Auden and Chester Kallman; and her young friend Chester Page and his partner, as well as many less famous individuals and couples, gay and straight, who enjoyed her transvestite performance mode—including film director Wheaton Galentine and his partner, Pratt institute design professor Harold Leeds, to whose house on Perry Street in the West Village Moore repaired after attending the NBC Opera Theatre production of Mozart's *Magic Flute* with Auden's English libretto on January 15, 1956. The visit is recorded in her 1956 appointment book: "7:15 69 Perry Street | Harold Leeds Wheaton Galentine | Loren Lloyd, Gertrude Flynn | Margaret Miller | G: 'An entrance!' tricorne | and cape."[26]

Lincoln Kirstein was another of these friends. Her friendship with him gave her special access to New York's ballet culture—as well as quite a few tickets and dinner invitations. She was also friends with Kirstein's wife Fidelma as well as his long-time lover Dan Maloney—the trio lived together for several years and Moore visited and went to events with them often, as their letters, some signed with "Love to Fidelma and Dan," attest.

Such groupings were not news to Moore in the 1950s. Kirstein also maintained a lifelong friendship with the art photographer George Platt Lynes (1907–55), with whom he had been at school,[27] and who took several iconic images of Moore, including the one in which she poses as George Washington in cape and tricorne with gloves.[28]

For the ten years from 1925 to 1935, Lynes, like Kirstein, was also part of a threesome: with Moore's longtime friends Glenway Wescott and Monroe Wheeler, the latter having published her long poem "Marriage" in his *Manikin* series in 1923. In 1935, Wheeler began work at the Museum of Modern Art, eventually becoming Director of Exhibitions, and, until Moore was bedridden in 1969, they attended countless events at the museum and around town together and often dined at one another's homes.

My point in outlining this history is to clarify that Moore was not being judgmental in seeing Mitchell as "outright," but descriptive—and even affirmative. In another letter to Kirstein, she makes a point of connecting herself and Mitchell, referring to him as a Blackamoor and signing herself off as likewise "A Moor," without the final E. Race, gender, and sexuality overlap here in ways I explore in *Apparition of Splendor*, and about which others will have more to say. That overlap offers a segue into examining Mitchell's second migration.

Migration to the Closet

If Mitchell's "outrightness" was recognized while he was with the NYCB, and hanging out with the ballet crowd there, it has since been erased from all public records. That is most likely due to the change in cultural location he made when, upon the assassination of Martin Luther King in 1968, he decided to travel back uptown to found the Dance Theatre of Harlem. He had previously formed dance schools in Washington, DC, and in Brazil, but the death of King convinced him it was important to make change at home. He invited Karel Shook, who had relocated to the Netherlands as ballet master for the Dutch National Ballet, to join him as a co-founder. Together they worked to give young Black dancers a chance to explore and excel at ballet, recognizing that "black children, given the same opportunity as white children, could be great dancers."[29] And they succeeded—the Dance Theatre of Harlem tours to sold out audiences to this day.

This decision led to Mitchell's second migration across Manhattan, this time moving back uptown—although he returned there mainly for work, not to live himself. He also visited with his family there, as he had all along—eventually buying his mother a brownstone across the street from the Dance Theatre of Harlem building on West 152nd Street, not far from where they'd lived in his childhood.

Either part of that migration/transition—to working with children or to moving uptown to a community most open to a straight-presenting man—could singly have pushed him into the closet, and certainly together they would have constituted a strong shove. The oral histories he recorded make no mention of any romantic life, and no inconvenient questions are asked. Though his lack of any female partners might have raised questions among those around him, he clearly made a concerted effort no longer to present as "outright," or effeminate. This might be perceived as necessary as he worked to engage young Harlem men of all persuasions (and their parents) to challenge stereotypes and embrace ballet. And it echoes the similar kinds of cultural pressure brought to bear on Alvin Ailey, strikingly parallel to Mitchell in the world of modern dance, as a gay man who kept his personal involvements secret, but who is at least acknowledged as gay on his Wikipedia page, where both Mitchell and Shook are not.

The New York Mitchell was born into was not the accepting Village that Moore entered in 1918. He was born just after New York's enactment in and around 1933 of regulations that "explicitly prohibited gay men and women from gathering in licensed public establishments, and ... systematized the exclusion of homosexuality from the public sphere."[30] Those rules emerged to quell what had been an increasingly bold gay presence in the nineteen teens and twenties. World War II again loosened some restrictions, as hordes of men came into close contact in the army, and the world had other things to worry about. But in the 1950s, the strictures came back strong—and it was against that backdrop that the young Mitchell danced his challenge to claims that Blacks could not "do" ballet and to anti-miscegenation laws, while complicating it with an actual lack of romantic interest in the women he was partnering.

In the 1950s and 60s, before Stonewall, New York was complex for gay men and women—and while the world of ballet offered an accepting enclave, that barely offset their precarity in most other spaces. Of course, Mitchell's precarity was doubled in being both the only Black man and a gay man in the New York City Ballet world while he was there.

It makes sense on moving back to Harlem as a kind of businessman, for whom respectability would be a key factor in attracting both students and donors, that Mitchell would become, at least in the public eye, a celibate, enabled to forward new ideas and make change by restraining his own self-expression, negotiating precarity. In that respect, he resembles the also celibate Moore, although for different but perhaps related reasons. From the start she understood the social calculation—the "mentality"—that was also a part of Mitchell's physical artistry, and she had made her own calculations about what could or couldn't be shown over the decades. Her oblique poems were "armored" against intrusive eyes from early days, although they featured their armoring in a way that called attention to itself, revealing and veiling her difference simultaneously, and actively combating bias against female authority and alternativity of all kinds. Similarly, Mitchell was able to "reveal and veil" his challenge to bias—clearly demonstrating his opposition to race bias, but veiling the challenge that he nevertheless made to anti-gay bias, and which was no doubt recognized by many in his orbit.

Migration toward a Better World

I will close with a quotation from another letter, this one from Kirstein to Moore right before the *Midsummer Night's Dream* premiere—in which he cites Mitchell:

> I got back from Russia a month ago, and have been trying to catch up, more or less, ever since. You will be happy to know that Arthur Mitchell had a stupendous personal success [in] the Mozart "Divertimento" when Johnathan Watts hurt his back; he never thought he was a "classic" dancer, but Balanchine worked at him, and he did it very well; I said, Arthur, you looked VERY well: He said "Well; I said to myself: Arthur: be elegant; think White.["] And after the crowds in the Lensoviet Hall in Leningrad shouted themselves hoarse: Meet- ell; Meeetch-elll; I saw him come back from his curtain bow; he said : honey; I'd be a good dancer even if I was WHAIT. In a steam-bath in Khiev, where he went to get warm; it was so cold outside, his skin was the marvel of the Ukraine; he was asked if he were not indeed … from … Ghana. He said to the interpreter: My grandmammy may have, but I'm from Old Noo Yawk.[31]

There are many migrations embedded in this telling: of a young New Yorker from Harlem conquering the cultural centers of Europe; of a young Black man being absorbed into an art form marked as white only, but which he transforms by entering; of an ancestor suffering through the

Middle Passage; and, at another level, Mitchell's skillful migration of affect and meaning through irony, from his apparently more deferential "be elegant, think White" to his franker valuation of his own skill and undercutting of the assumption that white dancers are better at ballet, in the comment, "Honey, I'd be a good dancer even if I was *White*," pronounced in a way to emphasize his difference.

Moore shares Kirstein's delight in that reversal. In her reply to this letter, Moore too savors Mitchell's in-control archness, asking in a handwritten addition to her typescript, "*Was he ever just a stripling in a ballet?*" The implied answer would seem to be "No."

For both Mitchell and Moore, migrations across geographies, cultures, economies, and contexts brought them both a high degree of canniness about negotiating the sharing of alternative perspectives early on, so they were never "just striplings." It propelled them to further migrations across decades of pro-democracy activism. Both of them moved across diverse communities within New York City, communities that sat close together but were nonetheless quite distinct and distant from one another. And each of these artists became a bridge, opening commerce across divides. While documentation of some parts of their lives was obscured in their public presentations, they both modeled the possibility and value of alternative perspectives and voices—in the combination of what they accomplished in the world and the meticulous style with which they carried it out. In that respect, in spite of pressures to obscure difference, they were both consistently "outright."

CHAPTER FIVE

"His Shield"
Prester John, Amphibiousness, and Black Fugitivity in Marianne Moore's Haile Selassie Poems

Ryan Tracy

Haile Selassie in Moore's Poetry

The Ethiopian Emperor Haile Selassie (1892–1975), also known as Ras Tafari, was a figure of profound importance to Marianne Moore (1887–1972). For the greater part of her adult life, Moore followed Haile Selassie's public persona, his belief system, his attempts to modernize Ethiopia, and, most importantly, his struggle against colonial aggression by fascist Italy in the 1930s and 40s. Selassie appears in at least three of Moore's poems, "In Distrust of Merits" (1943), "His Shield" (1944), and "Leonardo Da Vinci's" (1959). In "In Distrust of Merits," one of Moore's most anthologized poems, Moore briefly alludes to Selassie as a "black imperial lion of the Lord" who must "be joined" to other nations if cyclical violence wrought by war is to end.[1] In "Leonardo Da Vinci's," Moore meditates on sovereignty by connecting the "Leo" in Da Vinci's first name and the "lion" in his unfinished painting *St. Jerome and the Lion*.[2] At the end of Moore's blazon to the Renaissance artist, she turns to another lion—"Lion Haile Selassie"—beckoning him to "blaze on" "with household lions as symbol of sovereignty," a reference to the domesticated lions that Selassie kept as pets in his royal palace in Addis Ababa.[3]

In the poem "His Shield," which I will discuss later in this essay, Moore conjoins Selassie with the medieval legend of Prester John, a mythical figure who by the seventeenth century came to be represented by Europeans as both Ethiopian and racially Black.[4] This conjunction, both historical and poetic, asks us to reconsider Moore's lifelong evocation of amphibiousness, and amphibious skin—found in her published poetry and writing notebooks—as a racialized metaphor for fugitive being in the world. Moreover, I will show that Moore's interest in Selassie kept her attuned to domestic and global struggles for Black liberation insofar as Moore's representations of Selassie endorse contemporaneous African American celebrations of the Ethiopian monarch as a sovereign figure who embodied the promise of freedom for Black people around the world.

Selassie ascended to the Abyssinian throne in 1930 as Africa's only indigenous sovereign. He would be the last ruling monarch of the Solomonic Dynasty, which had claimed the Hebraic King Solomon as a patriarch for seven hundred years.[5] Selassie's reign was notoriously interrupted by Italy's 1935 incursion into Ethiopia. Italy's military aggression broke the League of Nation's injunction against armed belligerence between member nations, while threatening to complete Europe's colonial domination of the African continent. Selassie fled Ethiopia in 1936, taking refuge in England and rejecting Mussolini's proposal to allow him to return as a puppet of the fascist government.[6] From England, Selassie lobbied Western nations to support Ethiopia's liberation. Selassie would be restored to the Abyssinian throne five years later, in 1941, after Allied forces drove out the occupying Italian military. Selassie reigned until 1974, when a communist military coup deposed him, putting an end to the Solomonic dynasty, whose rule had given Ethiopia its sense of national identity for seven centuries.

Importantly, Selassie's celebrity—as the Black leader of a Christian nation in Eastern Africa, and the only African nation to have successfully repelled European colonization—gained widespread traction among people of African descent in the Americas, inspiring the Ras Tafari movement among Black Jamaicans, as well as a groundswell of grass-roots support among African American communities, especially during the Italian occupation.[7] While African Americans had developed an identification with Ethiopia via biblical references since at least the eighteenth century—an identification referred to by scholars as "Ethiopianism" when expressed in literary and visual culture—Ethiopia's 1896 victory over Italy at the Battle of Adwa, a triumph that put an end both to the first Italo-Abyssinian war and the decade-long European "scramble for Africa," imbued this identification with an anti-colonial register, as evidenced by the numerous "Abyssinian" churches that sprang up in African American communities at the turn of the century.[8] As Robert A. Hill has pointed out, by the time of the 1935 invasion, African American communities had developed a "deep psychological and ideological investment" in Ethiopia's struggles against colonialism.[9] Consequently, the 1935 crisis provoked "a remarkably unified African American response."[10] Moreover, the threat Italy posed to the Solomonic monarchy in the 1890s and 1930s resonated with the history of African American representations of slavery as a fall from premodern African aristocracies, such as the one recounted by Olaudah Equiano in his *Interesting Narrative* (1789). As Jennifer Wilson has recently argued, "many African Americans saw Italy's military campaign [in 1935] as a direct attack on black sovereignty by a white imperial power."[11] The loss of individual sovereignty under white supremacy therefore cannot be dissociated from a certain loss of state, or national, sovereignty.

To be clear, Selassie's reception among African Americans was uneven and contested, in part, as Nadia Nurhussein has argued, because "the desire to celebrate the grandiosity of a historic black empire" often conflicted with Black nationalism's "commitment to democratic ideals."[12] Imperial Ethiopia's continued practice of domestic slavery and Selassie's status as a monarch could create an impression of the Emperor out of step with everyday African American struggles. Langston Hughes's poem "Broadcast on Ethiopia," published in 1936, in fact offers an ambivalent portrayal of the Ethiopian sovereign. Hughes—a later in life friend of Moore's—imagines Selassie as an unprepared and somewhat uninspiring leader, "with his slaves, his dusky wiles, / His second-hand planes like a child's."[13] Yet Hughes's 1966 poem, "Emperor Haile Selassie" attests to the enduring value of Selassie as a symbolic figure of hope for African Americans and Black people worldwide. In the latter poem, Selassie appears as someone who, although a king, became "a symbol ... on which men who are neither King of Kings nor Lions of Judah" could "feed their pride" and nourish the undying dream of freedom.[14] This and other poems dedicated to Selassie demonstrate the "sense of profound diasporic connection" Selassie inspired among African American writers.[15]

Reciprocally, Selassie held a sympathetic view of African American struggles against domestic forms of white supremacy during the Jim Crow era. According to Robert Alexander Findlay, Selassie used his first diplomatic visit to the United States in 1954 to connect with African American communities and to acknowledge the contributions African American aid groups had made to Ethiopia's fight against colonization.[16] Though Selassie's visit was designed to celebrate Ethiopia's alliance with the United States during the Korean War, the State Department, cognizant of Selassie's celebrity among Black communities, did its best to manhandle Selassie's public appearances and to downplay his symbolic status as a Black sovereign touring a racially segregated America. Findlay argues that despite the State Department's intervening, Selassie's tour created "a new space for black Americans to debate Jim Crow laws, desegregation, and the oppression of peoples of 'color' worldwide" because it had "symbolically linked desegregation [in America] with African independence and decolonization."[17] Moore's Selassie poems draw their impassioned energy from this context.

It must be said that Moore's admiration for Selassie was unusual for a white American. America's mainstream press tended to indulge in racist caricatures of Selassie, even as American political leaders were attempting to align themselves with him.[18] Moore's celebratory, respectful representations of Selassie markedly depart from this tendency. Nor can I think of a single white peer of Moore's—other than Ezra Pound—who acknowledged the seriousness of the Italo-Abyssinian war, and the importance of Ethiopia's fate for the world of nations. As I have suggested, in terms of literary categorization, Moore's Selassie poems are best considered in the context of contemporaneous African American literary responses to the 1935 invasion of Ethiopia, such as Langston Hughes's aforementioned poems, Richard Bruce Nugent's experimental short story "Pope Pious the Only" (1937), George Schuyler's *Ethiopian Stories* (1935–39), Melvin Tolson's "The Bard of Addis Ababa" (1944), and *Amiable with Big Teeth* (ca. 1941), Claude McKay's recently unearthed novelistic account of

Harlem politics during the Italian occupation.[19] Put another way, the only other American creative writers devoting sustained attention to Selassie from 1935 onward would likely have been Black.

Such a claim puts pressure on scholars of Moore to be more willing not only to read for representations of racial blackness in Moore's poetry, but to consider the potential significance of Moore's poetry—and the ubiquitous theme of resistance to capture, or what I will call *amphibious fugitivity*—for Black American readers. "In Distrust of Merits," for instance, has rarely been read for its allusion to Selassie, and the meaning that that allusion would have had for African Americans confronting racial discrimination in America. Even when scholars have brought up this allusion, insufficient attention has been paid to the racial differences that produce different kinds of reading practices for differently positioned readers.[20] Bernard Engel, for example, is right to connect Moore's mention of Selassie in "In Distrust of Merits" to the anti-racist platitudes (or "vows") that appear in the middle of the poem.[21] But he strays when he claims that Moore's idealism linking war and everyday racial and religious relations is "naïve," and when he argues that "Neither the troops nor Roosevelt and Churchill could be said to have had in mind improved racial and religious relations."[22] Only in "hindsight," he avers, "[can we] say that the war did in fact bring home to public and politicians some recognition of the horrors of racial and ethnic prejudice."[23] We might question exactly for whom "hindsight" was necessary in order to "bring home" the horrors of racial and ethnic prejudice. Likewise, military service has long been a highly fraught but nevertheless important pillar of African Americans' struggle to be recognized as full citizens. The historical desire for state recognition for Black Americans through military service complicates Engel's claim that "the troops," in general, did not consider World War II a theater for improving race relations at home. Moreover, many Black troops, such as those who volunteered to fight in the Abraham Lincoln Brigade during Spain's Civil War (the United States government barred Black Americans from fighting in Ethiopia), viewed their participation in the global military conflicts of the 1930s and 40s as a fight against antiblack imperialism overseas.[24] Marianne Moore's allusions to Selassie, then, are aligned with the Emperor's reception among people of the African diaspora living in the Americas insofar as armed resistance to colonial aggression—or "fighting, fighting, fighting," in Moore's words—was directed toward a displacement of racism on a global scale.[25]

While this is not the place to offer a detailed account of Moore's reception among African American readers, it is worth underscoring Linda Leavell's claim that "Moore's concern for the racially oppressed did not go unnoticed by African Americans."[26] Such considerations may shed light, then, on why "In Distrust of Merits" was selected—twenty-five years after it was published—to be read by Sidney Poitier on an episode of *The Tonight Show* in 1968 the week it was hosted by Jamaican-American calypso singer and Civil Rights activist Harry Belafonte, whose mother was a Rastafarian.[27] I speculate that the poem's allusion to Selassie/Ras Tafari as the "black imperial lion of the lord" had a lot to do with this momentous cultural event. In other words, it wasn't just that "In Distrust of Merits" was an anti-war poem, but a poem that alluded to a still-reigning Haile Selassie, while articulating the role antiblack racism played in the continuance of global conflict, that made it an obvious choice to be read on this historic week of Afrocentric American television.[28]

Moore's archive at the Rosenbach Museum and Library in Philadelphia supports my contention that Moore took special interest in Selassie's life and political career, and that she was aware of his function as a pan-African symbol of Black liberation. Selassie ephemera in Moore's archive is primarily located in source materials for the poems "His Shield" and "Leonardo da Vinci's," the latter of which includes an autograph note on which Moore transcribed Selassie's "3 Priorities" of reform from a *Christian Science Monitor* article from 1950 (Figure 5.1), and two undated and uncaptioned images of the Ethiopian runner Abebe Bikila, who became the first Black African to win an Olympic gold medal by running the marathon barefoot at the 1960 Olympics in Rome, and by doing so provided a symbolic repudiation of Italy's aggression against Ethiopia in the late 1930s.[29] The images appear to be clipped from a 1965 *Sports Illustrated* profile on Bikila, entitled, "The Number Two Lion in the Land of Sheba."[30] The photos of Bikila evidence Moore's enduring concern for the fate of Ethiopia—six years after the publication of "Leonardo Da Vinci's"—while adding a global dimension to Moore's documented admiration for Black athletes.[31]

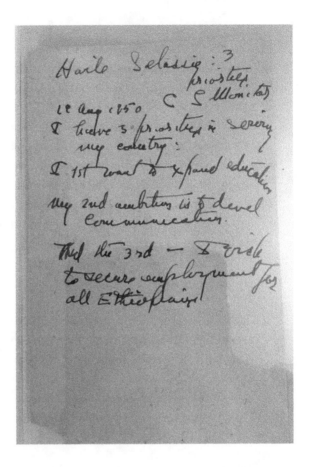

Figure 5.1:
Moore's transcription of Haile Selassie's "3 Priorities"

The source materials for "His Shield" include *Haile Selassie: Emperor of Ethiopia* (1936), a biography of Selassie published during the early years of the Italian occupation and written by Princess Asfa Yilma (alias Hannah Holland), a "distant relative" of Selassie, and an associated vertical file of interfoliata, consisting of clippings from newspapers and magazines, many of which post-date the 1943 composition of "His Shield."[32] (As I will discuss later, Asfa Yilma's historical accounts of the Solomonic Dynasty and the Prester John legend will play a major role in Moore's representation of Selassie in "His Shield.")

Importantly, Moore's archive demonstrates that Moore's interest in Selassie predates the Italian invasion of Ethiopia and the biography of Selassie she purchased shortly thereafter. A photograph clipping of Selassie's son-in-law on a diplomatic visit to the United States in the summer of

1933 can be found in Moore's archive in the subject folder "Africa and the Middle East."³³ This is the earliest Selassie-related clipping I have found in Moore's archive. The caption of the photograph mentions that Prince Desta Demtu was visiting the United States out of reciprocity for the U.S. delegation that traveled to Ethiopia for Selassie's coronation in 1930. Thus, it seems likely that it was Selassie's internationally celebrated coronation that first drew Moore's attention to the Ethiopian sovereign and was the root of her admiration for him as a Black leader.

Italy's 1935 invasion of Ethiopia, therefore, would have concerned Moore insofar as Selassie's sovereignty, and the political autonomy of Ethiopia, were under threat. Fiona Green has recently noted that Moore transcribed a news report about the invasion in one of her notebooks while visiting her brother Warner in Virginia:

> 4 July 1935
> Heavy Losses in Ethiopian Fight. Ethiopia to Concede Nothing to Mussolini, Haile Selassie Says. Emperor Signed Article Charging Italy with Arming Colonies and Provoking Trouble by Frontier Activities. …
> "Concerning an Armed Italian Protectorate over Ethiopia, an old proverb says 'One shouldn't sell the lion's skin before killing the lion.'"³⁴

Though Green credits Ezra Pound with stoking Moore's interest in the invasion, I think Green is perhaps giving too much credit to Pound. As I have mentioned, Moore's interest in Selassie predates the Italian invasion. Moreover, the transcription about the invasion in Moore's notebook suggests that Moore's representations of Selassie after 1935 are informed by her understanding of the Emperor as an African sovereign under siege by colonial violence—a fugitive "black imperial lion" whose proverbial fierceness might prove a foil to European imperialism. In other words, Moore is not necessarily taking cues from Pound, who strenuously defended Italy's invasion of Ethiopia in radio broadcasts at the time.³⁵ Rather, Moore's poetic affirmations of Selassie's right to maintain his "household" "sovereignty," and to protect Ethiopia from Italian aggression, might better be read as her tacit yet forceful disagreement with Pound's pro-imperial stance.

As I have argued, Selassie-related clippings in Moore's archive repeatedly frame him as an important Black figure both in international politics *and* in America's domestic racial conflicts. Moore was living in New York when Selassie's entourage rolled through the city on the northeast leg of the tour on May 25, 1954. I have not been able to determine whether Moore was able to see him in person, or, as people still do, take to the streets to watch as diplomatic cavalcades roll past. But the presence of six articles in Moore's archive clipped between 1954 and 1955 suggests that Selassie's visit reanimated Moore's interest in the Ethiopian sovereign. In fact, the majority of the clippings Moore kept about Selassie date from the time of his 1954 visit and years following. It should be remembered that the mainstream, or white, press's coverage of Selassie indulged in prejudicial stereotyping, often making fun of his hair and slight stature.[36] However, the articles Moore kept are by and large positive in their view of Selassie as an "autocrat" who had nonetheless prioritized social reform since the time of his coronation.[37] The 1950 clipping of a *Christian Science Monitor* article is not insignificant (Figure 5.2). According to Findlay, the *Monitor*—one of Moore's favorite journals—was rare among mainstream American publications in the way it did not portray Selassie in overtly racist terminology.[38] Selassie gave an "exclusive" interview to the *Monitor* for the article published on August 19, 1950, in which he laid out the aforementioned "3 Priorities" that Moore transcribed onto a notecard.

Moore collected clippings about Selassie and Ethiopia until at least 1965, and though most of this coverage portrayed Selassie in a positive light, at least one article gives a negative report of Selassie's reform efforts. Published in the *New York Times* in 1961, one year following an unsuccessful *coup d'état*, the article reports on the state of "feudalism" that continued under Selassie's rule, criticizing the way political power continued to lie with Selassie's family, the military, and the church.[39] The article also cites a United Nations report that Ethiopia registered the third worst literacy rate in Africa, noting that the "rank and file" of Ethiopia's "18 million subjects" are "illiterate and inhabiting mud huts," a situation the article deprecatingly describes as "still living as in the Middle Ages." Moore was thus likely aware of Selassie's limitations as a sovereign. The omission of any such critique from her poetic representations of him certainly leaves a racially romanticized impression of the Ethiopian leader.[40] But it

Figure 5.2: Photograph of Haile Selassie from item in *The Christian Science Monitor*. Moore's clipping of this article is held at the Rosenbach Museum and Library

is a romanticized vision informed by historical realities related to Selassie's reign, namely his brief status, between 1935 and 1941, as a fugitive king in exile from his own kingdom.

Fugitivity, Amphibiousness, and the African American Imaginary

To help think through the racialized resonance of fugitivity and flight across Moore's work, and her poetic representations of Haile Selassie in "His Shield," I turn to poet and scholar Fred Moten, whose thought traverses the fleeting and liberatory dimensions of blackness, or Black racial embodiment. In his monograph, *In the Break: The Aesthetics of the Black Radical Tradition*, Moten defines blackness as a "freedom drive" that exists prior to its subjection to, or encounter with, modern European economies of race.[41] For Moten, the fugitive impulse of blackness can be thought of as "the ontological and historical priority of resistance to power and objection to subjection," or, "the freedom drive that animates black performances."[42] Moten plays on the Freudian resonance of "drive," but sidesteps *eros* and *thanatos*, marking a drive for *freedom* that gives motion to embodied blackness. Elsewhere, Moten will refer to this animating drive for freedom as "fugitivity."[43] This fugitive drive for freedom does not simply follow the event of subjection, enslavement, policing, or the desire of the *slave driver* to abuse and enslave. Rather, Moten asks us to imagine an animating drive for liberation—something uncapturable, fugitive— that precedes the historical subjection of blackness by European cultures, both in the Americas and on the African continent. In this sense, Black fugitivity, as Moten imagines it, should be thought of as a racialized ontological inhabitation with global dimensions.

However, Moten notes that the term *fugitive* draws its rhetorical force from American political and racial history. Turning to Nathaniel Mackey's writing about the Black Arts poet Amiri Baraka, Moten explains that "Mackey speaks, with regard to Baraka ... of 'a well-known, resonant history of African-American fugitivity and its ... relationship to enslavement and persecution.'"[44] Indeed, the figure of the "fugitive slave" dominated American racial politics from the nation's founding, culminating in its legal instantiation with the "Fugitive Slave Act" of 1793 and its brutal reinforcement in 1850. During this period, the figure of the "fugitive slave" found its literary expression in the numerous autobiographical narratives published during the abolitionist era—narratives that dramatize scenes of flight that toggle between land and water routes, such as those found in works by Harriet Jacobs, Frederick Douglass, and William and Ellen Craft.⁴⁵ Harriet Beecher Stowe's fictionalized depiction of the fugitive slave Eliza running across a frozen Ohio River is perhaps one of the most famous of such scenes, demonstrating the power that the figure of the fugitive slave had to impress the imagination of white writers as well.

Here, I want to emphasize the way that the scenes of Black fugitivity in the American literary tradition Moten harkens to in his discussion of the "freedom drive" depict, time and again, land and water as avenues of trans-terrestrial escape and opportune locations for subterfuge and evasion. In other words, Moten's ontological notion of the freedom drive should be thought in relation to a topological *amphibiousness* that enables fugitive acts. Though primarily associated with a land–water binary (i.e., the *amphibian* class of animals), there is nothing in the etymology of the word "amphibian" that restricts its meaning to these two elements. According to the *Oxford English Dictionary*, "amphibian" derives from the Greek word ἀμφίβιον, which combines the roots *amphi*, meaning "both," with *bios*, or "life," connoting the ability to live in two opposing worlds.⁴⁶ Thus, the theme of flying that appears in the African American literary canon, such as "All God's Chillen Had Wings," or the "caged bird" metaphor dating back at least to Paul Laurence Dunbar's poem "Sympathy" (1899), can be read as expressions of *amphibious fugitivity*.⁴⁷ The countless scenes of flight and fleeing in the African American imaginary index trans-terrestrial subterfuge and escape as an indispensable if fraught strategy for survival in the project of Black liberation. In short, within American literary culture leading up to and contemporaneous with Moore's writing, scenes of amphibious flight would have been disproportionately associated with African American literature, or, in the case of *Uncle Tom's Cabin*, white literature featuring enslaved and persecuted Black characters.

Amphibiousness, and its association with escape (or flight), appears to have been an early poetic preoccupation of Moore's. The poem "Ennui," published in 1909 in Bryn Mawr's *The Lantern* while Moore was still a student there, first extols the mysterious powers of amphibiousness, which Moore records as the central occupation of a "curious wish." The poem, supposedly written by Moore during class, portrays the scene of a student succumbing to the relatable desire to be elsewhere:

Ennui

He often expressed
A curious wish,
To be interchangeably
Man and fish;
To nibble the bait
Off the hook,
Said he,
And then slip away
Like a ghost,
In the sea.[48]

The poem's student daydreams of an alternative mode of inhabitation that might allow him to flirt with capture, but ultimately to escape it.

Many of Moore's readers will likely recognize this amphibious "curious wish" from the mature poem "The Plumet Basilisk" (1933), in which the Central American lizard is described as embodying "mythology's wish to be interchangeably man and fish."[49] First published in 1933, "The Plumet Basilisk" largely celebrates an emerald-green lizard that can live on land and run on water. *Basilisk* derives from the diminutive form of βασιλεύς, the Greek word for "king," which Moore plays on when she depicts the "ruler of Rivers, Lakes, and Seas" retreating across land, air, and water: "He runs, he flies, he swims, to get to / his basilica."[50] Though Moore salutes the Plumet Basilisk (or "aquatic flying / lizard-fairy") as a "living firework," she does not portray him as a faultless conqueror, but as a fugitive "king," who succeeds by evading capture.[51] Thus, the poem, and its central "amphibious falling dragon," underscores the links between amphibiousness, fugitivity, and sovereignty that, I argue, will imbue Moore's representation of Haile Selassie in "His Shield."[52]

"His Shield" / Haile Selassie

"His Shield" is Marianne Moore's most extensive poetic meditation on Haile Selassie. The poem represents Selassie as both racially Black and a fugitive monarch who was able to maintain his sovereignty and "freedom" by paradoxically "relinquishing" his throne. The poem thus allegorizes

Selassie's narrative of flight-and-fight—his exile in 1936 and his militarized return in 1941. However, Selassie's image is also fugitive in the sense that Moore encodes him indirectly in her poem, paralleling the indirect strategy of amphibious resistance that Moore idealizes. For instance, the anagram that opens the poem—His Shield / Haile Selassie—although incomplete, still suggests that Selassie is the animating though unnamed figure behind the work.[53] In this sense, Moore produces, in a poetic register, the fleeting, momentary presence of a fugitive subject. Importantly, Moore's flighty representation of Selassie in "His Shield" is aided by a medieval legend about a Black Christian king who was thought to have reigned over an "unconquerable" land of unicorns and lions, thwarting the fires of subjugation with robes made of amphibious salamander skin. Known to Europeans, and eventually Ethiopians, as "Prester John," the legend would serve as a source for Moore, not only in her oblique representation of Haile Selassie in "His Shield," but also, as I will show, Moore's copious representations of amphibiousness as a fugitive inhabitation of the world.

First published in 1944, "His Shield" responds to the context of the accelerated military armament and head-to-head political opposition that characterized World War II and the decades of Cold War nuclear proliferation that would follow. Moore opens the poem by introducing a bevy of "battle-dressed" creatures—the hedgehog, porcupine, echidna, and rhinoceros:

> **His Shield**
> The pin-swin or spine-swine
> > (the edgehog miscalled hedgehog) with all his edges out,
> > echidna and echinoderm in distressed-
> pin-cushion thorn-fur coats, the spiny pig or porcupine,
> > the rhino with horned snout—
> > everything is battle-dressed.[54]

The poem's emphasis on spiny skin as a defensive shield departs from Moore's other "armored" poems, such as "The Pangolin" (1936) and "Nevertheless" (1943), in which the poet more or less celebrates the self-defensive capacities of thorny creatures as qualities of strength otherwise overlooked by common prejudices. Here, though, Moore seems prepared to criticize animals that, more ready-to-wound than willing-to-be-wounded, pose a threat not only to whatever they perceive as threatening to them, but also to themselves. Armed to the quill, the creatures enumerated at the beginning of "His Shield" are primed to engage in violent conflict.

In juxtaposition to these belligerent beasts, Moore introduces an amphibious means of sartorial self-defense—the "salamander-skin" of Prester John. "Pig-fur won't do," writes Moore:

> I'll wrap
>   myself in salamander-skin like Presbyter John.
>   A lizard in the midst of flames, a firebrand
> that is life, asbestos-eyed asbestos-eared, with tattooed nap
>   and permanent pig on
>   the instep; he can withstand
> fire and won't drown.[55]

Moore's menagerie of "ironshod" animals is displaced with the "firebrand" figure of an amphibious Prester John. Or, rather, inserting herself into the poem, Moore suggests that we follow her in taking Prester John—and his salamander-like ability to resist water and "fire" (here, I think we should hear the double meaning; fire as *flame*, and fire as *gunfire*, or attack with artillery, mortar, words, etc.)—as a model. To be "asbestos-eyed" and "asbestos-eared" suggests fire-retardant senses of perception, and, by extension, an ability to make sound judgments in times of "distress." By inserting herself into the poem, Moore takes a principled stance against spur-like weaponry, allying herself instead with "Presbyter" John (an alternation that is likely an allusion to her own Presbyterianism) and his attempt to shield himself as a means of fighting, rather than be egged into direct combat.

Prester John's legend dates back to the European Middle Ages. In the twelfth century, following the failure of the crusades to win back the Middle East for Roman Christendom, rumors began spreading about a Christian sovereign who supposedly ruled with an emerald scepter over a vast kingdom beyond the Mongol and Islamic worlds, which had by that time spread through Asia, the Middle East, and North Africa, effectively cutting off Europeans from trade routes and paths of cultural transmission to India and the Far East.[56] By the fifteenth century, after European explorers began to make and chronicle their contacts with the ruling Solomonic dynasty, Prester John was believed to have ruled over Ethiopia. The migration of the legend's kingdom from the "Indies" to Ethiopia turned out to be prescient. Despite the dubious European origins of the legend, Abyssinia had indeed been an isolated Christian kingdom for nearly a millennium. We might think of Prester John's land—to repurpose one of Moore's most well-known aphorisms about poetry—as *an imaginary kingdom with a real king in it.*

Early in the legend's history, a letter purportedly written by "Prester John" began circulating across Christian Europe. The letter, written in the first person and addressed to the Emperor of Byzantium (who was then in conflict with the church in Rome) presents the image of a sovereign ruler over a utopian realm with rivers overflowing with emeralds, happy and loyal subjects, and fantastical fauna commonly found in the medieval European imaginary, such as unicorns, dragons, and fireproof salamanders—the kind of myth-making animals Moore found so appealing.[57] The king boastfully presents himself as waited on by a staff of kings and possessing far greater wealth than the king of Byzantium. However, despite this superlative state of affairs, the king self-deprecatingly assumes the diminutive title Presbyter, or *elder,* indicating his place as a peer among Christian brothers.[58] The letter also mentions fire-retardant royal garments made of salamander silk that Moore mentions in "His Shield," and that she uses as a metaphor for Haile Selassie's fugitive strategy of indirect resistance.

The ethical and tactical question of how to defend oneself against aggression was at the center of Selassie's own response to Italy's attempt to colonize Ethiopia. Selassie's decision to flee at the beginning of the conflict, rather than remain in Ethiopia, was certainly a strategy that prioritized the self-preservation of the sovereign over the need to demonstrate heroism in battle. In fact, the decision drew criticism from some African American critics, such as the flamboyant Jamaican American leader Marcus Garvey.[59] Yet it was also a strategy that, in the long run, allowed Selassie to achieve victory and return to his throne, securing

Ethiopia's independence. Notably, Moore's truncation of the letters *h* and *s* throughout the first stanza of "His Shield" is emblematic of Haile Selassie's—or "His"—shielded, fugitive presence in the poem. The linguistic play between "hedgehog" and "edgehog" and "spine" and "pin" performs the play between shielding and revealing as stratagems of combat.

Moore refers to this perspicacious shielding as Prester John/Haile Selassie's amphibiously coded "humility":

> the inextinguishable
> > salamander styled himself but presbyter. His shield
> was his humility.[60]

Moore drew these lines from Asfa Yilma's account of the Prester John legend. "Do you ask why," Yilma writes, echoing the letter, "though ruling in such magnificence, [Prester John] styles himself only 'presbyter'? That is his humility."[61] Moore links Prester John's "humility" to amphibious "salamander" skin, an alternative armor (or "shield") that is an antidote to the prickly self-defenses raised earlier in the poem. As Moore would later write, in 1949, "Humility, indeed, is armor."[62] It is at this moment in "His Shield" when Moore introduces allusions to Haile Selassie:

> > In Carpasian
> > linen coat, flanked by his household lion cubs and sable
> > > retinue, he revealed
> > a formula safer than
>
> an armorer's: the power of relinquishing
> > what one would keep; that is freedom. Become dinosaur-
> skulled, quilled or salamander-wooled, more ironshod
> and javelin-dressed than a hedgehog battalion of steel, but be
> > dull. Don't be envied or
> armed with a measuring-rod.[63]

While the mention of "Carpasian linen" is likely borrowed from Asfa Yilma's account of Prester John, the "household lion cubs" clearly point to Haile Selassie, whom Moore celebrated in "Leonardo Da Vinci's" as a "symbol" of domestic autonomy, or, "household" sovereignty.[64] And the "sable retinue" likely refers to Selassie's royal entourage. By bringing Prester John and Haile Selassie together in the concluding lines of "His Shield," Moore asks us to rethink the value of "dull," or dulled (versus "quilled") defenses. However, Moore does not create an image of Selassie as passively non-violent. As Bonnie Costello has written, "His Shield" "celebrates humility, not repression or abdication."[65] Moore insists that we think of Selassie as a smart fighter who knows when it is more advantageous to disappear and wait for an ideal moment to engage in battle. In this sense, Moore asks us to think of flight, or tactical fugitivity, as a shrewd way to win. It is by fleeing, or disappearing, that Prester John/Haile Selassie paradoxically reveals a superior "formula" for victory.

To be clear, Moore was not alone in paralleling Prester John with Haile Selassie. Asfa Yilma notes that, although of European origins, the legend of Prester John had become "part of the national tradition," with Ethiopian emperors being regarded as Prester John-like warriors of Christendom.[66] The legend also appears to have drawn some attention from African American readers. The mention of Prester John in "The Land of the Burnt Faces," W. E. B. Du Bois's chapter on Ethiopia in *The World and Africa* (1947), suggests that Prester John's name was circulating in African American discussions of Haile Selassie contemporaneous with World War II.[67] Moreover, the entry for Prester John's "Letter" on the contemporary research website BlackCentralEurope.com indicates that the myth has also gained traction among those seeking to understand the relationship between the legend and European perceptions of racial blackness over time.

I also insist that Moore is consciously thinking of Prester John as racially Black and that we misread the poem when we do not imagine the poem's central figure as Black in the modern racial sense. By mentioning his "sable retinue" and "salamander-wooled" epidermal defense (*wooly* being a common description of kinky hair), Moore marks Prester John, and the off-stage presence of Selassie, with signifiers of racial blackness. Moore thus departs from Asfa Yilma, who, like many Ethiopian aristocrats, dismissed the notion that the ruling Amharic class were Black in the "Negro" sense (Du Bois addresses and counters similar attitudes among white scientists and historians in *The World and Africa*).[68] In contrast,

Moore remains true to a racially Black image of Prester John and Haile Selassie as fugitive sovereigns.

Critics have been right to question the limits of Moore's celebration of fugitive or "indirect" strategies of resistance for those facing persecution. While Bonnie Costello insists that Moore's affirmation of sovereign humility "is not directed at the powerless or undistinguished," she still worries that "[a]t its limit, such an ethos denies selfhood."[69] Cristanne Miller has likewise called into question the effectiveness of the indirect strategies, or tactical "by / play," that Moore sometimes idealizes in her poems.[70] Yet in "His Shield," Moore was playing off the historical reality of Haile Selassie's situation and his strategy for winning the fight for Ethiopia's freedom. Haile Selassie's fugitive defense was imperative *and* effective, and helped ensure Ethiopia's freedom from European colonization. To return to Moten, such methods of survival should be read as hallmarks of the freedom drive that animates Black fugitive being in the modern world.

Prester John: A Fugitive in the Background

If the unconquerable Prester John assisted Moore in thinking through the relation between racial blackness and a fugitive, amphibious resistance to capture in "His Shield," it should be no surprise that Prester John, in Moore's corpus, is not confined within the poetic lines of this poem. While Moore drew on Asfa Yilma's account of the Prester John legend for her fugitive portrayal of Selassie in 1944, archival evidence indicates that Moore was well aware of the legend before she had read Yilma's book. In fact, Prester John's name, and its racialized association with sovereign resistance to subjection, can be found both on- and offstage of some of Moore's most famous poems.

Take, for instance, the appearance of the motif of fire-retardant salamander skin in Moore's amphibiously themed "Sea Unicorns and Land Unicorns" (1924). Linda Leavell has described its central theme as "the dilemma of unity and difference."[71] I would add that the poem might also be read as a meditation on sovereignty and flight from captivity. Moore refers to the "white coat" of a unicorn as "unconsumed as if of salamander's skin," an allusion that is meant to evoke the unicorn's legendary resistance to capture.[72]

References to "Prester John" appear regularly in two of Moore's digitized writing notebooks, now available at the Marianne Moore Digital Archive (MMDA)—one kept from 1922 to 1930, the year of Haile Selassie's coronation. The other, kept from 1933 to 1940, overlaps with the years of the Italian occupation of Ethiopia. I argue that what we witness in these notebooks is Moore's nascent interwoven thinking of Prester John and Haile Selassie while Moore was at work on some of her most well-known poems. The 1922–1930 notebook contains numerous references to Prester John among lines drafted for the poems "Marriage" and "An Octopus," as well as poems associated with what is often considered Moore's incredibly generative period of publishing following her editorial leadership of the *Dial*, such as "The Hero," "The Steeple-Jack," "The Student," and "The Jerboa." The amphibious "wish to [be] interchangably [sic] man & fish"—from the poems "Ennui" and "The Plumet Basilisk"—appears among draft lines for "Sea Unicorns and Land Unicorns," a wish made by a fugitive creature "that never can be caught" or "taken alive."[73]

It is soon after Moore's reference to this amphibious "wish" that direct references to "Prester John" begin to appear in the journal. A few pages later, Moore refers to "swannes in England" with feathers "as blue as any cloth."[74] Next to these lines, Moore writes the marginal note: "Prester / John / w his scepter, of emerald." Ten pages later, among lines that may be attributed to "The Steeple-Jack" and "The Student," Moore writes a description of flying seagulls, likening them to "swans in Prester John's land blue as any cloth."[75]

Unsurprisingly, Prester John imagery continues to accumulate in the notebook as Moore begins drafting lines that will end up in "The Plumet Basilisk." Moore repeatedly characterizes the lizard in the emerald-green living-flame imagery associated with the Prester John legend. On page 0133-recto, Moore refers to the basilisk as "The undethroned emerald dressed king." "Emerald dressed" touches on the theme of defensive amphibious cloaking represented in the Prester John letter and might be heard in anticipation of the "battle-dressed" animals of "His Shield." "Undethroned" captures, in double negative, Prester John's status as both king and presbyter. Moreover, when modified by "undethroned," the flighty king portrayed here suggests a sovereign who has been restored to power, or perhaps one who, like Selassie, held onto his throne by surrendering it.

I insist, again, that we read Prester John and the networks of associations it generates in Moore's poetry as marked with Black African, or "Negro," racial specificity. Such a reading amplifies the denotations of racial blackness not associated with Prester John that also appear in this notebook, such as Moore's references to "Eubie Blake" and "the old time cake walk," as well as Moore's transcription of a Jim Crow minstrel song.[76] As a geographical locale connoting racial blackness, Ethiopia is also marked in this notebook by way of the word "Ethiope," which Moore associates with a giraffe, and which some readers may recognize as an alteration of the epithet Ezra Pound used when, after reading "Black Earth" (1918), he asked Moore if she were "a jet black Ethiopian."[77] A reference to "black skin" appears at the end of a line that begins "Porcupines, pins, edges," imagery that will end up in "His Shield," at least a decade later.[78] These notes indicate the presence of a conscious interrelated thinking of modern racial blackness, animals indigenous to Africa, and defensive epidermal coverings during a time when the legend of Prester John was significantly influencing Moore's writing.

The notebook Moore kept from 1933 to 1940 also includes allusions to Prester John, which appear alongside draft lines for both "The Buffalo" and "Virginia Britannia"—two poems in which racial blackness strongly informs Moore's poetics. Given that Moore kept this notebook after Selassie's coronation in 1930, and during the early years of his exile, it is very possible that Selassie's renown was retroactively influencing Moore's thinking of the Prester John legend during this period. The legendary king—with "scepter, of emerald," to borrow Moore's phrases—may have influenced, for instance, the "emerald shore" in "Virginia Britannia," a line that was drafted in the 1933–1940 notebook about a colonial "region not / noted for its humility."[79] As I have mentioned, Moore had paid attention to the invasion of Ethiopia in 1935. The event likely informed the anti-colonial sentiments found in "Virginia Britannia" and might also have influenced Moore's meditation on the history of African American liberation struggles, indicated by the poem's mention of "the Black idiom" (or southern Negro dialect), the forced transport of "the Negro" to the colonies, and the anti-racist dictum that the "black savage ... is not all brawn and animality."[80]

More obvious allusions to modalities of racialized epidermal resistance associated with the Prester John legend appear in draft lines for

"The Buffalo" (1934).[81] In her reading of the poem, Linda Leavell acknowledges that the poem evinces Moore's "ongoing concern with racial justice."[82] Though Leavell does not elaborate, the presence of references to Prester John in these draft lines support Leavell's racial reading of the poem. Published in 1934, this poem opens with a reflection on the "significance" of the color "black" in the vocabulary of European heraldry:

> **The Buffalo**
>   Black in blazonry means
> prudence; and niger, unpropitious. Might
> hematite-
>   black incurved compact horns on a bison
>   have significance?[83]

The poem, quite literally a meditation on the value of the color "black," toggles between two meanings, one positive and one negative—both related to the signifying grammars of blazonry, or armor. Moore first associates the color black with "prudence," which the *Oxford English Dictionary* defines as "acting with or showing forethought; having or exercising sound judgement in practical or financial affairs; circumspect, discreet, cautious; far-sighted."[84] We might understand prudence, in this sense, as caution manifested by wisdom. Moore counters this value of blackness with "niger," an obsolete word used to indicate a black stone, which signifies something unpropitious or unfavorable.[85] Moore then introduces a third term of blackness—"hematite," a mineral with a black metallic luster—to speculate on the "significance" of the bison, or buffalo, an animal with silvery black horns that are used for battle and self-defense.[86]

Draft lines for "The Buffalo" in the 1930–1940 notebook show Moore directly linking the meaning of blackness, as "prudence," to the buffalo's skin. In one entry, Moore writes the lines "coarse black guard hairs / on the prudent skin."[87] If "Black in blazonry means prudence," then "prudent skin" should be read as "black skin" that is defensively armed with the power of sound judgment and foresight, such that might lead, for instance, to a strategic decision to flee. In subsequent draft lines, the image of "prudent skin" links up with the sartorial theme that informs Moore's Prester John-derived amphibious fire- and waterproof imaginary, with its concentrated focus on skin as a protective shield. The phrase "fire proof salamander's skin" appears following a description of an "ox" in combat.[88] On the same page, alongside mention of the "cockatrix or basilisk" (likely a reference to Bulfinch's *Mythology*) and a reference to a "serpent / w skin the color of the shower," Moore writes the following lines: "Impervious to fire" / "There is nothing one cld [sic] be / better dressed in than the / skin of the giraffe." Moore here is likely thinking of the similarity between the smooth, checkered fur of the giraffe and spotted salamander skin, which she elsewhere associates with Prester John's fire-retardant and water-resistant coat. In this notebook, Moore again avers that it is better to be "better dressed" than "battle-dressed." Moreover, as an animal native to Africa, the giraffe carries with it a Black racial connotation, suggesting, again, that the "salamander skin" that the poet wraps herself in in "His Shield" should be read as "black" skin in the racial sense.

Lastly, Prester John's "humility" also seems to be circulating in Moore's thinking of blackness, freedom from capture, and prudent judgment in both of these digitized notebooks. In the 1922–1930 notebook, in draft lines for "The Hero," Moore can be seen reflecting on the heroic quality of self-restraint via cautious judgment. Moore twice mentions the name "Regulus," whom she describes as "patient under suffering" and "the warrior whom war does not intoxicate / not the heretic, the chooser."[89] Regulus—who appears as one of the published poem's named heroes—is the diminutive form of *Rex*, or "king," in Latin. Moore's heroic imaginary is thus linked to the humble, emerald-green Prester John-like falling "little king" of "The Plumet Basilisk." Regulus is also the name of the brightest point in the constellation "Leo," thus linking Moore's hero to her celebrations of leonine sovereigns, such as the genius Leonardo Da Vinci and the "Lion Haile Selassie" in "Leonardo Da Vinci's." In the 1933–1940 notebook, Moore specifically mentions "humility" in a passage that takes up the theme of power: "[A] man who has power," Moore writes, "can be humble as a man who has none and is crazed with the thought of it can't."[90] This line suggests that the "crazed" desire for power indicates a lack of real power drawn from the shield of humble self-restraint, or, as Moore will write in "His Shield," having the wisdom not to "be envied or armed with a measuring-rod."[91]

"S-like": Selassie, Salamander, Solomon; or, the "Sparrow-Camel"

Between the 1922–1930 and 1933–1940 notebooks, we witness the evolution of Moore's interwoven thinking of Haile Selassie and Prester John with poetic imagery—emeralds, amphibious fire-proof salamander's skin, and humility—in order to represent racial blackness as a fugitive mode of sovereign embodiment in "His Shield." However, like the fugitive Prester John, who works behind the scene of so much of Moore's poetry, Haile Selassie's absent presence can also be found outside of the poems I have so far discussed.

Take, for instance, one of Moore's later poems, "O to Be a Dragon" (1957). Moore opens this poem by evoking King Solomon, the patriarch of the Solomonic dynasty, reconfiguring the amphibious "wish" to be "man and fish" as the "wish" to be a shape-shifting flying lizard whose chief characteristic is its ability to evade capture by disappearing. Composed in the years following Selassie's 1954 visit to the United States, "O to Be a Dragon" was published in an eponymous collection of poems that also included Moore's blazon to the Solomonic king Haile Selassie, "Leonardo Da Vinci's":

> **O To Be a Dragon**
>   If I, like Solomon, …
>   could have my wish—
>   my wish … O to be a dragon,
> a symbol of the power of Heaven—of silkworm
> size or immense; at times invisible.
>   Felicitous phenomenon![92]

Read with "His Shield" and "Leonardo Da Vinci's," we can hear the "S-l" vocable of "O to Be a Dragon"—"symbol," "silkworm," "visible," "Felicitous"—run across Solomon, salamander, and Selassie (not to mention "basilisk"), a semantic skipping stone denoting an "S-like" amphibious sovereignty associated with the power of subterfuge—or the power to become "invisible" at will—and possessed by a drive for freedom.

I draw the phrase "S-like" from Moore's poem, "He 'Digesteth Harde Yron'" (1941). First published on the heels of Selassie's victorious return to

Addis Ababa, and anticipating the publication of "In Distrust of Merits" and "His Shield," "He 'Digesteth Harde Yron'" extolls the ostrich as a "solitary," persecuted African "rebel" and "symbol of justice."[93] The poem shares with "His Shield" both a masculine titular subject and a thematic focus on flight and strategic surrender. Moore depicts the male ostrich as a heroic protector presiding over a brood of chicks with "maternal concentration"—a phrase that alludes to Moore's poems, "The Paper Nautilus" and "The Hero."[94] While the ostrich appears to be a "nervous restless / bird that flees at sight / of danger," Moore corrects this first impression: "he feigns flight / to save his chicks, decoying / his decoyers."[95] Described as amphibiously gifted—a "quadrupedlike bird which flies on feet not wings"—Moore portrays the ostrich as strategically triumphing over tyranny via fugitive action: "The power of the visible / is the invisible; as even where / no tree of freedom grows, / so-called brute courage knows."[96] Gifted with the power of foresight, the ostrich courageously outwits those who would attempt to curtail his freedom, as well as the freedom of "his chicks"—that is, of future generations.

I suggest that the guardian ostrich of this poem is likely another allusion to Haile Selassie, and that the "S-l" vocable links this poem to Moore's broader racialized amphibious fugitive imaginary. Half-way through the poem, Moore describes the shape of the camel-sparrow as "S-like":

> Yes this is he
> whose plume was anciently
> the plume of justice; he
> whose comic duckling head on its
> great neck, revolves with compassneedle
> nervousness
> when he stands guard, in S-
> like foragings as he is
> preening the down on his laden-skinned back.[97]

This graphic articulation—"S-l"—bears on the remainder of the poem. Moore plays on the "s-l" vocable within the name of the solitary African bird by reversing the "l-s" in "camel-sparrow" to the "s-l" of "sparrow-camel," who is hailed in the poem's triumphant closing: "This one remaining rebel

/ is the sparrow-camel" (100). This chiastic about-face echoes the *Selassie-like* stratagem of deceptive reversal by which the ostrich appears to flee but actually "feigns flight." Like Haile Selassie, the one remaining indigenous African sovereign at the time of the poem's composition, the sparrow-camel fights and flies, throws himself (like a "Solomon," or a salamander) into the line of fire, but also knows when the fugitive power of invisibility is the best armor to don for battle.

As I have demonstrated, Moore's representations of Haile Selassie as a sovereign resisting capture draw from a culturally specific context in which Black liberation was frequently represented via the trope of fugitive escape catalyzed by what Moten calls the "freedom drive" that animates "black performances"—an expressive strategy still in use today. For one example, in the spoken-word track "Ghost" from Beyoncé's 2013 self-titled album, the singer expresses frustration with (and resistance to) the subjectivizing protocols of the music industry. She does this, in part, by deploying the "S-l" wordplay that runs between "Solomon"—the patriarch of the Solomonic Dynasty—and the amphibious "salamander." "I could sing a song for a Solomon or Salamander," Beyoncé speaks in monotone, as though intentionally trying not to sound like "Beyoncé."[98] The affectless vocal tone reflects Beyoncé's *ennui*, or boredom, in the face of the music industry's commodification of her music, and the negative impact it has on her perception of her own work: "I'm climbing up the walls cause all the shit I hear is boring / All the shit I do is boring / all these record labels boring."[99] While Beyoncé's use of the Solomon/salamander S-l wordplay is surely coincidental, the coincidence is no less meaningful. Moore's cognizance of Black biblical iconography, her familiarity with the Black king of the Prester John legend, her admiration of the Ethiopian emperor Haile Selassie, and the attention she paid to Black liberation struggles resonate with this moment of racial meaning-making in Beyoncé's music. And though "mythology's wish to be interchangeably man and fish" is, well, mythical, and not only relevant to modern notions of racial difference, Black amphibiousness clearly has a unique articulation within the American context of Black liberation struggles and Black expressive culture. By "climbing up walls," Beyoncé invokes the lizard or salamander-like habitus of a being who must find alternative routes of mobility through white mainstream society's perpendicular and hopelessly rational angles.

Moreover, by self-releasing her album—an act of subversive self-assertion—Beyoncé aimed to circumvent the boring and racially subjectivizing constraints of the predominantly white music industry. Like "Solomon or Salamander," Beyoncé's song (or *psalm*) performs a fugitive self-positioning—a temporary identificatory dislocation from dominant racial coordinates, enabling an alternative space of autonomous being and becoming to unfurl. Beyoncé's fugitive, amphibious ghosting evades such capture by refusing to disavail herself of the spectral powers of strategic flight, opting instead to flirt with what menaces her, then slip away—to recall a phrase from Moore's "Ennui"—"Like a ghost / In the sea."[100]

CHAPTER SIX

Archives of Excess and "power over the poor"
Marianne Moore's "The Jerboa"

Linda Kinnahan

During the 1930s, Marianne Moore's attention to notions of work and labor engage with socio-economic systems that cross time but speak to her particular moment.[1] "The Jerboa," which Linda Leavell identifies as speaking "more directly about the Depression than anything else Moore wrote for publication," does so by archiving a series of ancient artifacts.[2] Relevant to the Depression era's economic injustices, the poem counterpoints the visible display of possession and consumption with the invisible and dehumanized labor of making—and the body of the maker—promoted by the consumer culture emerging after the century's turn. While critical of the sacrifice of literary craft for political polemics that she saw in some of her contemporaries during the Depression years (as her letters suggest), Moore remained deeply concerned about the economic distress of her fellow citizens and cognizant of her own financial losses and increased dependence upon others for her needs as the 1930s progressed.[3]

Questioning the push for social welfare, several years into the Depression, she would write to Bryher that Franklin Delano Roosevelt's (FDR's) re-election demonstrated that "the majority of the people are willing to profit at the expense of others,—are in favor of spoils, that is to say. We have such an appetite for Relief that we are like the frogs who would have a king."[4]

107

However, Moore's opposition to the New Deal developed, Leavell argues, "not because she was unsympathetic to those harder hit by the Depression than she was. She believed rather that the New Deal would degrade the poor by denying them both dignity and freedom," qualities that Leavell attributes to the jerboa.[5] Moore's Republicanism, in the face of the Depression, invested faith in Hoover in the early 1930s, whom she saw as an exemplar of a man who "cares for another man's good as much as is own," specifying that "I ... am in that sense a Republican," although confessing to lack the wisdom to tell whether "his political economy is the best."[6] These equivocations about economy, capital, and labor suggest Moore's nondogmatic approach to economics, while the object archives of "The Jerboa" suggest her deep concern with displays of consumer potency, among the wealthy and non-wealthy alike, that make labor invisible. By the 1930s, this concern questions financial crisis as, in part, the elision of production and the bodies of producers within a rapidly growing consumer ethos.

The identification with a broader community suffering from economic "tumult," Odile Harter notes, led Moore to write poems in the 1930s that adopt a "more ... communal intent, and greater interest in describing humanity as a whole," enacting "the experience of a dissenting bystander who feels ethically obligated to identify with the collective."[7] This "collective" manifests in "The Jerboa" as a curation of material archives, a poem built of selecting and presenting a series of objects that speak to economic injustice across historical eras. The poem suggests Allan Sekula's concept of a "shadow archive," which Laura Engel defines as "an alternative record of the histories of marginalized individuals that exists alongside traditional histories" that are "reinterpreted and reenacted for larger audiences" beyond the archive.[8] In the act of (re)interpreting archival objects, the poem—especially its first section entitled "Too Much"—dwells upon the function of specular display in relation to narratives of power derived from the archive she assembles, while pointedly recovering the labor and laboring bodies left invisible. Amidst the economic discourses marking the early twentieth century's embrace of consumer culture and the subsequent hardships of the Depression, "The Jerboa" excavates a relationship of display and disembodied labor echoing monetary values privileging desire for possession and its visible proof above production and the bodies that produce.

Objects and Archives

First published in *Hound and Horn* in 1932 as a longish poem of 162 lines, "The Jerboa" divides into two sections entitled "Too Much" and "Abundance," suggesting a tense distinction between excessive consumption and human need, between possession for possession's sake and the rich satisfaction of life's hungers.[9] The poem's diptych structure counterpoints different organizations of knowledge as though offering a bifocal lens for viewing concepts of a bountiful life. The first section, "Too Much," constructs an archive of object artifacts to suggest a chronological and taxonomic basis for knowledge, a method other 1930s poems like "Virginia Britannia" share.[10] Originally entitled "Poverty," this section overflows with the ancient and precious artifacts but suggests a concurrent state of moral destitution. The second section, "Abundance," shifts modes from archiving artifacts to closely observing and reveling in the physical properties and environment of the desert rat, the jerboa. The picture drawn of the jerboa integrates naturalistic and empirical details to praise the creature's capacity for abundance in meeting its needs and living in accordance with its surroundings: Moore notes that he is constantly "seeking food" but "has / happiness" (l. 94), and "one would not be he / who has nothing but plenty" (ll. 101–2). As readers of the poem commonly note, two very different notions of "abundance" accrue in each section—one requiring possession and power, the other derived from a capacity to thrive without dominating others, to be content in one's place and meeting one's needs.

This archive's sourcing from material culture and its structural arrangement of objects continues a familiar strategy for Moore but one that intensifies in the 1930s. In "Too Much," Moore's customary fascination with material objects arranges the poem as an archival catalogue insistently material and visual, choosing an approach that functions differently from Moore's archival structure of quotations marking earlier poems like "Marriage" or "An Octopus." As Harter persuasively argues, "Moore's quotation practice ... undergoes an infrequently noted transformation during the 1930s. While the poems of the 1920s form a citational patchwork, the poems of the 1930s present just a few touchstones per poem."[11] Moreover, the citational quality of the 1930s poems develops a particularly object-oriented trajectory, complexly continuing earlier quotational and citational tendencies that surface the textual mediation of the object or image while foregrounding the assembly of objects and artifacts, archival-like. Sarah Berry likens this poetic process to the seventeenth-century "cabinets of curiosity," collections of objects curated and assembled in box-like structures "popular ... [among] aristocrats, doctors, or intellectuals" like Sir Thomas Brown, for whom such "collections were morally inflected."[12] Thinking through objects becomes a way of thinking through history, of interpreting a material archive to narrate our past while remaining aware of the non-neutral pressures shaping the act of interpretation.

The contexts of Moore's poetic processes and interests have generated rich interpretations of the poem, upon which I hope to build. Victoria Bazin's incisive study of Moore's textual sources, including for "The Jerboa," from the *Illustrated London News* explores the influence of a publication Moore read devotedly in the interwar years, compiling folders of clippings referenced in the 1930s poems. Bazin links the paper's "fascination with the otherness of non-Western cultures" with an imperial mindset that "The Jerboa" dissects through treating its artifacts as evidence of "the power relations underpinning all forms of cultural production."[13] For Moore, Bazin argues, this intervention into archival narratives of power reveals her preoccupation with justifying poetic labor, especially in a time of social distress, suggesting "an awareness of how language as a form of observation is capable of intervening in the object world" and evidencing "the literary labour of the poet engaged in restoring community."[14] Berry, also concerned with the poem's poetic ethics, highlights Moore's attention to the decorative arts in the poem's litany of objects, arguing that "it seems likely that her aesthetic interest in decorative arts might also be morally inflected" and that her interest in the "ethical implications of decorative art objects" provokes questions of "bad use," such as the use of luxury items to delight the owners and oppress those who make them.[15] Berry notes the common distinction of fine art from the decorative arts on the basis of use, a determination devaluing the object in relation to "art" and often relegating the creator—and their labor—to anonymous invisibility. Noting the poem's carefully obsessive detail describing the small and delicate objects it describes (toilet boxes, walking sticks), balanced by the poem's acknowledgment of the producers' poor treatment and forgotten status, Berry concludes that the poem forces "us to confront the tension present in all decorative art objects. ... the uneasy relationship between sensory pleasure one takes in an object and the mind's awareness of the circumstances of its production" in which skill and creative identity are elided.[16]

In Bazin's concern with the textual mediation of archival objects (how these objects present themselves to Moore through textual and media forms) and Berry's attention to the category of decorative arts, the poet is positioned as a reader of archives, interested in the ways knowledge is organized and produced through archival construction, exhibition, and attention. Intersecting these discussions of "The Jerboa" is the notion of Moore's engagement with archives and with archival method. And, indeed, Moore's fascination with collecting (collections), archiving (archives), and the viewing and arrangement of exhibition is commonly understood to shape her aesthetics, whether the focus be on her use of quotations or capacious catalogues of details and material objects and myriad textual sources. For Catherine Paul, the museum stands as a formative source and model for Moore's responses to modernity that stage poems as collections. As Paul fastidiously details, Moore's "long interest in museums and galleries" and her role as an "avid collector of art, textual objects, curiosities, clippings, and memorabilia" inform poems of the 1930s; moreover, these poems engage with museum practices such as curation and exhibit organization to investigate ideological formations of knowledge.[17] In 1932, the year she composed "The Jerboa," Moore wrote "detailed accounts" of museum visits, conducting research for both "The Pangolin" and "The Jerboa" at the Akkeley Hall of African Mammals (AKAM).[18] Her poetic processes of assembling "pieces from her textual collections" (her copiously maintained notebooks and files) into poems "reveal Moore thinking about the acts of collecting and curating" and "examining how material objects transmit knowledge and shape points of view," as in "Too Much."[19] The shift in focus of "Abundance," the second section of "The Jerboa," activates a different approach, empirically based in natural observation that focuses exquisite detail upon the titular jerboa, a "sand brown jumping-rat" of the desert (Moore, l. 106). This change in the poem's approach to "acts of collecting and curating" reflects what Paul identifies as the AKAM's pioneering method of exhibiting "habitat groups," poetically adapting the form of the "habitat diorama"—"the complex and realistic displays used at the AMNH to create impressions of animals and cultures."[20] The poem's structure, drawing from different methods of curation and exhibit, effectively contrasts a show of "too much" with the "plenty" of the jerboa in his austere desert home (Moore, l. 103).

Enumerating displays of wealth as signs of power, "Too Much" explores the narrative function to which conventional archives are subjected. Rodney G. S. Carter argues that archives "were created to preserve the lives of people considered to have value and other people were left out," constituting "spaces of power" that "allow voices to be heard" by "highlighting certain narratives and … including certain types of records created by certain groups."[21] Counter-narratives can unsettle the archive's relationship to power, as Laura Engel suggests, through reading objects in the archive as "constructed documents rather than unmediated authentic narratives."[22] Calling to mind Moore's persistent attention to processes of textual mediation in poems of the 1920s and 30s, this notion of the archive-as-constructed underscores her poetic engagement with the selective and narrative process of interpreting documents and material objects from history. As Engel notes in her work on archival research as a form of tourism, Griselda Pollack's concept of the "'virtual feminist museum,' a virtual exhibition of juxtaposed images," suggests the social determinations of archival construction, preservation, and narration.[23]

> The archive is selective not comprehensive. It is pre-selected in ways that reflect what each culture considered worth storing and remembering. … Vast areas of social life and huge numbers of people hardly exist, according to the archive. The archive is over-determined by facts of class, race, gender, sexuality and above all power.[24]

Like Moore, the reader of the archives "reanimates the discourses he or she discovers in the archives."[25]

"Too Much": Reanimating the Object Archive

Moore's poetic staging of object archives and exhibition methods gestures toward gaps and invisible bodies pertinent not just to the histories signified by her archives but speaking to economic hierarchies of power in her Depression-era moment. Although mediated through photographs and textual presentations, the object status of the archive of "Too Much" suggests the tangible but unknowable and contingent history carried by an object. How does one "read" the object archive? Theorizing the interpretive possibilities of an object archive, Laura Engel concedes that "[a]lthough it is not possible to access the authentic nature of the past, material objects, especially those that contain traces of the embodiment of particular individuals,"[26] there are nonetheless "strategies for thinking about archival gaps that employ creative and/or curatorial methodologies in order to make informed speculations about the invisible connections between materials."[27] Writing about contemporary poet Susan Howe, Julie Philips Browne understands her treatment of the archival object as "already a precarious trace, the result of a collector's unlikely effort to capture and preserve."[28] Illuminating the archival research process as a "re-animated" encounter with an object that has, by virtue of landing in the archive, been kept out of circulation until said encounter, Howe's words seem a gloss on Moore's poem and its "re-collected" objects:

> One historical-existential trace has been hunted, captured, guarded, and preserved in aversion to waste by an avid collector, then shut carefully away, outside an economy of use, inaccessible to touch. Now it is re-animated, re-collected (recollected) through an encounter with the mind of a curious reader, a researcher, an antiquarian, a bibliomaniac, a sub sub librarian, a poet.[29]

In "The Jerboa," the display of wealth, through material artifacts, is shown to accompany the elision of laboring bodies. While concern with exploitation of the poor and the colonized is well-noted in commentary on the poem, I want to consider the archival impact of inserting laboring bodies and processes of production back into narratives of economic power. The poem repeatedly notes how labor production is rendered invisible, a process reflecting the historical anonymity of many forms of labor (including labor of the enslaved). Importantly, though, the historical dislocation of acts of labor and workers' bodies also reflects the modern shift to a consumer culture, particularly glaring during the 1930s financial crisis. Corporate capitalism's dominant emergence in the early decades of the twentieth century regarded consumer desire as the driving force of value, downplaying and even erasing the labor of production from determinations of value. The labor, and the body of the laborer, vanish within the frame of desire and display promoted to the modern consumer. "The Jerboa," reaching back in time to speak to its present moment, archives the interplay of display and labor embedded in the material object or artifact. Again and again, the poem redirects our attention from the object to its possible maker and the process by which that maker and their labor vanish from view but remain as traces within the archived artifact.

The poem opens by citing a labor arrangement producing the sculptural Roman fountain, the "Fontana della Pigna," now located in a main courtyard of the Vatican gardens.[30] The pine nut or fir cone, the "pigna," is a colossal bronze sculpture, rising four meters high, that stood near the Pantheon in the classical age and was moved to St. Peter's Basilica in the Middle Ages before being relocated to its present location in 1608. The once-functioning fountain is now flanked in the Vatican Gardens by bronze copies of a pair of peacocks that decorated the tomb of Emperor Hadrian, now the Castel Sant'Angelo near St. Peter's. Moore's opening language and image derive from Duff's *Freedmen of the Early Roman Empire* (referenced in Moore's notes, which she supplies in her *Selected Poems* but not the *Hound and Horn* presentation) and an illustration entitled "Colossal Fir-cone of Bronze."

Moore's poem begins with the condition of its making:

> A Roman hired an
> artist, a freedman,
>   to make a cone—pine cone
>   or fir cone—with holes for a fountain. Placed on
>   the Prison of St. Angelo, this cone
>   of the Pompeys which is known
>
>   now as the Popes', passed

for art. A huge cast
   bronze, dwarfing the peacock
   statue in the garden of the Vatican,
      it looks like a work of art made to give
         to a Pompey, or native

of Thebes. ... (ll. 1–13)

In the image of the pine-cone fountain, Moore's poetic movement across history—from classical to medieval to modern—bridges the power of empirical Rome with the power of religious institutions. The artist, once an enslaved laborer, is a freedman but still subject to the whims of the mighty: he makes a giant, intricate bronze pine-cone, now situated in the Vatican Gardens, having once (as Moore presents it) been for the powerful Pompey (Caesar's rival). Moore reads power rather than art into the sculpture, for although it "passed for art" with the Popes, "it looks like a work of art made to give / to a Pompey," a work that inscribes power now grossly out of proportion with its surroundings. Suggestively, the artist's work is warped by such a dynamic, rendering the piece no longer art, and the artist reduced to an anonymous functionary.

The poem's archival catalogue proceeds to trace this kind of power and its display through material wealth back to the Greeks (with a reference to Thebes) and the ancient Egyptians, referenced as the "Others" who understand, as builders of the pyramids, "making colossi and / how to use slaves" (ll. 15–16). Leavell notes that Moore worked from notes on ancient Egypt in developing this poem, and Moore's notes identify one of the objects, a toilet-box elaborately decorated, as dating from the twenty-second Egyptian Dynasty. These "Others" "understood / ... / how to use slaves" in ordering and displaying ownership as power (ll. 13–16). They "kept crocodiles and put / baboons on the necks of giraffes to pick / fruit, and used serpent magic" (ll. 16–18). Gardens for "impalas and onagers, / / the wild ostrich herd" and "cranes, / storks, anoas, mongooses, and Nile geese" are built with "avenues" of tropical fruit and "pools of pink flowers, tame fish, and small frogs," a showplace for what "They looked on as theirs." (ll. 23–34). As Bazin comments, "the speaker acknowledges that the Egyptian sense of ownership ... leads to the exploitation of both human and natural resources."³¹ Moreover, emphasizing the *spectacle* of possession, the poem briefly but pointedly notes that such display must enlist the labor of "their men," who "tie / hippopotami" and perform other such jobs to keep the show of wealth going (ll. 19–20).

While Moore's poem focuses on ancient Egypt, her descriptions of spectacle and the display of wealth as a means of conveying power resonate within the context of America's explosive capitalism, from the wealth gaps and ostentatiousness of the Gilded Age, through the growth in modes for enticing consumer desire (department store windows, advertising, etc.) and heightening profit through consumer activity, to the crash of 1929 of a lightly regulated economy. When Thorstein Veblen popularized ideas of "conspicuous consumption" in his 1899 critique of capitalism, *Theory of the Leisure Class*, he identified forms of display as the primary means for communicating pecuniary strength, signifying cultural shifts from traditional values of thrift and modesty to a more modern equation of character with material wealth evidenced through its display. Significantly, his gender analysis of conspicuous consumption recognized the heightening of the wife's role in a marriage to serve, objectified through her displays of fashion and jewelry, to visually substantiate her husband's wealth. Moreover, Veblen discerned a cross-class contagion of "conspicuous consumption," as those without financial means nonetheless desired to emulate the upper class's habits of display. Conversely, other economists like Simone Patten advocated consumerism as an important tool of assimilation for immigrants, equating consumer strength (and its visible evidence) with Americanism and membership in the American community. The migration of economic theories of consumption into poetry's domain during this period lands in diverse places. Harold Loeb, editor of *Broom* (where Moore published poems in the early 1920s), writes in a 1922 issue on the "The Mysticism of Money," connecting America's "formative-creative art epoch" to its obsession with the pursuit of money as the "good life" and "the rule of conduct for the devout is *Competitive Ostentation*," likening the display of wealth to a "new era" stimulating America's artistic ascendence while Europe declines.³² Mina Loy would attribute America's poetic innovations, a few years later, to the culture's monetary energies ("Modern Poetry" 1925) and the contribution of immigrant populations to this drive. Loy's economic picture, presented in the 1925 essay "Modern

Poetry," published in *Charm* magazine, invests in the creative energy of the seller—the public circulator of goods—rather than the consumer or the consumption of goods (pretty much leaving the worker out of the picture).

For Veblen, and I would argue for Moore, the impact of consumerism and its display harms the community and privileges a hierarchy of power, while labor and the worker strengthen the communal basis. Whether Moore read Veblen's initial theories or not, his ideas popularly circulated and formed the basis for the relatively progressive worker-centered economic theories of the American Institutional School, ideas that Veblen developed further while publishing a series of articles in the late 1910s in the *Dial* and briefly serving as editor (1918–19), alongside John Dewey and Randolph Bourne. In his *Dial* period, which engaged Moore as a reader, Veblen developed connections between creative labor and communal histories, advocating community value as the instinct of workmanship—the desire to produce goods well and meet human needs—as opposed to the business (profit-oriented) value of stimulating desire for the consumption of goods. Veblen's ideas, relatively dormant in the 1920s, were rediscovered in the 1930s, newly relevant to the Depression era and contributing (through his advocates by this decade) to the design of the New Deal.[33]

In Moore's poem, display designates hierarchy as precious objects and environments speak of power but must be visually seen to do so. Presenting the garden and its animal inhabitants as a microcosmic spectacle of consumption and possession, the poem describes further domestic items, the "toys" of "Lords and ladies," each serving as a "royal totem" or emblem of power (ll. 43–46). The "toilet-boxes marked / with the contents" (ll. 45–46), such as

>   goose-grease
> paint in round bone boxes with pivoting
> lid incised with the duck-wing
>
> or reverted duck-
> head (ll. 46–50)

are listed with the "buck / horn and rhinoceros / powders" "kept in horns" (ll. 50–51). Detailing the picture of the Nile and a "pig-tailed monkey on /

slab-hands" (ll. 57–58) decorating one box—its "poetry of frog grays, / duck-egg greens, and egg-plant blues" (ll. 63–64)—Moore steps back from the close-up detail to speak, a third of the way through the poem, to the visual display as an ideological mechanism supporting the world view of the powerful and the economics of wealth disparity, issues intensely relevant to her own decade and, indeed, century. The charming painting of the Nile, decorating a domestic vessel, offers both

> a fantasy
> and a verisimilitude that were
> right to those with, everywhere,
>
> power over the poor. (ll. 64–67)

Bazin eloquently notes the relationship between labor and power conveyed in these lines: "Questions of power become central to an understanding of the production and consumption of cultural objects. More specifically, such ornate and intricate objects bear the traces of exploited human labour."[34] As I read these lines, I keep getting stuck on the word "right"—the "rightnesss" or "a right" understood by those with power over the poor, justifying their oppressed condition.

I want to come back to this particular line in a moment and contemplate its placement amidst the archival abundance of material objects in the poem, but first notice how the poem rapidly tabulates the invisible labor behind such power in the ensuing stanzas. We are told that

> Those who tended flower-
> beds and stables were like the king's cane in the
> form of a hand, or the folding bed-room
> made for his mother (69–72)

The laborers are useful and innovative but equated to objects in this field of power. The folding bed, Moore's notes (in the *Selected Poems*) tell us, is the "portable bed-chamber of Queen Hetepheres presented to her by her son, Cheops," which Moore saw photographed in the *Illustrated London News,* and the "complexity of the relationship between these Egyptian objects and the history of human exploitation" is "embedded" in these lines.³⁵ The queen's tomb, excavated in 1925 after two decades of archaeological work, included many treasures such as the bed and a queen's chair. Cheops, as the ancient Greeks called King Khufu, is thought to have commissioned the Great Pyramid of Giza in the twenty-sixth century BC, one of the "colossi" built with the labor and engineering skill of slaves but remembered as the accomplishment of a ruler. Rendering these small objects as though "excavating" like an "archaeologist," "Moore's speaker finds evidence of the human industry and creativity of those *without* power in small things" and remains "[a]lert to the ways in which 'those with power' construct an image of the past that negates or silences 'the poor.'"³⁶ The object's archival evidence suggests how the "excavated artifact reveals the secrets of its culture, the power relations underpinning all forms of cultural production."³⁷

The poem's emphasis on archival objects reflects, as well, the function of the visual archive as an organization of knowledge that is selective and constructed in relation to power. The poem's intervention into the archives manifests as a process of noting not only what is left out of the narrative of power—making visible those without power but responsible for the production of labor to make the object—but also suggesting how the power of claiming the labor of others ensures visibility through history. The visibility of power, then, persists in the archive by modes of appropriation and concealment. The poem's examples of such an archival privileging of those in power extend to agricultural and spiritual realms particular to early Egypt. As the first civilization to practice bee-keeping, Egypt considered bees sacred, with oblong temple hives managed by a hierarchy of beekeepers whose overseer reported to the pharaoh. Cattle, important for both practical and religious purposes, supplied a form for several gods, including the female goddess Hathor. Laborers in Moore's poem associate with these agricultural and spiritual labors that the king then appropriates: the

> bee-man and milk-
>
> maid, kept divine cows
> and bees; limestone brows,

> and gold-foil wings. They made
> basalt serpents and portraits of beetles; the
> king gave his name to them and he was named
> for them. (ll. 78–84)

Here, the pronoun "them" remains ambiguous about whether the king gives his name to the laborers or the objects they produce, further collapsing the human worker into an objectified (and anonymous) state while granting the king's name to accomplishments and even divine connections. The labor of the anonymous workers produces the visible proof of their master's power in Moore's object archive.

Alongside the poem's direct use of objects from ancient cultures, the poem's Depression-era resonance distils in the lines of commentary that step back from the historical moments being archived. We are not meant to remain in those moments of ancient Rome or Egypt, but to consider, like the pine-cone fountain in its modern placement in the Vatican, the disproportion of power based upon wealth as a twentieth-century problem alongside the heightened regard for consumption as a form of modern agency. Let's return to that line—"power over the poor"—that operates like Roland Barthes's notion of the "punctum" in a photograph. The punctum is a detail or conveyance that "bruises" or "pricks," that "rises from the scene, [and] shoots out of it like an arrow" to pierce or break the individual consciousness and contextual field—in this case, the material culture archives—to produce an affective meaning, to allow a subjective response.[38] The line "power over the poor" invites an identification with the powerless and poor, while commenting upon the signifying power of material objects, enabled by the elided labors of the poor.

One can think of this line as part of an archive of poetic lines within Moore's oeuvre, those moments when a line cuts into the reading of a poem, stopping us head-on. In "Marriage": "experience attests / that men have power / and sometimes one is made to feel it";[39] in "Virginia Britannia": "colonizing" and "tyrant taste" constitute "taking what they / pleased";[40] in "Black Earth": "... Black / but beautiful, my back / is full of the history of power."[41] This chorus of incisive socio-historical commentary might well leave us pleased with the archives making up these poems.

"Abundance" and the Unresolvable Archive

And yet, thinking back to the body imagined in "Black Earth" as "full of the history of power," how can we view the curation of the *raced body* amidst the archives of power that "The Jerboa" collects and arranges? A second "punctum" line appears, for me, early in "Abundance," comparing the "free born" and "untouched" jerboa (like the free-born artist) to "the blacks, that choice race with an elegance / ignored by one's ignorance" (ll. 106–8). If "Too Much" describes the "human tendency to use art and collected objects to display power," "Abundance" offers a corrective to the archives, both through this comment and the shift in formal presentation of the second section.[42] Nonetheless, while the archival structure of the first section is, in large part, replaced by more naturalistic observation in the second part, it is nonetheless observation framed by archival readings that raise further questions about display and specular economies of meaning: the opening lines position the jerboa by historically referencing the conquering, colonizing, and enslaving march of Western history; the final lines evoke one last archival object, a carved foot of a Chippendale stand that resembles the jerboa's. I'd like to muse on these archival instances in concluding this essay.

The initial lines of "Abundance" offer a corrective to the archival evidence of power that has been enumerated up to this point. These lines move from a reference to Roman imperialism, to the contrasting freedom of the "sand brown jumping-rat," to the suggestion of contemporary circumstances affecting the "choice race" of "blacks":

> Africanus meant
> the conqueror sent
>   from Rome. It should mean the
>   untouched: the sand brown jumping-rat—free born; and
>   the blacks, that choice race with an elegance
>   ignored by one's ignorance. (ll. 103–8)

Here, Moore references the Roman general Scipio, who, leading an African campaign in the early second century BC, gained the name "Africanus" after a victory against Hannibal in Carthage that led to the expansion of

Roman territories into Africa. Scipio's appropriation of the continent's name, an act of naming that signals an idea of conquest, is refuted as the poem lights not only on the jerboa as true "Africanus" but seeks to recognize "blacks" in response to an "ignorance" that, through global disregard for African history, New World and American slavery, and Jim Crow conditions of the twentieth century, has "ignored" or made invisible these archives of "elegance." While the jerboa is "happy" without the extravagant wealth of the ancients, the present-day disparities of wealth and equality, especially as organized around race, rely on a continued elision of archives long ignored, the poem suggests.

As a "choice race," the distinction or "elegance" of "the blacks" assumes a visual economy of race, one that early twentieth-century America anxiously struggled to keep intact. In Moore's time, despite the Supreme Court's "separate but equal" decision in *Plessy* vs. *Ferguson*, the assumption of the visual as a register and boundary of racial identity proved unsustainable for maintaining with complete assurance the Jim Crow forms of segregation and discrimination that held to the "one-drop" concept of racial difference and purity (i.e., that "one drop" of "black blood" or heritage defined one as Black). Anxiety over racial passing reached a zenith during Jim Crow, signifying the insufficiency of a visual display of physical characteristics defined as racially distinct to determine "identity" within America's system of racial difference. Moore's reference to "blacks" carries a long history—an archive—of visual signification as socially determining, constituting a racial difference that the poem interprets as an "elegance" that only "ignorance" misunderstands. In other words, these lines legitimately press a progressive viewpoint regarding race and racial history in America, while also carrying the assumption of a visually defined racial difference, an archive of laws, customs, and economic systems reliant upon, and frustrated by, clear boundaries readable through a visual apprehension of "Black."

For the critic, at this point in reading the poem, another kind of archival consciousness is activated, a sprawling collection of letters, reading notebooks, conversation notebooks, poem variants, essays, clippings' files, footnotes, and other materials that swell the Marianne Moore archives. Critics routinely confront Moore's copious extra-poetic materials, whether stored at the Rosenbach and other libraries, or identified in her footnotes, or accessible digitally on the Marianne Moore Digital

Archive site, all of which increasingly inform Moore studies, a scholarly environment certainly invited by the poet's methods of quotation, citation, collection, and archival arrangement in the poems themselves. And so I find myself modestly in the Moore archive, pondering Moore's letters as I read and reread the poem's visualized and racialized embodiments. I feel like the "archival tourist," theorized by Laura Engel: "as researchers we are all tourists in the archive, curating materials according to our own subject positions and contextual performances. ... [that] emphasize that creative ways of engaging in critical speculation are crucial in piecing together marginalized histories."[43]

Like the archival tourist taking a detour from the poem into the letters Moore wrote while working on "The Jerboa," I read letters reflecting her concern about contemporary issues as the Depression persisted, war threatened, and social upheavals characterized America's direction. A letter to Kenneth Burke in November of 1932, responding to a long letter from him criticizing the economics of capitalism, notes a dissonance between FDR's racial politics and his support for labor.[44] She is critical of the newly elected president's "grateful co-operation ... with the anti-Negro south," linking his racial politics to her impatience with polarized debates between labor and capital: "we are subject to illusions about labor as well as about capital. ... So whether capital or labor has the power, there is a deadlock," demonstrating a refusal of people who "think well in one direction, dodge thinking about the whole."[45]

Strikingly, vexingly, her critique then chooses a racialized metaphor to encapsulate what she defines as a "disharmony" in the "inward characteristic" of both FDR and Norman Thomas, the Socialist presidential candidate (1928 and 1932, and four elections thereafter) and Protestant minister: these two men "are, to me,—like the spotilly pigmented offspring of a Negro and a white parent, biologically inept, and we don't want them—or rather, need not want them."[46] Offensive on many levels, this disparagement of racial mixing strikingly emphasizes the affront to clear visual understandings of race in the "spotilly pigmented offspring" while designating visual signs of mixing as evidence of inferiority (biologically inept) and waste (we don't need them). This "disharmony," expressed in racial terms, associates an aesthetics of appearance with inner character and physical vigor, a dependence upon the visual to determine the integrity of self that the "elegance" of "blacks" in "The Jerboa" convey, assuming (in the poem) a purity of African being and inheritance and, therefore, a visual aesthetic confirming America's racial categories.

Reading the archival relation of letter and poem animates connections between the jerboa, Africa, contemporary racial issues, and concepts of "visibility" and power explored through the poem's archival structure. Evoking a body that makes visible America's long and abusive history of racial miscegenation, this body also blurs racial lines throughout America's history that legal definitions of slavery and iterations of Jim Crow tried to solidify in privileging white power. Moore's comments are troubling, not the least in suggesting an awareness of how racial lines operate in a visual economy but nonetheless participating in an aversion to the racial "taint" of mixed blood. While she distances herself from the "anti-Negro" element of the south, she articulates a preference for clear and separate racial categories, for the elegant "blacks" of "The Jerboa" and not the "spotily pigmented" affront of the mixed offspring.

This unresolvable archival moment seemingly pits contraries against each other. However, as much as I want to read Moore's letter and the poem's call to admire Blacks as a paradoxical contradiction, the complexities of racism point to a continuum of logic in her capacity to hold progressive notions about a race she considers unjustly oppressed while wanting to preserve boundaries between her own whiteness and their blackness. The pigment of the offspring visually upsets that boundary, spiraling as it does into an apprehension of the body as itself an archive challenging racial categories and hierarchies.

In thinking about "The Jerboa" in relation to this archival vexation, we might question then the role of empirical observation stressed in "Abundance" through the detailed descriptions of the creature making up the majority of its stanzas. Despite this emphasis, the poem questions the primacy of empirical knowledge even as it engages in its methods, both in the processes Moore undertook in writing the poem and in its published form. Certainly, the work of critics like Catherine Paul or Victoria Bazin in establishing the media and museum resources for the poem clarifies how text mediates experience in the compositional process and the poem's presentation.

The poem suggests this mediation when, after several stanzas stressing the natural body and home of the animal, its final lines return evidence of human labor, looping back to the poem's first section. After an extended observation detailing the body, habitat, and movement of the jerboa, the last stanza returns to human-made objects, the flageolet (a small wind instrument) and a decorative art furniture piece. In part, these objects pay homage to the creature while also memorializing it in more permanent form:

> Its leaps should be set
> to the flageolet;
>   pillar body erect
>   on a three-cornered smooth-working Chippendale
>   "claw"—propped on hind legs, and tail as third toe,
>   between leaps to its burrows. (ll. 157–62)

Writing to Monroe Wheeler on November 30, 1932, soon after "The Jerboa" was accepted by *Hound and Horn*, Moore thanked him for a "Christie catalogue," commenting that "I look on the Chippendale tripod stands as acquaintances also," signaling that she too had been inspecting this style, which becomes a visual source for her poem.[47] Neatly, the naming of Chippendale furniture after the London cabinet maker Thomas Chippendale in the mid-eighteenth century is the first instance of naming a furniture style in England after its maker rather than a monarch. It is lovely to imagine that Moore knew this fact, although it is mere speculation that she knowingly ended her poem with an artifact that recognizes its creator and the labor of the production in contrast to the "shadow archives" of anonymous laborers of "Too Much."[48] Another reading might suggest that, as a furniture style that became popular in colonial America, the Chippendale contrasts the "free" jerboa as an echo of the section's opening gesture toward Scipio and histories of colonizing power.

And yet another reading emerges from archival conjunctions. Moore had earlier written to Wheeler that year (on July 11) about an image of a hunting-leopard:

> The hunting-leopard is a delight—rightly speaking, a study; and the production itself is so very remarkable in *harmonious contrasts, and definiteness*. The whole concept—bony frame and dog claws, with the "useless" claw on the foreleg so well depicted—is more interesting to us than I can tell you. Strange to say, I had just been thinking about this beast in connection with something I am trying to write for *The Hound & Horn*—"The Jerboa."[49]

The "useless claw," Bazin argues, signals her disdain for modern Western cultures that "defined the value of objects in terms of their price and that failed to appreciate forms of human labor that produce 'things' with apparently no economic value (such as poems)" or decorative carvings.[50] Here, the useless claw contributes to a "harmonious" whole, creating aesthetic value for the viewer. I am struck by the reference to "harmonious contrasts, and definiteness," the language echoing the pointed lack of harmony—the "inharmony"—characterizing political strategies and figures Moore criticizes through a metaphor presenting racial mixing as inherently disharmonious. The archives again unsettle me.

The Chippendale carving joins and ends the poem's archive of objects that revel in spectacle and display, gesturing toward the ostentatious showing off of wealth through possessions that are meant to be viewed. In its curation, the poem considers its objects in relation to a contemporaneous circulation of ideas of display, wealth, and consumerism, particularly in recognizing the disappearance of production and the laboring body under the pressures of what Veblen calls "conspicuous consumption," a culture of consumption fully emergent by the 1920s, and conditions of labor by the 1930s. The poem's archival re-inscription of laboring bodies works to lay bare the relationship of consumer spectacle and economic oppression relevant to these pre-Depression and Depression-era years. At the same time, the framing values that Moore brings to her archive reveal her own complex attitudes shaping how some bodies, especially racialized bodies, are perceived in thinking about the "harmonious" design of either creature or society. It seems fitting that our own readerly curation of the archive making up "The Jerboa" (and existing beyond the poem) mitigates the easy resolvability of interpretation and challenges assumptions of the neutral archive. In this sense, the "processes of archival thinking and practices of curation" undertaken by this poem and by interpretations of it jointly "project an archival imaginary" that, finally, reflects upon the process of archival engagement rather than seeking final answers in the archives.[51]

Archives and Meanings

CHAPTER SEVEN

"Possible Meaning"
Marianne Moore's Anagogical Reading of Rilke, Herbert, La Fontaine, and Hölderlin

Luke Carson

In a lecture she attended in April of 1940 entitled "The Lyric of Condensed Experience," Marianne Moore was taken with a distinction made by the speaker, W. H. Auden, between a poem's "immediate meaning and possible meaning."[1] No trace of this distinction appears in Auden's writing and although she uses it twice in her published work, Moore never provides a clear gloss on it; characteristically, she only provides examples.[2] Its appearance is particularly striking in her Reading Notebook 1938–1942, which she kept in preparation for the many academic obligations she had committed herself to beginning in 1940.[3] This notebook consists primarily of transcriptions of major texts—mostly of contemporary literary criticism, such as T. S. Eliot's essays, but also of editions of works by Robert Burns, Emily Dickinson, and Stéphane Mallarmé. As we will see shortly, among these writers is Rainer Maria Rilke, whose work had been translated in the 1930s by J. B. Leishman, sometimes with the assistance of Stephen Spender. In the margin of her notes on Leishman and Spender's commentary on Rilke's poetics, Moore draws a parallel to Auden's distinction. The distinction becomes a key critical concept for Moore in spite of remaining, as I will argue, theoretically indeterminate; in spite of the opportunity presented by the notebook's expansive literary-theoretical readings, Auden's distinction undergoes no clarification or displacement or subsumption by the conceptual apparatus of the influential texts from which she cites. She never, for example, clarified the difference in meaning between the "immediate" and the "possible" in terms of metaphor, which, as she knew from reading and taking notes on *Philosophy of Rhetoric*, had been reconceived by I. A. Richards in terms of tenor and vehicle. Even the expansive key concepts proposed by F. O. Matthiessen in his just-published *American Renaissance* (1942), which restored concepts such as metaphor and symbol to their context in the visionary and redemptive cultural ambitions of a Romanticism disparaged by Moore's contemporaries, had no perceptible effect on this formulation. In fact, she notes a deficiency in Matthiessen's comments on Eliot when he is unable to see that when Eliot uses the word "triumph" it has what she calls a "special meaning." While the problem Moore identifies may be attributed to a lapse in Matthiessen's reading, it may also indicate for Moore a deficiency in his theory and method: "special meaning" may have some relation to the enigmatic category of "possible meaning," a concept that allows Moore to posit an ultimate anagogic meaning that critics such as Matthiessen and, as we will see briefly, William Empson, foreclose by means of the protocols of their interpretive discipline.[4]

The medieval concept of anagogy and the related notion of ultimate meaning may seem alien in the context of Matthiessen's humanism, but the religious context of Moore's response to Matthiessen, which is her most detailed and engaging critical observation in this notebook, is clearly established by the topic of Eliot's religious poetry and the challenge it posed to secular modes of meaning.[5] Matthiessen observes that "the faith voiced in *Ash Wednesday* and *Murder in the Cathedral* is scarcely triumphant; it is often nearly obscured in doubt, and beset by the most subtle of temptations, that in which spiritual pride masks itself as humility."[6] Moore marks the passage with several question marks and offers a theological critique: "triumph has a special meaning here. M. is being too practical. It won't be/isn't in the 'end' but in the outcome that faith triumphs."[7] While this is a complex comment to parse, it would seem that the difference between "end" and "outcome" indicates the difference between Matthiessen's "practical" understanding that Eliot's poetry would have the option of occupying a position of "triumph" when that word only has meaning in an anagogic sense as the "end" under the aegis of eschatological vision. Matthiessen "is being too practical" in thinking that the triumphant "end" is a position that can be embodied in literary form; the "outcome" of faith, on the other hand, would seem to be its works, which include poetry as what Moore calls (referring to Blake) "a special kind of seeing." Citing Ruskin, Moore says that "[t]o see clearly is poetry, prophecy, and religion all in one."[8] But poetry itself—as work that is one of the outcomes of faith—implies the "end" as triumph beyond works: Moore's distinction is eschatological and marks the boundary between poetry and theology where the visionary mode of writing comes into play, a boundary where eschatological poets such as Dante, Milton, and Blake interest Moore. In this essay, I hope to deepen our sense of Moore's relationship to the visionary tradition with which she affiliated herself by considering first her reading of Rilke and Herbert as poets of "possible meaning"; second her extension of that literary concept to her reading and translation of the fables of Jean de La Fontaine; third and finally, I will demonstrate the idea at work as Moore reads Hölderlin for the first time in her 1943 *tour de force* review of Frederic Prokosch's translations of a selection of his poems.

I

"Immediate meaning" is not a concept readily available either in the literary criticism contemporary with Moore or in the history of criticism or theories of meaning. It tends to be quite casually used rather than theoretically determined. I would include among these more casual uses Eliot's 1942 lecture, "The Music of Poetry," in which he touches upon a word's "immediate meaning in ... context."[9] It has a more theoretical formulation in the concluding "summary" of I. A. Richards's *Practical Criticism*, in which he discusses the process of "understanding"—the philosophical notion of *verstehen*—in terms of the apprehension of thought, feeling, tone, and intention in a communicative act.[10] Leaving out for his present purposes the problem posed by understanding figurative language, Richards says that "the other [that is, the non-figurative] meanings are best received, when possible, each in its appropriate more direct and immediate manner."[11] Richards's notion of the "immediate" is of course not a simple one—like Auden's "immediate meaning," it is not as simple as the idea of "literal meaning"—since the goal of practical criticism is the social and aesthetic education of understanding so that its immediacy may become richly meaningful as it approaches the horizon of the ideal reader. "The gift [of understanding]," Richards writes, "reaches its heights perhaps only in certain favorable social settings," such as the world in which Julien Sorel finds himself and in the criminal underworld, with its requirement of indirect communication, to take two of Richards's examples.[12]

Such complexity in the notion of the "immediate" is also the case with Eliot. My isolation of his apparently common-sense formulation of "immediate meaning" above misrepresents the phrase by stripping it of its resonant context:

> The music of a word is, so to speak, at a point of intersection: it arises from its relation first to the words immediately preceding and following it, and indefinitely to the rest of its context; and from another relation, that of its immediate meaning in that context to all the other meanings in which it has had in other contexts, to its greater or less wealth of association.[13]

As Richards would say, there is a certain point at which "thought" must intervene in order to mediate or to "understand" but the end of such thought is clearly the intensification of "immediate meaning" in the form of its closely related and perhaps even synonymous category of "immediate experience."

None of these formulations of what is beyond the "immediate meaning" understood in a narrow sense related to "literal meaning" addresses what I think Moore understood by "possible meaning." Moore's interest was not in Richards's pedagogical goal of clear communication of complexes of feeling, intention, and thinking as a process of hermeneutical and empathetic understanding in which, ideally, communication is a form of "immediate experience." What Moore understood by "possible" was not a hermeneutical category subject to debate among interpreters in the classroom or the institutions of literary criticism seeking protocol for legitimacy of interpretation, an issue explored so richly by William

Empson, whom I will discuss shortly. Instead, "possible meaning" is perceived at the threshold of the work, where it encounters or crosses into a region of significance not delimited by the unifying frameworks of, for example, the genre or mode by which readers and critics have oriented themselves within the work. As I suggested above and as I will now argue, "possible meaning" provides a passage from genres and modes such as lyric and fable to eschatological vision and to the threshold of literature and theology.

This becomes clearer when we read the passage that inspired Moore's marginal note. In the introduction to their translation of Rilke's *Duino Elegies*, Leishman and Spender write that while in "the greatest poetry ... there may be many layers of meaning, what may be called the primary meaning is always immediately apparent."[14] In the margins, Moore writes: "Auden / immediate / meaning & possible."[15] She appears to have found a confirming explanatory power in the context of their comments:

> Rilke often finds himself confronted with the limitations of language: sometimes the particular shade of meaning, the particular tone of feeling he wants a word to bear is not naturally and immediately determined by its particular position; it will only, as Hopkins would say, "explode" when the reader comes to it with recollections of it in other contexts, even, perhaps, in other works. Sometimes a word or phrase which at first seems puzzling or odd is found to be charged with concentrated or subtle observation of some quite ordinary phenomenon, looked at from Rilke's peculiar angle of vision: we are like amateurs gazing at something through a microscope; at first everything is blurred, but we keep on focussing and adjusting, and then, suddenly, everything is clear.[16]

In "Humility, Concentration, and Gusto" Moore appears to quote, perhaps from her lecture notes, Auden's application of this distinction to define the "concentration" of her title—although one suspects that the presentation of the idea is her own rather than a transcription from Auden's talk—and we might suspect a memory of Leishman and Spender's image of the telescope in the gloss Moore provides on her textual example when she first introduces Auden's distinction into her published work:

> [A] poem is a concentrate and has, as W. H. Auden says, "an immediate meaning and a possible meaning; as in the line,
>
>   Or wedg'd whole ages in a Bodkin's eye
>
> where you have forever in microscopic space; and when George Herbert says,
>
>   I gave to Hope a watch of mine,
>   But he an anchor gave to me,
>
> the watch suggests both the brevity of life and the longness of it; and an anchor makes you secure but holds you back."[17]

Moore's (or Auden's) interpretation of the line from Pope's *Rape of the Lock*, which describes one of the many punishments to which the sylphs tasked with protecting Belinda's lock will be subject, may be the best way to consider what she means by "possible meaning," what region of experience and thought it occupies, and how it is one begins to approach it. Notice first Moore's sleight of hand as she translates the indeterminately hyperbolic "whole ages" into the concept of "forever," and then shrinks "forever" into "microscopic space." What we are asked to comprehend is not the verbal concepts that guide us to this place but a vision of the suffering at the intersection of the eternal and an invisible point of near-nothingness; an idea from the domain of theological speculation abruptly intervenes in our reading process and we find ourselves contemplating a damnation of the sort associated with Dante. What I am arguing is Moore's leap into the domain of "possible meaning" cannot be validated by a process of interpretation constrained by immediate context; in this case, the context of Pope's satire delimits its relationship to the theological depth that licenses Dante's depictions of suffering. But the minute gap opened in Pope's line permits Moore to glimpse the "possible meaning," as if through a "Bodkin's eye" or through a microscope, of the suffering of the damned.[18]

Moore (or Auden) performs a similar operation on the lines from Herbert she cites in the passage above, an example Auden may first have come across in *Seven Types of Ambiguity*, in which William Empson writes:

> You may regard the poem [Herbert's "Hope"] as chiefly about the soul's irritation and despondency at the slowness with which

it can achieve perfect union with God; so that the *watch* is the brevity of human life, and the length of time already spent in waiting (since it means both these, a symbol of time, not of time considered either as long or short, was wanted); the *anchor* either the certain hope of resurrection, or an acquired power of endurance, of holding on to the little that has already been gained.[19]

While Moore's (or Auden's) interpretation of the watch corresponds to Empson's in identifying the simultaneity of brevity and length, which implies the despair that time will never end and the anxiety that it moves too swiftly, their interpretation of the anchor differs significantly. The difference may derive from Empson's understanding (in Richards's sense, implying *verstehen*) in contrast to Moore's, which presumes the more primary and fundamental relationship to theological meaning that makes an anagogical leap possible. To say as Moore does that "an anchor makes you secure but holds you back" includes and enhances Empson's meaning, but the enhancement is primarily a darkening of the feeling; if security, however necessary for the soul's survival, holds one back, the only thing one can do is raise the anchor and head into the winds again in what we can infer is a terrible insecurity. The figure of Hope's anchor is illuminated by one of Moore's crucial maxims: "hope [is] not ... hope / until all ground for hope has / vanished."[20] The feeling and idea we get from this interpretation is not so much "about the soul's irritation and despondency at the slowness with which it can achieve perfect union with God" as it is about the discontinuity of the moments in which the ground of Hope is touched—consider also the depth to which the anchor has to plunge to touch that ground—and the terrible burden and weight of the moments of exposure to despair, in which the weight of Hope is a burden and which may be indistinguishable from despair itself.

Moore's interest in the lines from Herbert may remind us of her own use of abstract terms for moral and spiritual states; her work consistently leans towards even as it draws back from the allegorical meaning that she found in one of her favorite works, Bunyan's *Pilgrim's Progress*. One example bookends her writing career: a poem called "Fear is Hope" that appeared in her first book, *Observations* (1924), is a revision of a 1916 poem entitled "Sun" that has the allegorical epigraph, dropped in 1924,

"Hope and Fear—those internecine fighters—stop fighting and accost him."[21] When it is published again in 1966 as the concluding poem of *Tell Me, Tell Me*, and then again in 1967's *Complete Poems*, it has recovered its 1916 title, "Sun," and the epigraph is restored in abridged form: "Hope and Fear accost him."[22] Between title and epigraph the words move back and forth from moral or spiritual concept to allegorical figure; the allegorical tendency of the poem remains unresolved under the pressure of theological concern on the one hand and lyric resolution on the other. By lyric resolution I mean the poetic mode in which psychological and spiritual dilemmas or crises are dramatized in a process of reflection culminating in some form of emotional or argumentative equilibrium. By theological concern I mean the pressure of signification that poetry and language experience when they broach questions of the ultimate meaning of such terms as Hope and Fear in eschatological terms, which, I will argue, is what Moore has in mind when she thinks of the meaning of the word "possible." Like Herbert's, Moore's interest in the experience of Hope and Fear touches upon their possible meaning in relation to eschatological vision, in this case the experience of hope and of fear as ultimate infernal and purgatorial states. As hope and fear become "hope" and "fear," which then become Hope and Fear, private modes of feeling and experience become guides to the final things toward which the medieval system of the four levels of meaning oriented readers, in which the mystery of those final things themselves could be properly contemplated in the mode of anagogy.[23]

Thomas Aquinas's formulation of the mode of anagogy quickly gets us to the eschatological level of contemplation: anagogy, he writes, "relates to eternal glory." While "hope" and "fear" can retain a full meaning without an appeal to final things, the idea of "eternal glory" is not merely conceptual but asks that we imagine modes of being beyond such human experiences as hope and fear; but it also asks that we see "hope" and "fear" in light of such anticipated glory. For medieval thinkers, the fulfillment of such glory is to be found first in the incarnation of Christ, then in the words and events of the New Testament, which fulfill the Old with the fullness of meaning, and then finally in the last things of revelation. For Moore, on the other hand, in addition to the New Testament there are certain texts at the threshold of the literary and of revelation, such as Richard Baxter's *The*

Saints' Everlasting Rest, Milton's *Paradise Lost*, and, perhaps less obviously or frequently, Dante's *Divine Comedy*. Baxter's work probes relentlessly at what everlasting rest must be like as a mode of glory; Milton provided Moore with a way of imagining, for example, the innocence of Adam and Eve in the glory of creation; and, as I will argue here, Dante can be glimpsed in Moore's imaginings of despair, which "relates to eternal glory" as its deprivation. Anagogy breaks the circuit of allegorical meaning that goes from concepts (hope and fear) to figures (Hope and Fear) and back to concepts without making contact with the spiritual and experiential state of hope or of despair. These ultimate states are what Moore saw in the idea of "possible meaning," in which, as she writes at the end of "Virginia Britannia," one might experience "an intimation of / what glory is."[24]

II

Moore's anagogical moments occur when a poem has built into it a synaptic leap to another text or image with which it is discontinuous and which, I argue, discloses or indicates a spiritual state that the poem itself cannot present in its immediacy. The first of these moments I will establish is a Dantesque vision of damnation that appears with the shock of what she calls the "not said" in her highly attentive and detailed, although often wayward, translation of La Fontaine's fables. The critical concept of the "not said" appears in Moore's 1951 essay, "Impact, Moral and Technical; Independence versus Exhibitionism; and Concerning Contagion," where she claims that "we are the most eloquent by reason of the not said."[25] To illustrate this idea she first turns to Lafontaine for two examples of what she considers, in her intriguing and obscure distinction, his work "go[ing] out of date" and so failing to achieve its proper eloquence. Both examples focus on the pun as a form of "terseness." I will start with her second example, which is a passage from "The Dairymaid and her Milk-Pot," in which a dairymaid on her way to market counts the money she will get for her milk until, in Moore's translation, "her head [has] grown light" as her summer dress. Moore comments: "the word 'light' is literal."[26] This may seem counterintuitive, since the zeugma has two meanings, and forms a kind of pun. But if we are to follow Moore, we might say the word has two literal meanings and each lacks "the shimmer of the unsaid."[27] Both of these meanings are readily available in the dictionary and do not require recourse to the figurative.

When we turn from Moore's second example from La Fontaine to her first, a similar problem emerges, but Moore's reasoning discloses a move she makes to supplement the poem with an outside element. In "The Cobbler and the Financier," a cobbler sings at his workbench, and the music is so beautiful that anyone hearing it stands still to hear the arpeggios "sink / Deeper than the seven sages think."[28] In this passage, Moore claims, "'deeper' is literal," and again the reason may be that there are two literal meanings present simultaneously: the depth of the music is the cobbler's voice sinking to *basso profondo* and the depth of profound aesthetic appreciation is associated with contemplative wisdom. Oddly, however, if we turn to La Fontaine's original text we see that the word "deeper" does not appear there. Instead, his cobbler is described as "plus content que les sept sages"—happier than the seven sages.[29] Though the word *plus*, or "more," suggests a quantitative increase, Moore's "deeper" is not a "verbal transcript," as she will say in her review of Frederic Prokosch's translations of Hölderlin, but is a translation based on an understanding of the experience of happiness described by La Fontaine with the literal word *content*. Moore's translation offers a phenomenological correction of La Fontaine's original: it understands "happiness" to be, when intense, an experience of depth, and Moore therefore provides that metaphor in order to appeal to an understanding of the experience outside the poem itself. She thereby silently indicates where La Fontaine falls short.

In contrast to these failures of what I take to be "possible meaning," which Moore considers to be "out of date," Moore turns to one example of La Fontaine when he is not "out of date [but is] ahead of it"—a phrase that, as I mentioned above, remains very enigmatic. La Fontaine "succeeds," as Moore sees it, in "The Fly and the Ant," a fable in which a fly proudly asserts his superiority to the industrious ant on the basis of, for example, his freedom to land on a king's head and to take the first few tastes of a sacrifice prepared for the gods. But the central claim that interests Moore is the fly's claim that, as Moore summarizes it, his superiority is recognized at court because an artificial beauty patch is called a "fly," or in French a *mouche*:

"the court belle adjusts her artificial fly-freckle," intensifying her complexion by a little patch before she goes forth to conquer; and where the ant says to the fly, "but flies are spies and sure to be hung"—playing on the word *mouche* with which the word "patch" is identical, and it is so compact that it is a desperation because we are not often able to achieve such simultaneity ourselves.[30]

The ant retorts that flies that land on the king's head are subject to a quick death and that the ones that eat the gods' food taint it; but the ant reserves his scorn particularly for the idea that a beauty patch being called a *mouche* implies recognition of the fly's nobility. As the ant says, the patch "is as black as you or I," but he would prefer it be called a "fly-speck" than have it be named after him.[31] The ant then proceeds to denounce the "langage si vain" of the fly, a phrase that makes clear that the poem is thinking about language.[32] Moore translates the phrase as "boasts that are inane,"[33] which misses the emphasis by narrowing the concern to the vanity of the fly and his "notions so lofty" (*hautes pensées*). The ant promptly subjects the fly's metaphorical extension of the word *mouche* into a devastating series of overlooked "immediate" meanings, that is, meanings for which a certain word, with all of its punning and metaphorical potential, is routine currency: "Are not parasites also known as flies?"[34] This insult is intended to remind the fly of the range of the "immediate meaning" of the word *mouche*, and the ant's interpretive verve with meaning clearly establishes the moral truth about the fly's misplaced pride.

The ant is rhetorically adept with the resources of words. But the wordplay operates on another level as well, which is the level of Moore's translation. To take one example, consider how the word "inane" in the line previously cited recovers and preserves the French word *âne*, the donkey or ass the ant invokes in contrast with the king invoked by the fly: "Pre-empting the head of a king or an ass [*âne*]."[35] The *âne* that persists in "inane" as an echo of La Fontaine's *Ane*, a word Moore translated faithfully in its first appearance in the fable, suggests the metamorphic power by which a human or even a fly may become an ass. Moreover, the word "inane" stubbornly occupies an ambiguous place between translation and the original language, perhaps reminding us of Shakespeare's Bottom ("How thou art translated!") and further suggesting that such metamorphosis may not always be reversible. In contrast, Moore almost entirely effaces La Fontaine's twice-used verb *hanter*, meaning "to frequent" or "haunt" a place, a word used by the fly to describe the freedom he has to enter palaces at will: *Je hante les palais* ("Frequenting mansions," in Moore's words).[36] By translating *hanter* as "to frequent" Moore leaves out the ghostly sense that is one of its "immediate meanings" in English. While Moore rightly if narrowly translates it as "frequenting"—narrowly because in French too it has the sense, to the point of spookiness, of not being quite appropriately or fully present, of lingering where one may not quite belong—she does echo it when the ant scornfully throws the fly's phrase back at him: *Vous hantez les palais; mais on vous y maudit*.[37] Moore's somewhat homophonic translation loses the immediate meaning of *hanter* as it converts the phrase into an epithet for the fly: "My haughty palace fly! scourge loathed by royalty!" The ant points out that the fly is promptly expelled from the courts he haunts and is considered among the *profanes*, La Fontaine's rhyme word for *Ane*. The ant's religious language is hyperbolical; his own position remains that of a moralist using the "immediate meaning" of words for his rhetorically sophisticated moral condemnation. Moore indicates that the ant's level of rhetoric and meaning is confined to the socially determined register of "immediate meaning" by identifying the fly as "the economist." As an economist rather than a moralist or a priest, the ant may himself be on insubstantial moral or ethical ground in his self-righteous tirade. We might distinguish this "economist" and his "spirit of capitalism," to quote Max Weber, from the "rapture and labor," as Moore writes in connection with Blake, of La Fontaine's cobbler.[38]

To summarize the first part of the analysis above, we could say that the fly's understanding of the "immediate meaning" of the word *mouche* is deficient and that the ant corrects him by saturating the immediate meaning with the lesson he provides the fly. On the level of translation, however, another region of meaning is perceptible. The language of the fable is restricted to the dimension of the moralizing "economist" so that the religious language of damnation (*maudire*) and profanation has a merely social meaning, and the word "haughty" is merely a social judgment lacking the eerie otherness implied by *hanter* and "to haunt," which is only echoed distantly in Moore's "haughty." Yet that ghostliness has been displaced to a definite region that is still perceptible in the poem, which is haunted by something that is there but not in its proper rhetorical, figurative, and semantic place. Recall that "we are the most eloquent by reason of the not said."[39] At the end of this poem is silence: the fly is not permitted to reply to this crushing denunciation. But if he was receptive to the degradations landed upon him by the ant, he might experience, in his silence, a horrifying self-recognition. The anagogical moment of this poem emerges under the pressure of Blakean vision: if the fly were to arrive at the horrified self-recognition the ant offers him, he would see himself as William Blake's "Ghost of a Flea," which for Moore is an example of "[a] special kind of seeing" that is "poetry, prophecy, and religion all in one."[40] La Fontaine's "parasite," subjected to Blakean vision, achieves its anagogic form as the flea depicted by Blake and described by him in the text by John Varley from which Moore here cites:

> During the time occupied in completing the drawing, the Flea told [Blake] that all fleas were inhabited by the souls of such men as were by nature blood-thirsty to excess, and were therefore providentially confined to the size and form of insects; otherwise, were he himself, for instance, the size of a horse, he would depopulate a great portion of the country.[41]

With his failures, Moore writes, La Fontaine "goes out of date," but with his successes he is "ahead of it"; the obscurity of that statement is illuminated somewhat when Moore reiterates the phrase "out of" at the end of her paragraph as she admits her "desperation" at trying to achieve such an effect of what she calls "simultaneity" as La Fontaine does with his *mouche*: "Robert Bridges insisted that words be in keeping—or, we might say, deliberately out of keeping."[42] Bridges borrows the word "Keeping" from painting, in which it means, according to the *Oxford English Dictionary*,

> The maintenance of the proper relation between the representations of nearer and more distant objects in a picture; hence, in more general sense, "the proper subserviency of tone and colour in every part of a picture, so that the general effect is harmonious to the eye" … the maintenance of harmony of composition.[43]

Blake's vision of the ghost of a flea haunting a palace certainly disturbs "the maintenance of proper relation," a disturbance once again associated in Moore's presentation with a distortion, as through a microscope or telescope, of the large and the small. G. K. Chesterton describes it as a "tall vampire stalking through tall corridors at night," or haunting, we might say, "some silent castle of giants."[44] Moore's abrupt revision of Bridges with her idea that words may also be "deliberately out of keeping" indicates the break in continuity, a threshold "out of" the "immediate meaning" of literary context, where the opportunity for the anagogical leap of "possible meaning" is held out as the text gives us a glimpse of what Moore, after Eliot, calls "depths of 'degradation.'"[45]

III

As we can see from both Eliot and Richards, the notion of "immediate meaning" is very closely related to the idea of immediate experience, which in Richards is explicitly related to the hermeneutic problem of understanding, or what the German philosophical tradition after Kant called *Verstehen*. Rather than being a reductive notion of the immediately accessible or the disciplinary literal as the "actual," for example, it is an aesthetic notion of experience. For Moore, however, such experience amounts to "poetry, prophecy, and religion all in one."[46] Moore's understanding of "immediate" when she heard Auden's talk may have identified it with the meaning she was familiar with from her Bible classes in 1914–15. According to her instructor, Rev. E. H. Kellog, "you know the truth in an immediacy."[47] This concept of aesthetic experience is also illuminated in her 1943 review of a translation of selected poems of Friedrich Hölderlin, whose work she praises for its "interpenetration of the literal and the figurative," which I take to be one way of formulating her understanding of "immediate meaning." While this interpenetration should be understood as a maximal form of aesthetic experience, it also implies the further question of "possible meaning," which I will explore in the rest of this essay by focusing on Moore's understanding of Hölderlin's sense of the presence of the divine. Just as La Fontaine's saturation of his poem with the immediate meaning of *mouche* arrives, in Moore's translation, at the eschatological vision of the soul in damnation—or in irreversible metamorphosis—as a vampiric flea, so Hölderlin's poetry discloses the reverse face of what Eliot calls "the depths of 'degradation,'" namely the eschatological vision of redemption and grace that is immanent to the New Testament in its typological fulfillment, according to its medieval Christian interpreters, of the Old. While this is in itself is less surprising than arriving at the anagogic level in La Fontaine, it is instructive for what it discloses about Moore's own practice as a visionary poet.

Moore's review appeared in the centenary of Hölderlin's death, which also saw two translations of his work—one in England and one in America. The more well-known and enduring of these was *Poems of Hölderlin*, a generous edition with a ninety-seven-page introduction and 140 pages of poems published by a nineteen-year-old Michael Hamburger. The other, entitled *Some Poems of Hölderlin*, was a slim collection of fifteen poems published by New Directions. The translator, Frederic Prokosch, was the American-born son of a German-speaking émigré professor who raised his children to be fluent in German. Prokosch is mainly remembered today for his 1935 novel *The Asiatics*, but at thirty-seven years old he was a well-known and accomplished poet and novelist. Prokosch's translation was reviewed very favorably by Moore in *Accent*, the quarterly magazine, and her review is a *tour de force* piece of Moore's idiosyncratic criticism. Reading Prokosch, Moore looks carefully at the German on the facing page, and is attentive, as one would expect of her, to "accent, syllable, and rhyme," and she comments on Prokosch's attempts to render Hölderlin's experiments in Greek quantitative verse. The review is written a little more than a year after Moore presented the earliest version of what would eventually be published as "Humility, Concentration and Gusto" at Harvard in December of 1941, and it is notable that what comes in for particular praise is Prokosch's inventive enjambment, which implies his recognition of what Moore calls "an impassioned humility in [Hölderlin's] run-over ending."[48]

While praising Prokosch, Moore twice revises his translations in what she calls "an eager loyalty of disagreement."[49] Both of Moore's revisions focus on scenes of "knowing" and "understanding" in Hölderlin, and the idea of an intimate difference and distance between the self and what it seeks to understand. Moore clearly recognized how important these questions were to Hölderlin's conception of the task of poetry and we can observe her making decisions about reading and translating Hölderlin in intimate detail. Her first revision is to the translation of the poem "Man" (*Der Mensch*), which is about the birth of the human being as "the fairest of [the Earth's] children"; while in his youth "the boy [has] the sacred vine as / / His nurse ... soon he is fully grown." Eventually, as he grows up, "the beasts / Avoid him, knowing man for a different kind."[50] In her revision of Prokosch's translation, Moore introduces a strong enjambment after the word "the" in order to achieve a "more informal" syntax that more clearly expresses, as she says, "impassioned humility." Oddly enough, however, Moore retains Prokosch's verb "to know" even though it is not in the original text, which reads: "ihn scheun / Die Thiere, denn ein anderer ist, wie sie, / Der Mensch."[51] Rather than any of the several verbs frequently translated into English as "to know," Hölderlin's only verb is "to avoid," as Prokosch writes. That this is closer to a revision of Prokosch on his own terms rather than a nearer translation of Hölderlin makes it apparent that she is not looking simply for what she calls "a verbal transcript."[52] But it may also suggest an implied interpretation of the idea of "understanding" that Moore figures in terms of her own representation of animals encountering the difference of humans.

I will return shortly to the implications of Moore's retaining the verb "to know" for the animal awareness of human difference, but first I will turn to her second major revision to Prokosch's translation, where because of her more active intervention we begin to suspect that the idea of "knowing" in Hölderlin's work holds a special interest for her. The passage, which is from Hölderlin's "Da ich ein Knabe War" ("When I was a child," translated by Prokosch as "Youth"), recalls being "spared ... from the clamor and violence of men" by "a savior" who kept him "safe and serene" in nature. Looking back at this moment, the speaker recalls the presence of the deities of nature:

True, not yet did I call	Zwar damals rief ich noch nicht
You by name, nor did you give	Euch mit Namen, auch ihr
Me a name, in the manner that men give	Nanntet mich nie, wie die Menschen sich nennen
Names, as though they *knew* one another.	Als *kennten* sie sich.

Yet I *knew* you far better	Doch *kannt'* ich euch besser,
Than I ever *knew* men;	Als ich je die Menschen *gekannt*,
Stillness of ether I *understood*,	Ich *verstand* die Stille des Äthers,
But the words of men never.	Der Menschen Worte *verstand* ich nie.

It is difficult not to notice the rich play of "to know" (*kennen*, as in "to be familiar with"), which in each of its forms (*kennten, kannt, gekannt*) echoes *nanntet*, "named" (Prokosch's "gave me a name"), which in turn rhymes with *verstand*. While humans give each other names "as though they knew one another," the speaker reserves "knowing" for his nameless relation to the deities, even as he hesitates in calling it "knowing"; when it was a nameless relationship it was not yet knowing, but we are presumably to take this poem, in which the deities are named as Helios and Luna, as a poetic advance on that early familiarity (although these are not names that would appear in Hölderlin's mature work). In the meantime, he has never been able "to know" men, or even, in the last two lines of the second quatrain, "to understand" their language:

Stillness of ether I *understood*,	Ich *verstand* die Stille des Äthers,
But the words of men never.	Der Menschen Worte *verstand* ich nie.

Note Prokosch's decision to reduce the chiastic repetition of "verstand" to the one use of "understood." Moore, on the other hand, takes the chiastic structure to introduce a difference in the meaning of the verb, as if two different modes of understanding or "Verstehen" are involved: "I *understood* the soundless air / Human speech I could not *grasp*."[53] The opportunity for this distinction lies in the previous lines, in which Hölderlin's speaker looks back at a childhood favored by the gods and, in composing his poem in gratitude to them, concedes that he was unable at the time to call them by name, and that he himself had no name "in the manner that men give / Names, as though they knew one another." The speaker's immediate relation to the gods seems to require no speech, and yet he has in this poem the capacity to call them by name; his disorientation in the world of human language, the medium he could not grasp, has been overcome in poetic work within that language. Yet even as the poet has acceded to poetic speech, the question remains of what posture human language will have when it approaches the gods. Though this poem is an early one,[54] it has within it the name, here only in noun form, of the god who would become so important to the later poems: *Äther*. The quasi-scientific concept Hölderlin uses in this work has yet to become the name of the god; here it remains as an uncomprehended possibility. As I will argue, Moore's word for the stance toward the god implicit in this poem is figured in the word "grasp."

What Moore introduces with "grasp" is of course the English word associated with the German word for idea, notion, or concept, *Begriff*, which has its roots in *greifen*, to seize, catch, or capture—and to grasp. I think it is safe to assume that this etymology is commonly known; if not, then Moore may have known it from her reading in German thought at Bryn Mawr, or perhaps from John Dewey, who describes a moment of theoretical knowledge as the subject "put[ting] forth his grasp, his *Begriff*, and arrest[ing] movement."[55] However Moore arrived at the verb "to grasp," she finds a sanction for it in reading Hölderlin's work in Prokosch's translation of the opening lines of the 1803 poem "Patmos," which are now among Hölderlin's most well known: "Near, near and / Difficult to grasp is the Almighty. / Where the danger lies, there / Likewise lies the salvation." Hölderlin's verb here is *zu fassen* and not *verstehen*, but in transferring the word from the one poem to the other and in some sense effacing the difference, Moore seems to have been sensitive to Hölderlin's complex sense of what it means to understand and to know. With her sensitivity to dialectical crossings, Moore sees how the struggle to "grasp" provides a dramatic image of the dialectical situation of willing or desiring and understanding.

The word is of course Moore's own, to a significant degree, and that dramatic sense of willing and desiring in the gesture of grasping is evident in the related images in Moore's own work: the "Hands that can grasp" in her definition of poetry in 1919; the grasping hand of Psyche contrasted with the "spread out" hand of Zephyr in the mid-1930s version of "Half-Deity"; the "hairy paws" that "hacked out" the alphabet with an axe in "Armor's Undermining Modesty"; above all there is the image, not explicitly of a hand, but of the human self as the "writing- / master to this world, [who] griffons," as if with the claw of an eagle, its angry and dark adage towards the end of "The Pangolin."[56] Moore's implicit use of "greifen" in her translation of Hölderlin, which recognizes, respects, and brings to the surface the implied dialectics of his chiasmus, suggests that she recognized something of her own concerns as a poet in him. Each of Moore's hand images has some degree of relation to animality—I have left out the inspired scribe who "wrote as with a bird's claw" in "Smooth Gnarled Crape Myrtle"[57]—and Moore deploys this relation in using "grasp" to translate Hölderlin. In doing so, she offers a presentation of Hölderlin's vision as she saw it in the passages she revises; linking these two passages allows her to disclose what in Hölderlin she recognizes as the discovery of her work as well. In "Poetry" the "[h]ands that can grasp" are associated with experiences such as Hölderlin's animals might have when they sense that "man is different": "eyes / that can dilate, hair that can rise"; but the potential difference lies in the qualification Moore adds in the next line: "if it must," which is a playful allusion to human pride in its assumed difference from the animals: the human imagines their hair rising only out of consent to an imperative, as if the will is involved. The figurative implication is that upon being commanded to "rise" to demonstrate respect, the human considers for a moment disobeying: I *can*, but I may choose not to. The phrase asks us also to revisit the "[h]ands that can grasp" and see in them a concise figure for a moment of incipient action and ethical potential. It is not an error when Moore defines the "mammal" in "The Pangolin" as having "two pairs of hands" rather than one:[58] one pair might be the actual hands that can grasp, but the other pair is the "possible" pair that is poised to grasp the god.

Moore does not often widen the aperture on her microscopic visionary moments, but much is disclosed when she incorporates a biblical visionary in "The Jerboa," in which Jacob, "cudgel staff / in claw-hand," saw "steps of air and air angels."[59] This appearance of the "claw" extends far. We can first note that, although he sees "steps," he cannot climb them with his feet, and, as in a dream, his sleep may intensify the frustration of any wish to. That hint is present, if it is, in the "claw-hand," which, however "terrestrial," may imply his "celestial" potential for wings like those of the angels (for example, in Blake's illustration of Jacob's ladder). But from the perspective of Moore's reading of Hölderlin, the most important use of his claw-hands is to build. At sunset, on his way to Haran, Jacob "lighted upon a certain place ... and he took of the stones of that place, and put them for his pillows, and lay down in that place to sleep." Waking the next morning after his vision, he "took the stone that he had put for his pillows, and set it up for a pillar ... [that] shall be God's house."[60] In her review of Hölderlin, Moore says that "German word-masonry ... defies translation," and, citing examples from his translations of lines from "Remembrance" and "Half of Life," praises Prokosch for his "valuable presentation—a Jacob's ladder for the heart that is not hard."[61] The implied figure of Hölderlin's activity in this juxtaposition is of Jacob's basic masonry as he makes a pillow out of stones and then the next morning sets up a stone as the foundation of God's house. Moore would have come across an image of Hölderlin in Leishman's translation of Rilke's *Later Poems*, which is among the books she transcribed from in her Reading Notebook. In "To Hölderlin," Rilke writes: "Oh, what the loftiest long for, you laid, with never a wish, / stone upon stone: it stood. And when it collapsed it left you / unbewildered."[62]

For Moore, the lucidity of Hölderlin's work lies in "the interpenetration of the literal and the figurative," an observation she may have had confirmed in Leishman's commentary on Rilke's "To Hölderlin," in which the word "interpenetration" also appears:

> In his perpetual aspiration after "something ever more about to be," in the originality of his sense of values, in the ardour with which he pursues his subtlest and farthest intuitions, in his interpenetration of mind with nature and of nature with mind, as well as in the very style and diction of his poems, Holderlin, more nearly than any other German poet, resembles Rilke.[63]

The conclusion of Moore's review draws attention to what is also beyond "the interpenetration of mind and nature" in which even "the stones" can be "friends" of the spirit, as Moore has it in "The Jerboa."[64] The "friend" in the New Testament is, of course, Christ, and Moore's Hölderlin is Christian. In Hölderlin, Moore writes, "[there] is nature worship we cannot resent; or to speak more exactly, the forces of nature embodying worship as set forth in the New Testament."[65] With the rare clarity of vision in Hölderlin's work, "the background becomes the foreground" as the apocalyptic figures of the New Testament—the Word—interpenetrate with the poetic word. The final lines of Moore's review are a carefully assembled climactic vision of the biblical allusions in Hölderlin's work, which are left to speak the final word:

> Near is the Lord "if haply we may find him." "And when I saw him, I fell at his feet as dead, and his voice as the sound of many waters saying, ... I am he that liveth"; "they shall mount up with wings as eagles, they shall run, and not be weary; and they shall walk, and not faint."[66]

Though this is the final word, Hölderlin's phrase—"Near, near ... is the Almighty"—introduces it, and we recall that the god is within reach of the "grasp." Moore's climactic vision also echoes her earlier reference to Jacob's ladder with the figure of "mount[ing] up"; but in the fulfillment of the image of Jacob's claw, the mounting is that of an eagle rather than of the foot on a ladder; the wings implied by the claw assume their power of ascent. Finally, the "griffon[ing]" creature of "The Pangolin" finds its redemptive and liberating "like" or likeness in this ascending eagle, which betrays no hint of the temptation not to "rise" when called, even though the eagles at the beginning of Hölderlin's poem "In darkness dwell," presumably with their claws gripping and their wings folded, in a state of possibility only.

CHAPTER EIGHT

Questioning Categories to Revitalize Words
Meaning and Mottoes in the Poetry of Marianne Moore

Jeff Westover

In memory of Cheryl Hindrichs

In *The Order of Things*, Michel Foucault cites Jorges Luis Borges as an inspiration for his investigation of taxonomies. Borges claims to quote from

"a certain Chinese Encyclopaedia" in which it is written that "animals are divided into (a) belonging to the Emperor, (b) embalmed, (c) tame, (d) sucking pigs, (e), sirens, (f) fabulous, (g) stray dogs, (h) included in the present classification, (i) frenzied, (j) innumerable, (k) drawn with a very fine camelhair brush, (l) et cetera, (m) having just broken the water pitcher, (n) that from a long way off look like flies."

As Foucault goes on to explain, "the wonderment of this taxonomy" provokes an awareness of "the limitation of" one's own "system of thought."[1] This semifictional comparative cultural analysis seems relevant to Marianne Moore's poetry, which often mixes fantastical creatures with more mundane ones. In terms of its wild variety and encyclopedic reach,

Borges's scheme of classification finds parallels in Moore's often paradoxical characterizations, while the exotic quality of its types would please a poet who sometimes showed her skepticism about the validity of received wisdom. Moore's sense of the inadequacy of taxonomies also partially accounts for her lifelong practice of revision.

Throughout her work, Moore often questions categories. By doing so, she unsettles assumptions and challenges her readers to join with her in rethinking them. She thinks critically about the sufficiency of categories and considers their limitations as well as their value, frequently preferring fuzzy sets to classical ones.[2] For knowledge to be serviceable and valid, its contours must be permeable enough to allow for growth and change. Errors can be corrected and new discoveries interpreted. As she writes in "The Student," "science is never finished."[3] New insights emerge as readers come to terms with the poet's ways of framing reality. By challenging readers to decipher the details of her poetic canvases, she pushes them to experience her subject matter in a complex and personal way.

Moore demonstrates her enthusiastic curiosity as well as her skepticism about the scope of human knowledge in a reading notebook she maintained from 1930 to 1943. Like her published writing, the notebook shows that Moore heartily agrees with Aristotle's claim that "All human beings by their nature desire to know."[4] Moore's notes are so wide-ranging that one of her entries sums up her attitude toward learning: "an impotent voracity for desultory information" is a "most desirable, and a not too common, form of mental appetite."[5] Moore identifies the author as Arthur James Balfour, who is repudiating Frederic Harrison's denigration of such voracity. For Harrison, to be a powerless (perhaps even sterile) reader of aimless information is clearly bad, while Balfour can see the value of a helpless passion for reading widely without a prescriptive plan. Just as Moore appropriates and adapts the words of others in her poems, Balfour appropriates Harrison's showy phrase and reinterprets it in a positive manner, putting a different spin on "impotent" and "desultory" than Harrison did. Moore's recording of the phrase in her notebook indicates her predilection for reading widely and freely, but it also shows her pleasure in looking at things awry, sympathetically adapting multiple perspectives, and reconceiving prevailing views in the process. As Barry Ahearn observes, "Moore privileges curiosity not just for its own sake but also for its tendency to defamiliarize and thus rout us from our complacencies."[6]

An example of the way Moore troubles the boundaries between categories may be found in her animal poems. Moore characteristically uses parts or qualities of many other animals and objects to describe the key creatures of her poems. One of the bovine avatars in "The Buffalo" has a "soot brown tail-tuft on / a kind of lion- / tail." Compared to the ancient Augsburg ox, latter-day cattle have "decreased / to Siamese-cat- / / Brown Swiss size."[7] Her Frigate Pelican isn't even a pelican. In Moore's rendering, it is "A kind of superlative / swallow" with a "scissor swallow- / tail" and an "eagle / / of vigilance."[8] Moore's jerboa "has chipmunk contours and "hops like the fawn breast," while Peter the cat has "katydid legs about each eye" and whiskers that look like "shadbones."[9] The Plumet Basilisk has "spider-clawed fingers."[10] Papuan pigeons have "lead-colored ostrich-plumes" and "cat-whisker-fibered battleship- / gray lace,"[11] while the cardinal in "Smooth Gnarled Crape Myrtle" sports "a hatchet crest."[12] Moore's compound modifiers reveal the complex structures, qualities, and behaviors of animals, but they also hint at the drawbacks of relegating them to discrete categories. Indeed, some cases are so extreme as to baffle classification altogether. In the unpublished poem "You, Your Horse," Moore is driven to admit that "It could not be described as either one / Thing or the other."[13] If one insists on an either/or logic, the consequent pigeon-holing can have a deadening effect. Friedrich Nietzsche makes this point in "Truth and Lying in a Nonmoral Sense" when he compares "the great edifice of concepts" to "the rigid regularity of a Roman columbarium," or catacomb.[14]

Sometimes Moore's animals have features in common with other animals in the same category to which they belong, but they often show features of quite different kinds of animals. She compounds the complexity of her references by including real as well as fictitious creatures. For example, although a "tiger-horse" evidently refers to an actual breed of horse, Moore adapts the phrase to characterize the "tiger swallowtail" butterfly in "Half Deity," so that the phrase retains an air of the exotic.[15] While the "camel-sparrow" or "sparrow-camel" of "He 'Digesteth Harde Yron'" may seem as fantastically mixed as a gryphon or

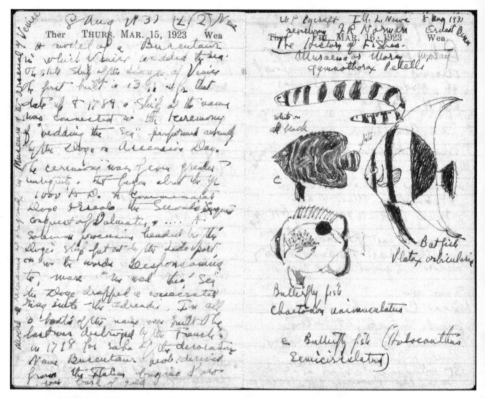

Figure 8.1: Moore's drawings of butterflyfish and batfish from her Reading Notebook 1930–1943 (www.moorearchive.org.Notebook 7.02.02). Thank you to the Moore Estate for permission to print this image

chimera, Moore shows that the names of some real animals also reflect the kind of hybrid profusion she loves.[16] In addition to the extravagant name for the ostrich in "He 'Digesteth Harde Yron,'" Moore draws images of creatures whose names reflect the same kind of heterogeneous combinations in an entry in her 1930–1943 reading notebook. The drawings include a batfish and two butterflyfish (Figure 8.1). The sketches appear among notes she took about W. P. Pycraft's review of J. R. Norman's *A History of Fishes* in *The Illustrated London News*. Moore identifies the fish by their Latin names.[17]

Moore's reliance upon compound modifiers referring to other animals and things reveals her concern to challenge the legitimacy of categories when it comes to perceiving, appreciating, and comprehending the world.

She expresses her enthusiasm for mixtures in a letter to her friend Hildegard Watson, rhapsodizing, "What an El Greco! I have never seen anything by him to which I was indifferent and this is a maximum peak of sensibility. What magical mixing up and differentiating of major minutiae."[18] The qualities Moore prizes in El Greco are hallmarks of her own writing. (After all, when she reaches for a way to characterize a supreme value near the end of "The Hero," she dubs it "the rock / crystal thing to see—the startling El Greco / brimming with inner light."[19]) As Robert Pinsky observes, "Moore likes to keep everything shifting and vibrating. That the reader is never completely sure suits her purpose."[20] Such scrambling of categories can rattle readers, driving them to focus diligently and determine what is being described. Fluid situations force them to reconsider their assumptions and to work through the scenes and contexts Moore strategically "present[s] / / for inspection."[21]

In keeping with this open-minded outlook regarding categories, patterns of inquiry and redefinition characterize many of Moore's poems. From the challenging of received meaning to the citation and investigation of mottoes in "The Student," "Frigate Pelican," "Walking-Sticks and Paperweights and Watermarks," "Virginia Britannia," "Smooth, Gnarled Crape Myrtle," "Then the Ermine," and "Elephants," Moore systematically identifies traditional ideas, questions them, and recasts them to rejuvenate her cultural sources. This is in accord with Ezra Pound's rallying cry to make it new and Moore's contributions to modernist innovation in general, but it also demonstrates something unique about Moore's habit of incorporating other people's words into her poems.

Moore unmoors terms from their conventional, assigned, static meanings so she can open possibilities for emergent meanings—where the sense of a word or image arises from its specific context, as the result of an interaction between a depicted situation and the reader. This is especially evident in two poems from *Observations*. In "Injudicious Gardening" Moore rebels against a given meaning based on a catalog in a book: "If yellow betokens infidelity; / I am an infidel."[22] As Robin G. Schulze explains, "In championing organic forms deemed 'impure' by the Victorian dictionaries, Moore's poem openly challenges a hypermasculinized Victorian conception of Man's place in Nature."[23] The *I* in this poem is proudly defiant, simultaneously appropriating and disputing the validity of the floral symbolism, since it arbitrarily imposes a meaning in an inflexible way. Like Robert Browning, whom she addresses as "you" in the second stanza, she will not brook "Effrontery." The undue limitation or fossilization of meaning offends her sensibility. In the poem, Moore opposes lived experience to book-learning. As she writes in a notebook she kept from 1922 to 1930, "Philosophy should help one to live not to stop living."[24] Moore's speaker takes a stand for the sovereignty of personal experience in engaging directly with the world.

Through spry sound-play, Moore reframes words and expands the possibilities of their meaning in relation to perception and experience. Her slant rhyme of "ill" and "well" indicates the arbitrariness of the incriminating judgment against yellow flowers by emphasizing the phonic difference between the words. "Ill" and "well" are what linguists call a "minimal pair," meaning that a single sound articulates the semantic difference between these polar opposites.[25] Moore begins to transform the color's significance by subtly contrasting the short i-sound of *ill* and the short-e sound of *well*. She continues this transformation through the exact rhymes between "will" and "ill" and "infidel" and "well" (together with the chiming of the last two with the first syllable of "yellow"). These exact and slant rhymes create an atmosphere of phonic similarity, but they also slyly help reshape meaning by semantically allying *infidel* and *well*. In this poem, Moore's skillful rhymes exemplify her ideal of "diction that is ... galvanized against inertia."[26] Over the course of the stanza, Moore turns infidelity into a sign of heroic resistance. In the ironized lexicon of this "injudicious" poem, an infidel turns out to be an Emersonian rebel against constricting social conventions.

In keeping with such reversal of judgment, Moore embarks on a series of meditative questions to open up meaning in "A Fool, A Foul Thing, A Distressful Lunatic." In the context of her descriptions of each animal, she infuses the questions with such innuendo that they are practically rhetorical. The effect of each question is an assertion of the undeniable. By tripling the questions, she builds a case for the wrong-headedness of an unthinking, continued commitment to dead metaphors that impugn the dignity and obscure the reality of the animals she identifies.[27] As Moore's descriptions of each animal show, the proverbial wisdom about geese, vultures, and loons oversimplifies each creature. The poem supports the view that "man prefers to believe in a simple truth; but ... the whole truth is the most complicated thing in the world."[28] Moore culled this statement by Josef Löbel from a 1934 review of his book *Whither Medicine?* Despite the fact that Löbel's book postdates "A Fool, A Foul Thing, A Distressful Lunatic," his insight aptly characterizes its situation. In her poem, Moore scores the pages of "folly's catalogue" with the nib of her forceful pen, reframing her readers' understanding of the creature she carefully redescribes and demonstrating the dangers of anthropomorphic thinking. In doing so, she configures a new "alphabet" of meanings in her latter-day bestiary.[29] As Ahearn observes, Moore's "poems put pressure on conventional definitions. We may come away from them less certain that the meaning we had taken for granted is adequate."[30]

The work of redefinition also occurs in a key passage in "The Jerboa" as well as more broadly in the contrast between the two parts of the poem (subtitled "Too Much" and "Abundance"). Moore writes,

> Africanus meant
> the conqueror sent
>   from Rome. It should mean the
>   untouched: the sand-brown jumping rat—free-born; and
>   the blacks: that choice race with an elegance
>   ignored by one's ignorance.[31]

Moore's appropriation of "Africanus" invests the military title with a meaning that jibes with the poem's overall values of freedom and self-reliance. By redefining the historical term, she satirizes the hubris of military conquest and asserts the dignity of the indigenous. "Untouched" implies pure and pristine, suggesting that the jerboa is beyond the reach of corrupting human influences. Honoring its environment by adapting so admirably to it, the creature embodies a heroic integrity worth emulating.[32] Like the addressee of "Bulwarked against Fate," the jerboa remains "inviolate."[33] The rhyme that rounds out the passage drives home the ideal of Black elegance through the semantic contrast with "ignorance," a benighted state that is intensified by the polyptoton in the final line.

Along with the redefinition of specific terms, Moore sometimes investigates or ironizes the language she quotes or cites. She incorporates mottoes in several poems, although she never sets them off in quotation marks in the way she sometimes does with other phrases.[34] Moore took notes on various coats of arms and the mottoes associated with them in the reading notebook she maintained from 1930 to 1943.[35] She even culled mottoes from the bookplates of prominent people. Her notes on bookplates suggest that she found the mottoes on them by research she conducted at the Pratt Institute Library.[36] Such notes seem relevant to the many poems addressing armor as well as to the poems featuring mottoes, although the mottoes in her poems do not overlap much with the ones in the notebook. In some cases, Moore incorporates mottoes to reinforce the key idea of a poem, but in most she treats them as expressions of received meaning, questioning and correcting them in favor of a primary value or principle that emerges over the course of the poem.

The latter seems to be the case in "Conseil to a Bacheler," a found poem from a motto on an Elizabethan trencher. In the motto, young and old men alike are warned away from marriage.[37] "A motto," writes Pamela White Hadas, "is a condensation of the world's complexity and often a defense against forces one does not understand very well."[38] According to this line of reasoning, the bachelor seems to need a warning against women because he cannot understand them well enough if left to his own devices. Moore presumably recontextualizes the verses to invite her readers' critical reflection on the institution of marriage by slyly hinting at the complacent self-interest reflected in the motto. (After all, Moore addressed Bryn Mawr alumnae when the poem first appeared in a college publication.[39]) In this respect, "Conseil" is a kind of prelude to her more wide-ranging treatment of the topic in "Marriage." Along similar lines, in such poems as "The Frigate Pelican," "Virginia Britannia," "Smooth Gnarled Crape Myrtle," "Then the Ermine," and perhaps "The Jerboa," mottoes are considered, corrected, or contrasted with alternate meanings that Moore develops.[40] In other poems, including "The Student," "Walking-Sticks and Paperweights and Watermarks," and "Elephants," Moore integrates mottoes into her poetic arguments as a culmination of meaning, in the form of an epigram that condenses an overall point as a general truth about the world. (In "Elephants," for instance, she offers Socrates' claim that "the wisest is he who's not sure that he knows."[41]) For Jonathan Culler, this feature may exemplify one of the defining qualities of lyric as a genre.⁴² In such cases, she emphasizes the benefit of inherited wisdom, but articulates it in a new context that reasserts its value. Proverbial wisdom resonates not only as moral desiderata, but also as ancestral insight newly reconfirmed.

In the case of the first group, Moore demonstrates the limitations of certain perspectives by citing common phrases. In "The Frigate Pelican," for example, she characterizes her emblematic bird by differentiating it from the industrious ambitions of would-be social climbers inspired by Poor Richard's advice in Benjamin Franklin's famous almanac: "Make hay; keep / the shop; I have one sheep; were a less / limber animal's mottoes."⁴³ Two of the three mottoes are so familiar that Moore feels justified in supplying only the beginning of each of them: Make hay while the sun shines; Keep thy shop, & thy shop will keep thee;⁴⁴ and Now I've a Sheep and a Cow, every body bids me good morrow.⁴⁵ Moore suggests that her abbreviated versions suffice because they are virtually proverbial, lodged as they are in the minds of many Americans. As Franklin explains in his *Autobiography*, he succeeded in his new business by making a show of his labor before he even secured a stable clientele.⁴⁶ By creating a general impression of his industriousness, he convinced prospective customers that his business had a lot to offer. By contrast, Moore's bird makes a nest for his offspring so it can enjoy leisure. Moreover, the bird secures much of its food by stealing the prey of other birds. Her heroic bird is a bandit, not unlike herself when she integrates the words of others in her poems.

Moore's bird is not even correctly named, as she points out to her readers. Its strategic observation makes it "an eagle // of vigilance" to such an extent that it "earns the term aquiline."⁴⁷ By pointing out the scientific name of the bird in a note ("*Fregata aquila*"), she implicitly justifies her act of poetic renaming. Moreover, like the music of Handel, Moore's bird embodies the sublime: "the unconfiding frigate bird hides / in the height and in the majestic / display of his art."⁴⁸ The bird transfigures "turbulence" into "seemingly bodiless" flight.⁴⁹ In its effortless motion, it embodies sprezzatura. Despite the bird's large size, the poet tries out the names of other birds (swifts, swallows, and eagles) to try to capture a sense of its majesty. Moreover, the comparison of the bird's trajectory to the movement of "charred paper" may suggest the inadequacy of language to communicate the grace of the bird's motion and the exhilaration it arouses in the viewer.[50]

Moore features another motto in the poem, one which she mentions in her reading notebook in an entry about a famous printer's mark: *festina lente*.[51] The phrase means "make haste slowly." In "The Frigate Pelican," she renders it as "be gay civilly," perhaps by way of a macaronic pun linking the Latin *festina* with the English word *festive*. The command to be gay replays the contrast between the elegant panache of the Frigate Bird and the earthbound, industrious-minded mottoes from *Poor Richard's Almanac*, not to mention the plebeian amusements of the "merry-go-round" and the circus act led by Artemis in her leopard-skin.[52] As Margaret Holley writes, "the contrary mottoes relativize one another and together point to the uncertainty that livens and deepens the poem."[53] The advice to "be gay civilly" complicates the forthright lesson of "making hay while the sun shines," giving a rakish tilt to the "hampering haymaker's hat" worn by Artemis.[54] The apparent non sequitur arising from the disjunctive command is a good example of Moore's recasting of meaning in her work.

While Moore cites cropped mottoes to refer to the idea of the Protestant work ethic in "The Frigate Pelican," she uses even simpler terms in "The Jerboa": *Too Much* and *Abundance*. The first phrase may be an allusion to the Greek proverb *mēden agan*, which could be glossed as "nothing too much" or "nothing in excess," a negative formulation of the more familiar English command to exercise moderation in all things. The prominence of mottoes in other poems and her notebook may suggest that Moore was thinking of the classical ideal of the golden mean as part of her strategy to celebrate the accomplishments of her desert rat.

"Virginia Britannia" might provide a better example of Moore's use of mottoes to enhance the signifying power of her poems. She refers to John Smith's coat of arms and its motto without quoting it. However, the meaning of the phrase is relevant to the poem as a whole, which emphasizes the inherent violence of colonization and decries the rapacity embodied by Smith's "Latin motto."[55] Although Moore refrains from quoting the motto in the body of her poem, she does provide it in a note, writing that "the ostrich with the horseshoe in its beak,—i.e., invincible digestion—reiterates the motto, *Vincere est vivere*."[56] The motto means "to conquer is to live," and it emphasizes the fact that conquest is Smith's defining ambition. In *A-Quiver with Significance*, Heather Cass White provides a diagram of Smith's coat of arms, without the motto. It features three heads of Turks, indicating his prowess in battle against them.[57]

The mottoes from bookplates and coats of arms in Moore's reading notebook seem especially relevant to her portrait of Smith and colonialism in "Virginia Britannia." Moore records mottoes from the bookplates of Dewitt Clinton (*Patria cara carior Libertas*) and William Bolts (*Virtus sub pondere crescit*).[58] The first motto means that "one's homeland is precious but freedom is even more so," while the second may be rendered as "character grows when one is confronted with a burden." In addition, she includes *mors mihi vita est* (death is life to me) and *repulsae nescia virtus* (courage knows nothing of defeat).[59] In her notes on the book plate of George, Earl of Macartney, Moore recorded "*Tria juncta in uno*," a motto especially relevant to "Walking-Sticks and Paperweights and Watermarks."[60] As the mottoes I have quoted show, her notes frequently feature variants of the Latin word *virtus*, and some of the examples seem to emphasize the concepts of manliness and bravery as well as such other meanings of the Latin word as virtue, character, and excellence. I mention the first definition because of its connection to the Latin root of *virtus*, which is *vir*, meaning "man." Perhaps the Latin mottoes reminded Moore of Roman republican virtues and the U.S. founding fathers' admiration for them. Another relevant meaning stems from the Renaissance ideal of *virtù*, an Italian word which can emphasize martial forms of valor. The military dimension of the Latin term is especially germane to Moore's depiction of John Smith in "Virginia Britannia."

"Smooth Gnarled Crape Myrtle" is the last poem Moore arranged into a sequence of four when she collected it in *The Pangolin and Other Verse* (1936). She named the suite "The Old Dominion" and began it with "Virginia Britannia," followed by "Bird-Witted" and "Half Deity." The title of the sequence alludes to the colonial history of the United States (the phrase is a nickname for the state of Virginia). By arranging her poem in this series, Moore invites readers to consider colonial history and national identity in "Smooth Gnarled Crape Myrtle." The poem features two mottoes in conversation with one another. The first one is "joined in friendship, crowned by love." As Moore points out in a note, this inscription is taken from a Battersea enamel box, an artifact that had its heyday in the middle of the eighteenth century. This "patch-box pigeon-egg" depicts a bird and its mate on a limb, with a single male cardinal between them.[61] A patch-box holds patches to decorate the skin or cover blemishes, a personal adornment people used in order to attract partners.

One expects the cosmetics box to harmonize with its picture of the pair of birds and the hopeful motto accompanying it. Instead, the poem depicts the cardinal as out of place, which disrupts the coherence of the motto and undercuts its relevance to the picture. Hence, Moore writes, "Art is unfortunate." In the scenario of the poem, there seems to be a mismatch between the picture on the patch-box and its accompanying caption. The meaning of "unfortunate" as unsuitable or inappropriate makes Moore's curt three-word judgment more forceful than it may seem at first. Moore treats a species as a genus, reading the particular artifact as a figure for art in general. The epigram appears to be an acknowledgement of the difficulty of capturing complex experience in adequate language.

In her earlier days, Moore might have called this poem "Pat Picture with Dunderheaded Caption," but she would probably not have closed it with the second motto, which responds to the discrepancy between ideal and reality embodied by the patch-box with an acknowledgement of the discrepancy between prayed-for peace and a world in conflict: "'By Peace / Plenty; as / by Wisdom Peace.'"[62] As Holley points out, "the poet's questioning and anxious response to the final emblem and motto ... does not try to replace them with any completing claim."[63] Instead of masking flaws with cosmetic patches, Moore acknowledges the unhappy facts of poverty and conflict: there was neither peace nor plenty in the era of the Great Depression. In both Thomas Lodge's *Rosalynde*, where Moore encountered her second motto, and Shakespeare's *As You Like It* (which is based on Lodge's plot), conflict abounds. Brother plots against brother, and lovers encounter obstacles before they win their mates.

By closing her poem with an adaptation of a motto from a publisher's mark, Moore suggests that the semiotic discrepancy of the patch-box applies to the world beyond both the artifact in the poem and the poem itself. This accounts for her lamentation at the end. "Alas!" expresses Moore's sense of personal failure to live up to ideals, but it also attests to the inadequacy of language to convey complex human conditions.

The closing exclamation shares this insight with her readership, and the lament grows in scope in the context of worldwide economic depression, racial injustice in the United States,[64] and the German military build-up that would eventuate in World War II.[65] Whether the "clasped hands" of the poem are folded in prayer or joined with another in friendship, both efforts come up short.

In keeping with some of the other poems I have discussed, "Then the Ermine" addresses an established antithesis. It does so by shifting from the assertive purity of the ermine's white to the opposite extreme of intense jet-black. Without explicitly committing herself to absolute assertions or harsh asseverations, Moore manages to represent change in positive terms and to designate the color black as a sign of this revaluation. As she explained in an interview published in 1967, "growing up means being able to change from a fixed opinion."[66] An entry in Moore's 1930–1943 reading notebook similarly attests to the value of actively rethinking things. In it, Moore quotes from *Rule of the Road*, a 1937 publication by Anne Byrd Payson:

> It may be that certainty is too
> static for human development & that
> minds devel. best in uncertainty,
> that trying to find truth is better than
> than leaning hard on demonstrable
> fact.[67]

In terms of its substance and speculative syntax, Payson's suggestion is relevant to Moore's work. By avoiding a definitive assertion, Payson embodies the open and dynamic posture she proposes. Moore finds the posture congenial and invites her readers to adopt it.

"Then the Ermine" opens with a motto ("rather dead than spotted") that Moore puts in conversation with another ("*Mutare sperno / vel timere*").[68] Instead of consigning herself and her readers to a black and white view of things that forecloses nuance, she recodes the negative extreme of the polarity by recasting blackness as beautiful (be it a bat's color, the color of the upholstery on a rosewood piece of furniture, the sheen of a crow's feathers, or the hue of a great artist's violets). This reconfiguration comes about through the critical investigation of the Latin motto (which she briskly translates as "I don't change; am not craven"), in dialogue with the English motto that launches the poem. Moore deftly shifts from white to black in a way that valorizes blackness, and she does so without damning whiteness in the process.

The line acknowledging that "Nothing's certain" shows off Moore's poetic brio to handsome effect.[69] It marks a turning point in her argument between the absolutes of both mottoes and the open-minded self-questioning broached by her response to the Latin motto, reminding readers that the mind is not a deadly "Herod's oath that cannot change."[70] As Hadas observes, "a motto is personal and has more to do with possibility or ideal than with fact."[71] By stepping back and asking whether she is fearless and what it means to be afraid (which she does more overtly in an earlier version of the poem),[72] Moore allows for an alternative to the polarizing outlooks summed up by the mottoes. This leads to a rich proliferation of otherwise unforeseen possibilities, possibilities first articulated by the "wavering," "weaving" bat near the beginning of the poem. In "Then the Ermine," "wavering" accrues strongly positive connotations, whereas in the context of "Apparition of Splendor," the poem that appears just before it in *Like a Bulwark* (1956), to be a "waverer" is reprehensible.[73]

Although Moore is committed to questioning categories throughout her work, there are also cases in which certain categories appeal to her. Moreover, the fact that she produced an index for *Observations*, edited the *Dial*, and worked as a teacher and librarian show that she appreciated the pragmatic importance of categories.[74] "The Student" and "Walking-Sticks and Paperweights and Watermarks" are two poems that exemplify some aspects of Moore's less skeptical approach to mottoes. Mottoes help her drive home points in a pithy, aphoristic manner. At the same time, Moore also challenges assumptions associated with familiar categories even in these poems.

In "The Student," Moore cites a few college mottoes to help develop her argument on behalf of the value of widespread college education in a comparatively young democracy such as the United States. By identifying the mottoes of Yale and Harvard, she singles out two prestigious members of the Ivy League in her effort to rebut the French view that higher education is not for the masses. In the process of developing her argument,

Moore goes on to identify a series of critical distinctions in biology that reflect the need for ongoing advancement in all areas of learning.

The distinctions are among allied species, so taxonomical categories provide a meaningful tool or guide for analyzing similar creatures to differentiate them from one another in terms of anatomical characteristics and genealogical heritage. This can provide the basis for establishing a new, although related, species. It is a process that establishes a legitimate new category in the context of contemporary biology:

> But there is more to learn—the difference between cow
> and zebu; lion, tiger; brown and barred
> owls; horned owls have one ear that opens up and one that
> opens down.
>
> The golden eagle is the one with feathered legs. The penguin
> wing is
> ancient, not degenerate.[75]

A source for the last item may be found in Moore's notes on "X-Ray Photos as Aids to Science: Studies of Antarctic Birds." The article appeared in the *Illustrated London News* of January 24, 1931. In her reading notebook of 1930–43, Moore writes, "Penguins are an ancient order of birds, & consequently show primitive characters. They are backward rather than degenerate."[76] This is a reflection on the evolutionary status of the creature, which is why Moore includes it in her list of "more to learn."[77]

As Moore writes elsewhere in "The Student," "It is a / thoughtful pupil has two thoughts for the word / valet, or for bachelor, child, damsel."[78] This passage wittily corresponds to the notion of having two words for one thought earlier in the poem: "tree-of-life" and "arbor vitae." It also complements the joke about the initials D. D., which offers "dishonorable discharge" as an incorrect solution to what the initials stand for while withholding the "correct" solution, "Doctor of Divinity." All the references allude to the polysemy of language, the role of context in signaling meaning, the possibility of miscommunication, and the ambiguity inherent in signification. Meanings of terms are grounded in their context, or at least considerably restricted to fewer definitions. And as the reference to the medieval meanings of her series indicates, the meanings of words change over time, with some older definitions growing obsolete. The biblical contexts for the tree of life point to the field of Christian theology, while the oriental arbor vitae, or Asian Thuja, may designate species of evergreen trees, phenomena germane to biology. Later in "The Student" Moore explicitly mentions theology and biology as two kinds of "science," or knowledge. This gives credence to the equation of Doctor of Divinity with the capitalized initials D.D., but in the naval context, dishonorable discharge is not just pardonable but could be correct. Given that Moore's brother was a Navy chaplain, both the military and theological contexts would have loomed large in her thinking. The successful student must be able to decipher cultural codes that define or delimit the meanings of specific terms. The codes of theology or biology operate differently, and the successful student must be able to identify them as well as determine when and how to apply them.

The distinctions between the kinds of animals belonging to similar categories (order, family, or genus) are distinctions based on anatomical and evolutionary data, but that data must be interpreted by using language. Moore attests to the centrality of signification in the production of knowledge. Moore's last motto in "The Student," *sapiet felici*, means "with luck, one will be wise."[79] It applies not just to learning information, but also to the manipulation and interpretation of signs. By placing wisdom rather than knowledge at the heart of the motto, Moore makes a case for a wholistic approach to learning. Knowledge can be useful, but education should not focus exclusively on developing instrumental reason or the skills to acquire wealth.

As for categories in "Walking-Sticks and Paperweights and Watermarks," only one example of each of the first two items in the title are featured in the original version of the poem. Nevertheless, all three words of the title designate categories of things rather than specific instances of them. In *Museum Ideals of Purpose and Method* (1918), which Moore took notes on in a notebook covering 1916 to 1921, Benjamin Ives Gilman explains that each item on display in a museum could be viewed as both a specimen representing other items like it and a unicum, or an item chosen for its distinctiveness.[80] Along a similar line of logic, Moore portrays specific instances of each item in her poem, but she also designates their respective categories by using their plural forms in her title. In this way, she blurs the boundaries between categories to revitalize her readers' perceptions of the world and invite them to reflect on what poetry should do.

A central dichotomy in "Walking-Sticks" is the one between the living and the dead. This is signaled in the first sentence of the first published version of the poem, where the interaction between the two is prominently portrayed. The relationship between them remains integral to the poem, and the borders between them become porous. This is partly the result of the salience of writing-metaphors. Moore's imagery of paper and inscriptions makes her readers mindful of the intimacy, vulnerability, and transmission of literature. In time, all literature becomes a library of letters from the dead addressed to the living. One aspect of literature is that it can unite the living with the dead, if only obliquely and temporarily. In this regard, Moore's poem scrambles the categories of the living and the dead.

Three mottoes play an important role in "Walking-Sticks and Paperweights and Watermarks": "difficulty is ordained to check / poltroons"; "courage achieves / despaired of ends";[81] and "'For those we love, live and die.'"[82] The second motto may be a version of *repulsae nescia virtus*, a phrase on a bookplate Moore recorded in a notebook.[83] The phrase appears in Horace's Ode 3.2, which features another passage relevant to walking and to Moore's reference to "trivia" as a convergence of three roads: "Virtus ... negata temptat inter via."[84] This can be rendered as courage makes its own way, or bravery risks the journey on a blocked-off road. Moore cites the first two mottoes when she describes the making of a seal, emphasizing the resistance involved when forming the wax inscription and paralleling the hardships of life. Since the action is a form of representation that is comparable to printing texts with type (an item Moore explicitly mentions), the seal can be interpreted as a metaphor for the production of literature.

Moore unites the action of making paper and glass in her comparison of the shape of the paperweight to a fool's cap. This phrase puns on *foolscap*, a common form of writing paper whose name derives from one watermark Moore does *not* mention in the poem. In addition, she allies glass-making with printing when she compares the paperweight to "typemetal" that has been "emory-armored / against rust."[85] As Aurore Clavier points out in her contribution to this volume, Moore's comparison of the paperweight to type-metal derives from notes she took about an article by Paul Koch. Koch describes the making of punches to produce type-metal: "The hardened punches are laid for ten minutes in a saucer filled w vinegar, then thoroughly dried w a rag, the face & conical surfaces cleaned w an eraser & all the filed surfaces polished on emery cloth to perfect brightness."[86] Koch also specifies each of the three ingredients in type-metal identified by Moore in the poem. By likening the glass object to type-metal, Moore reinforces the poem's self-reflexive metaphors of writing and publication.

Moreover, the metamorphosis of molten glass into solid paperweight parallels the making of paper from the wet pulp of rags as well as the transformation of unformed wax into a seal in the shape of the pelican with its chicks in a nest.[87] The nest is described as a "cartwheel," making the symbol parallel to the figure of the triskelion. Through sacrifice and bravery, the skillfully crafted work of art can be offered to the world. A poem can provide a way of celebrating the world's vitality. As the magnifying power of the paperweight shows, poems can also enhance readers' perceptions.

Moore's closing reference to juniper as an "unburdensomely / worthy officer of charity" unites the trinitarian symbol of the evergreen tree to the pelican's nest. These symbols focus on "true love."[88] In her reading notebook of 1930–1943, Moore copied the following passage from *The Magic Mountain* by Thomas Mann: "In the most raging as in the most reverent passion, there must be caritas, The meaning of the word varies? In God's name, then, let it vary. That it does so makes it living, makes it human; it would be a regrettable lack of 'depth' to trouble over the fact."[89] This passage provides a good gloss on Moore's reference to "charity" in "Walking-Sticks and Paperweights and Watermarks." Her portrayal of love as a communally sustaining and sacrificial force in the symbol of the "pelican in her piety" (as the emblem has come to be known) exemplifies the revitalizing of language in other poems I have discussed. So does one of the inscriptions of the official seal of Columbia University, an institution Moore leaves out of "The Student" when mentioning mottoes. Quoting Acts 7:38, the seal refers to *"logia zonta,"* a Greek phrase meaning "living words." Moore seeks to make "charity" a living word in "Walking-Sticks."

The reference to the pelican corresponds to Moore's subsequent treatment of maternal nurture in "The Paper Nautilus." ("Walking-Sticks" was first published in 1936, while "The Paper Nautilus" was originally published in 1940). Moore even refers to the Latin term in the passage from Mann's novel in "Charity Overcoming Envy," which first appeared in 1963. In light of this and the additional fact that Moore uses the term *charitive* in "Marriage" (first published in 1923),[90] charity, or love, might be regarded as a key issue throughout Moore's poetry. Luke Carson and Heather Cass White make a strong case for viewing "Walking-Sticks" as an important turning point in her poetry, so my charting of Moore's references to charity might be considered in light of their argument as well. They stress the fact that Moore gave up her ambition to write "visionary poetry" in the mode of Ralph Waldo Emerson in order to address the network of social obligations pressing upon her and her contemporaries during the 1930s.[91]

As I have shown, Moore reflects on proverbial wisdom by adapting mottoes of various kinds in many of her poems. She does this frequently enough that it is worth consideration and should be viewed in light of her poetic practice of quoting and adapting the words of others. Just as she researched topics in periodicals and reference works, culling phrases for her poems, she took notes on heraldry and mottoes that informed her poetic composition. Passages in the reading notebook of 1930 to 1944 document such research. While I have focused on the linguistic features of her notes on blazonry and bookplates, it is possible that her interest in its iconography may also have had an impact on her writing, especially given the recurrence of armor imagery in her poems and her fondness for ekphrasis. At any rate, the triads (instead of dichotomies) at work throughout "Walking-Sticks and Paperweights and Watermarks," along with the poem's writing metaphors, highlight Moore's ongoing efforts to redefine categories and reframe meanings, moving beyond antagonistic dichotomies while avoiding simplistic syntheses of them. Moore's emphasis on love in this and the other poems I have identified reveals the driving motive for such work.

Archive as Product and Process

CHAPTER NINE

"This is how the mind works"
Marianne Moore and the Aesthetics of Notebooks

Roger Gilbert

Most poets rely on notebooks as compositional tools, convenient receptacles for lines and phrases that may eventually find their place in a finished poem. The literary equivalent of artists' sketchbooks, notebooks give us intimate access to the process of creation in its early stages. But their appeal can be more than intellectual: like the rough sketches that precede a painting, poets' notebooks often possess their own distinctive beauty. In part this is simply the gestural beauty of handwriting, whether elegant or crude, when contrasted with the bloodless uniformity of type. The movements of the hand across the page find a correlative in the motions of mind they record, the slides and leaps of association and invention that form an essential substrate of poetry.

Among the richest and most revealing of poets' notebooks are those of Marianne Moore, archived at the Rosenbach Museum and Library and now in the process of being digitized and transcribed by a team of editors under the direction of Cristanne Miller. Moore's notebooks constitute an invaluable resource for scholars, who can use them to trace the evolution of her work from fragments of conversation, reading, and reflection to their coalescence in passages and entire poems. But I want to suggest that these notebooks are valuable not just for the insights they afford into Moore's compositional practices. My reading of the notebooks that have already been digitized and transcribed has convinced me they're also independently beautiful works that deserve to be enjoyed in the same way we enjoy the preparatory drawings of great painters along with their finished canvases. For the purpose of this essay I'll focus on two notebooks, labeled in the archive 07.04.04 and 07.04.07, that contain draft material for poems Moore published between 1922 and 1940. The online archive also includes two digitized reading and conversation notebooks that often shed light on her poetic activities but lie beyond the scope of my discussion.

"This is how the mind works," Moore writes in her 1933 notebook, and while she may not have meant the line to be self-descriptive, it captures the spontaneous eloquence and quicksilver wit that shows itself on every page of that notebook.[1] The tonally ambiguous cry "Neatness of finish! Neatness of finish!" that appears near the end of "An Octopus" and on the first page of 07.04.04 may define one crucial dimension of Moore's aesthetics; yet just beneath her neatly organized stanzas and sentences lies the prodigiously generative clutter of the notebooks.[2] A recent trend in interior design called "cluttercore" offers itself as a gemütlich alternative to Marie Kondo-esque austerity. Whether or not Moore's living room (lovingly preserved at the Rosenbach) qualifies for the term, her notebooks certainly do. Frugal as she was, it is hard to believe her habit of cramming as many phrases as possible onto each leaf of a small notebook was motivated purely by economic concerns. Putting heterogeneous particulars into close proximity is an essential practice of Moore's poetry, one her notebooks display in its purest form.

The porous relationship between notebook and finished work has often been exploited by poets wishing to espouse values of spontaneity, authenticity, and candor. Indeed, the term "notebook" has become something of a generic marker, occurring in the titles of many volumes. The most famous instance is Aimé Césaire's 1939 *Cahier d'un retour au pays natal* (*Notebook of a Return to the Native Land*), which records in a mix of prose and verse the psychic effects of confronting colonial racism in Martinique. The tension between the looseness of notebook writing and the demands of poetic form is foregrounded in Robert Lowell's *Notebook 1967–68*, which comprises unrhymed sonnets on public and private themes that were later revised and separated into two volumes, *History* and *For Lizzie and Harriet*. Other works that incorporate the word in their titles include Anne Sexton's *The Death Notebooks* (1974), John Ashbery's *The Vermont Notebook* (1975), and more recently Gabriel Gudding's *Rhode Island Notebook* (2007) and Campbell McGrath's *Seven Notebooks* (2008). All these poets use the term to evoke a less mediated relationship between compositional process and published text. Even works that don't call themselves notebooks implicitly align themselves with the form, e.g., Wallace Stevens's *Notes toward a Supreme Fiction* (1942) and Jorie Graham's sequence "Notes on the Reality of the Self" (1992).

Of course, many poets keep actual notebooks with no intent of publishing them.³ Moore clearly belongs to this latter group, for whom notebook and published work are entirely distinct. Given her penchant for precision and control, she seems an unlikely adherent to what I'm calling the notebook aesthetic. Yet I'd like to suggest that her published work is not as far from that aesthetic as one might suppose. The affinities may be most evident in her first authorized collection, *Observations* (1923). The most salient physical fact about a notebook is that it is bound and therefore can't be reordered except by physically dismantling it (as seems to have occurred with some notebooks in the Moore archive). Moore's decision to arrange the poems in *Observations* in their order of composition, an unusual choice for its time, suggests her desire to maintain the kind of visible connection between process and product that notebooks epitomize. The book's title also evokes the paratactic miscellaneousness of notebook writing; one could easily imagine the word "observations" being written on the cover of a budding author's journal.

Formally, the poems in *Observations* range from epigrammatic squibs in its early pages to the elaborately shaped syllabic stanzas that Moore develops and perfects in poems like "The Fish," "Peter," and "Those Various Scalpels." Such shaping entails a level of precise craftsmanship incompatible with the spontaneity of notebook writing. And in fact Moore's notebooks contain almost no hints of the process by which their contents are transmogrified into the rigorously counted and rhymed lines of the published poems. Yet what might be called the deep grammar of the notebook form can be discerned even in her intricately patterned stanzas. In "Poetry," one of her most famous syllabic poems, she proclaims her allegiance to "the raw material of poetry in / all its rawness," material that may include such cultural odds and ends as baseball fans, statisticians, business documents, and schoolbooks.[4] In the later pages of *Observations* that raw material becomes increasingly visible, as the poems shift from syllabic stanzas to a looser free verse that permits a more fluidly improvisational movement among bits of original and found language. A poem like "Bowls" feels especially close to notebook writing in its concatenation of apparently unrelated statements:

> on the green
> with lignum vitae balls and ivory markers,
> the pins planted in wild duck formation,
> and quickly dispersed:
> by this survival of ancient punctilio
> in the manner of Chinese lacquer carving,
> layer after layer exposed by certainty of touch and unhurried
>   incision
> so that only so much color shall be revealed as is necessary to
>   the picture,
> I learn that we are precisians—
> not citizens of Pompeii arrested in action
> as a cross-section of one's correspondence would seem to imply.
> Renouncing a policy of boorish indifference
> to everything that has been said since the days of Matilda,
> I shall purchase an Etymological Dictionary of Modern English
> that I may understand what is written
> and like the ant and the spider
> returning from time to time to headquarters,
> shall answer the question
> as to "why I like winter better than I like summer"
> and acknowledge that it does not make me sick
> to look playwrights and poets and novelists straight in the face—
> that I feel just the same;
> and I shall write to the publisher of the magazine
> which will "appear the first day of the month
> and disappear before one has had time to buy it
> unless one takes proper precaution,"
> and make an effort to please—

> since he who gives quickly gives twice
> in nothing so much as in a letter.⁵

Unlike other list poems in the book—e.g., "People's Surroundings," "The Labors of Hercules"—"Bowls" doesn't name a category, but meanders through a series of offhand observations and things-to-do ("I shall") whose connections remain largely opaque. The poem begins with one of Moore's trademark titles whose meaning shifts when revealed to be the first word of a sentence. Conjoining a lawn game and an ancient Chinese art, the opening sentence associates precision with unhurried movement rather than the stasis of Pompeii's petrified citizens. The thread that loosely connects the rest of the poem is correspondence; one could imagine it as a list of letters to be written in which room is made for associated tasks like buying an etymological dictionary. Here, as in other late *Observations* poems, Moore seems to be challenging herself and us to find a principle of order in a seemingly random assemblage of items that might easily have been jotted down in the pages of a notebook.

The two magnificent long poems that appear near the end of *Observations*, "An Octopus" and "Marriage," have an especially intimate connection to Moore's notebooks. In a groundbreaking 1984 article, Patricia Willis suggests the two poems originated as a single draft that eventually bifurcated.⁶ That process can now be traced in fascinating detail thanks to the Marianne Moore Digital Archive, which offers access to the 1922–1930 notebook (07.04.04) in which Moore drafted both poems along with "Silence," "Sea Unicorns and Land Unicorns," and post-*Observations* poems like "The Steeple-Jack," "The Jerboa," and "The Plumet Basilisk." The very first page of the top-bound notebook (technically a stenographer's pad) includes material that appears in both "An Octopus" and "Marriage," as well as what may have already been intended as provisional titles for the three longer poems that end *Observations*: "Marriage," "Mt. Rainier" ("An Octopus"), and "Tropics and Unicorns" ("Sea Unicorns and Land Unicorns"). Willis's suggestion that Moore initially planned "a single long poem" on the themes of "Adam, paradise, love, theology, divorce, woman, and hell" that "ultimately became two poems" may slightly oversimplify the compositional process visible in the notebook, which from the start distinguishes between the two poems' large subjects. That division is repeatedly blurred, however, as lines and phrases that appear in "Marriage" and "An Octopus" are interspersed throughout the early pages. By the time we reach the verso of the third leaf, the two poems have fully detached themselves:

> An Octopus
>   of ice—a stranded iceberg—
> translucent gray
>   pseudopodia indistinguishable fr the tailors chalk
>   & the torrents of glacial water heart   of the ~~mountains~~
>   valleys
> the cyclamen red dots on its pseudopodia
>   violet velvet rosettes around the waist
> & rosettes on the shoulder
>   I breakfast at home
>   I breakfast at home
>
>   <u>Marriage</u>
>   I don't know what Adam and Eve think of it by this time
>   I don't think much of it
>   Turn to the letter M and you will find ~~that~~
>   that "a wife is a coffin⁷

It is possible, of course, that these passages represent a later stage in the drafting process than their placement in the notebook would suggest, although in general Moore seems to have written continuously from recto to verso. What the notebook clearly shows is that the two poems were drafted concurrently, and that their final forms are intimately tied to their origins in jotted lines and fragments, many of them borrowed from other sources. Moore herself characterized "Marriage" as a series of "statements that took my fancy which I tried to arrange plausibly." "An Octopus" too relies heavily on quotations from various guidebooks, travel memoirs, and Park Service manuals. Moore's use of quotation has been the subject of much scholarly discussion; I'll simply add that the notebook form plays a crucial mediating role in her compilation, arrangement, and synthesis of quoted material. That role is especially visible in the later poems of

Observations, which in form and texture feel closer to notebook writing than her stanzaic poems.

As Cristanne Miller observes in her introduction to 07.04.04, much of the pleasure of reading Moore's notebooks comes from their recursive rhythms:

> For the general reader, the joy of reading this notebook will be in following Moore's repeating and sometimes wholly unexpected thoughts in relation to published poems they know. For the scholar, the primary interest of this notebook may have to do with Moore's pursuit of ideas or even particular phrases (for example, "eagles w tigers in their eyes & feet") that she repeats across the drafting of more than one poem.[8]

The specific phrase Miller cites appears more than ten times in the notebook, often at wide intervals. Here are some of the chief variants:

0002-verso: eagle w tigers in its eyes & feet
             eagles w tigers in their eyes & feet
0024-verso: curious rustic eagle w tigers in its eyes & feet
0025-recto: this eagle w tigers in its eyes & feet
0050-verso: eagle
             launched downward towards achievement
             w tigers in its eyes & feet
0055-recto: of this eagle w tigers in his eyes
             love & ambition & ferocity & greed & feet
0056-verso: Perched like the eagle w tigers in its eyes & feet—
0064-verso: She sees him as the eagle perched securely on
             achievement
             w tigers in his eyes & feet[9]

In itself the "eagle with tigers in its eyes & feet" is an astonishing trope, a chimeric image of pure rapacity. When encountered repeatedly with incremental variations across many pages of the notebook, it takes on a kind of fugal insistence. The variant on p. 61 that begins "She sees him" suggests the phrase was initially intended for "Marriage," an ambivalent characterization of the predatory instinct manifested in both the male gaze and body. As to why Moore ultimately abandoned the line despite its evident hold on her, my guess is that she concluded its Blakean intensity would have overwhelmed the subtler shades of irony at play in the poem.

The two poetry notebooks are full of scintillating lines and phrases that never found their way into Moore's published poems. In her introduction to 07.04.07, Heather Cass White confesses "If I had my wish she would have used more of those chosen-against lines," and every reader will come away with their own favorite hidden gems. One of mine is a beautiful descriptive fragment that appears amid material for "Marriage": "The acacia the personal filigree / w the angles of the starfish & the sinews of the cat."[10] Other epigrammatic lines are more obviously related to "Marriage": "It is not displeasing to be disliked / by an enemy" (07.04.04, page 0009-recto); "Marriage Is it not like a road uphill / in the sand for an aged person?" (07.04.04, page 0011-recto). Another phrase that recurs several times, "Behold the Tom cat & his enemy" (07.04.04, page 0023-recto), is also clearly intended for "Marriage," although it links to a series of feline images scattered throughout the notebook, one of which ends up in "Silence" ("Self-reliant like the cat / that takes its prey to privacy").[11]

We often see Moore try out an idea, then revisit it a page or two later, as with these lines that invoke an eccentric vision of paradise:

> if there is a par. upon earth
> it is this it is this it is this
> this profusion of ~~unaccounted for~~
> the ~~non~~un essentials
> the cradle of the race
> that custard apple swamp wh was ~~the~~ our cradle

The incantatory repetition of "it is this" recurs two pages later with a very different emphasis:

> He is amiss and I worse than don't like him
> If there is a paradise upon earth it is this,
> it is this, it is this?

From the American Eden of the Custard Apple Swamp (an actual place in South Florida, long ago supplanted by sugar fields) to the false paradise of marriage to a man who is "amiss," these fragments show Moore examining her theme from all angles, making the most elemental terms speak in radically different tones. The notebooks abound in such verbal modulations; Moore rarely sets down a phrase just once.

Of course in reading through the notebooks it is impossible to exclude our knowledge of Moore's published work. At least some of the pleasure they offer comes from recognizing phrases and lines we already know from the printed poems. The chief revelation the poetry notebooks afford is how radically non-linear Moore's compositional practices were. At times in reading them one almost has the impression that a familiar poem has been cut into strips and tossed in a hat. Lines that will eventually play a key structural role often appear in isolation; for example, the wonderful closing exclamation of "Camellia Sabina," "O generous Bolzano!" appears at the bottom of one page and the top of another, in neither case in any proximity to the lines that precede it in the poem. Pages containing draft material for "The Jerboa" intersperse descriptive passages that Moore eventually separated into the poem's two sections, "Too Much" and "Abundance," reproducing on a smaller scale the initial intermixing of lines for "Marriage" and "An Octopus." Here and elsewhere the notebooks show that for Moore the generation of poetic language and imagery often preceded the development of framing structures, whether prosodic or thematic. Her first compositional acts produced a kind of rich verbal magma she could then mold into stanzas and sections.

Then there are the startling outcroppings amid material for one poem of phrases that end up in another poem entirely. The most striking example is the inscription of two lines from "What Are Years"—"all are naked, none is safe," and "Satisfaction is lowly. How pure a thing is joy"—on a page containing notes for "The Frigate Pelican" and "The Buffalo." (These lines may have grown from the same aphoristic milieu that produced the phrases "Festina lente," "Be gay / civilly," in "The Frigate Pelican.") As Heather White points out in her introduction to 07.04.07, "What Are Years" was published six years later than the other two poems and marks a major turn in Moore's poetics toward rhetorical directness. It is fascinating to see the seed of that turn already emerging alongside the very different impulses toward dense concatenation and tonal complexity in her poems of the 1930s.

The distinction I've been exploring between unused material and lines we recognize from published work leads me to propose a thought experiment: suppose a reader who had never read a poem by Moore were shown one of her poetry notebooks. How would they experience it? Would it seem a mere jumble of disconnected phrases? Or would the lack of formal and syntactical coherence be offset by the pointillist brilliance of the phrases themselves and the associative links among them? Readers accustomed to the disjunctive styles of modernist and postmodernist poets from Ezra Pound and Gertrude Stein to John Ashbery and Susan Howe would surely have little difficulty navigating Moore's fluidly constellated word clusters. A more extreme thought experiment might imagine Moore herself as a different kind of poet, one who did not feel the need to recast her initial acts of writing into hypotactic sentences and tightly worked stanzas. *That* Moore might have published poems much closer to the notebook drafts—indeed, might have published the notebooks themselves. Needless to say, I greatly prefer the real poet to this bizarro Moore; my point is simply that looked at from a particular angle the notebook writing is already poetry. In fact, I'll go a step further and say that it is often dazzling poetry.

To support this extravagant claim, let me share pages from Notebook 07.04.07 that seem to me especially beguiling (Figure 9.1). As Heather White notes, they show Moore beginning to work on "Half Deity," although much of their content doesn't appear in the published poem. A striking feature of this notebook as a whole are the many first-person statements it contains, which are quite rare in Moore's published work. On other pages we encounter phrases like "I am a buffalo / or is this something else that I don't know about," followed by "I am a baby is that what I am to the universe ... a baby that has decided to cry"; and, in a more metaphysical vein, "I am a body & I have a soul? / I am a soul that has a body." On page 31-recto we find an even more disarmingly confessional sentence: "I am not 'quiet.' I am morose—a violent leopard with a pain in its head, flung into a net from the top of a tree."[12] While the net suggests Moore is contemplating the butterfly narrative of "Half Deity," the opening phrase is a sardonically personal utterance in which "quiet" and "morose" seem to have traded places. One can easily imagine someone being told "you seem morose," and replying, "I'm just quiet"; reversing the adjectives creates a more barbed effect. This is followed by a sentence that appears almost intact in "Half Deity," "One has often been thankful to a stranger for looking very nice—," although the line takes on a very different resonance when followed by another first-person declaration: "I am not prepared for modern romance."

We then get two heavily revised attempts at a sentence about masculine power and humility that sounds like an outtake from "Marriage": "a man ~~with~~ power ~~should~~ be ~~more~~ as / humble ~~than~~ a man who has / none & is crazed with the thought of it can't." Next comes an odd

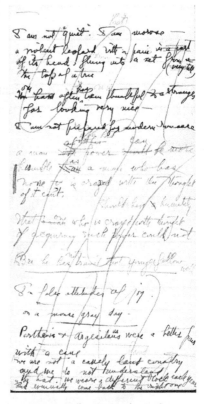

Figure 9.1: "I am not 'quiet.' I am morose—" www.moorearchive.org. Notebook 7.04.07, page 31-recto

sentence that Heather White glosses as a reference to Pound's mentorship of Louis Zukofsky, "Ezra he has not trained that younger fellow well," in which "not" has been inserted. This reference raises the intriguing possibility that the figure of Zephyr in "Half Deity"—the "quiet young man with piano replies," whose "talk was as strange as my grandmother's muff"—is an oblique portrait of Zukofsky, whom Moore may have met at Pound's behest. Another sentence included in "Half Deity" appears next, "No we are not a canely country," followed by additional observations on America's flawed sense of fashion:

> and we do not understand
> the hat. We wear a different block each year

so eventually come back to the right one
and fleetingly achieve a style.[13]

These playful comments on homespun Americanness might have found a place in "England" or "The Student," poems Moore had already written. They are followed by two versions of a wonderful Dickinsonian parable about a bee who, "confused by happy feelings when alone [and] working too late, had to spend the night in a flower." The second version contrasts the bee with the butterfly, again linking the lines to "Half Deity":

>   the butterfly they say has a finer nose than
>   the bee for flowers—
>   but the good bee will delay
>   & work so late   he has to
>   till its so dark   that he must
>   stay out overnight

A few lines later we get another delicious aphorism:

>   Strength perhaps is best defined
>   by strangers not ~~by~~ a friend~~s~~
>   by, shall one say, the wind.[14]

These two pages, like the notebooks as a whole, display the astonishing fecundity of Moore's imagination as she moves between sustained exploration of her chosen topics and wayward digression in pursuit of stray associations. The haphazard character of her notebook writing is far removed from the rigorously integrated discourse of her published poetry, but, as she writes in another context, "It is a privilege to see / so much confusion."[15] Reading the notebooks helps us appreciate how much the published poems rely on, and to some degree retain, that loose-jointed associative fecundity, even as they organize it into well-wrought sentences and stanzas.

My primary aim in this essay has been to echo and expand on Miller's and White's eloquent accounts in their editors' introductions of the deep pleasures these notebooks afford. Scholars will of course find them indispensable tools for reconstructing Moore's compositional processes, yet I want to reiterate that they reward a different kind of reading as well. There is sheer joy to be had in observing a great poet's mind at work and at play, throwing off images, tropes, and aperçus in a messy but gorgeous scatter and scrawl. Even the look of the pages is, to my eye at least, visually opulent, no two exactly alike in their dense hatching of scribbles, crossings out, overwriting, and sideways inscriptions. What a gift it is to have these notebooks easily available to scholars, teachers, students, and lovers of poetry, and how wonderful to know there are more on the way.

CHAPTER TEN

Robert Duncan, "On Reading Marianne Moore"
An Introduction

James Maynard

Sometime in the early to mid-1950s, the San Francisco-based New American poet Robert Duncan drafted a poem entitled "On Reading Marianne Moore" in one of his reading–writing notebooks. Now housed as part of the Robert Duncan Collection in the Poetry Collection at the University at Buffalo Libraries, The State University of New York, this undated, previously unpublished, and possibly unfinished thirty-seven-line poetic sketch demonstrates the influence that Moore had on a younger writer like Duncan (born on January 7, 1919, he was thirty-one years younger than Moore) who in 1957 organized a reading for her on behalf of the San Francisco State College Poetry Center. One of many examples of poems by Duncan that translate and respond to his experience of reading other writers, "On Reading Marianne Moore" engages with "her avid / sense of the quality of things." For Duncan, Moore was an important early source of his poetics as he acknowledged in both his published and unpublished writings. The details of their brief relationship are evident in their surviving correspondence, which, along with other archival sources, provides some background and a particular context for approaching Duncan's poem about reading Moore's poetry.

Throughout his writing life, Robert Duncan consistently characterized his poetics as derivative of a variety of writers and traditions, and in particular he constantly positioned the work of the modernists as his formal, spiritual, and cultural inheritance. In his biographical note that appears in Donald Allen's 1960 anthology *The New American Poetry*, for instance, Duncan writes that "the sources of my *virtus* lie among those immediately preceding me in Stein, Lawrence, Pound, H.D., William Carlos Williams, Marianne Moore, Stevens, and Edith Sitwell."[1] Such lists, when they appear, are sometimes longer and sometimes shorter but always include H.D., Pound, and Williams. A re-engagement with these modernist "sources" is the primary task of his *H.D. Book*, the issue, as Duncan puts it elsewhere in a 1953 poem written for Denise Levertov, of:

(how to brew another cup
in that Marianne Moore -
E.P. - Williams - H.D. - Stein -
Zukofsky - Stevens - Perse -
surrealist - dada - staind
pot)[2]

While Duncan scholarship has focused primarily on his relationships with Pound, Williams, Zukofsky, and especially H.D., little has been written about Duncan and Moore. From the material evidence of the bookplates in his personal library, also housed in the Poetry Collection, Duncan owned several of Moore's publications and had been reading her since at least as early as 1939 at the age of twenty. Biographically, Duncan's first interaction with Moore presumably occurred in 1957 when, as Assistant Director of the San Francisco State College Poetry Center (now part of San Francisco State University), he wrote to her on June 17, 1957, inviting her to give a reading. After teaching at Black Mountain College during the spring and summer of 1956, Duncan had returned to San Francisco in September to become the Poetry Center's Assistant Director, a position he would hold for only a short period of time before resigning. As Assistant Director, Duncan organized the Center's poetry readings and wrote and circulated introductions for the visiting writers.

Moore's first surviving letter to Duncan is dated July 28, 1957, although we know she likely had written previously, as there are two different carbon copies of a letter dated June 22 among Moore's papers at the Rosenbach Museum and Library.[3] In the July 28 letter she thanks him for helping to specify what she might read in San Francisco and also for sharing with her a copy of "The Maiden," a poem from *The Opening of the Field* that explicitly references Moore. After cycling through different literary and mythological maidens as figures of renewal, including at one point a photograph of Moore and her "elderly-maiden's face," the poem ends with a short section called "The Close," which begins: "Close to her construct I pace the line, / the contain homage arranged, reflections / on Marianne Moore's natural style, an artifice / where sense may abound."[4] In her response, Moore describes the work as "composed with such extreme care and with a charity that includes me as well as Rachel, Dame Edith, Wordsworth; and indeed Dante."[5]

Moore sent postcards to Duncan on August 20 and August 29, 1957, both of which seem to be responding to Duncan's poem "Poetry, a Natural Thing," which in some ways is his most Mooresque animal poem (in this case referring to salmon and a painted moose), but there's no evidence in the Rosenbach of exactly what correspondence from Duncan, if any, prompted the notes.[6] The entirety of the former reads: "I wish that poetry could be a 'natural thing', Mr. Duncan, and thank you for emphasizing it."[7]

The only other correspondence from Duncan among her papers is a letter dated October 1, 1957, just prior to Moore's trip to California, in which he included his two-page introduction featuring "Notes on the Poetics of Marianne Moore." In it he refers to her as "an ever-ready student" "characterized by her ability to respond." He writes: "In the root meaning she is an amateur as a student; it is her love of certain qualities that guides her. From this she has constructed a conglomerate form; eschewing connectives, she achieves her unity as it springs from her genius, her unsurpassed intuition for coherence." Naming her a "master" "for those of us who are concerned with the articulation of the line in the poem and its notation" and praising her "intimations of coherence that depend not upon the conscious convention or invention but upon the organic complexity in unity of sensibility, emotion, will, and intellect," he quotes in particular lines from her early poem "To a Chameleon" from *Observations*.[8]

Moore begins her response dated October 4, by stating: "It is a very great encouragement to have something liked that was a prime excitement to me when written. I must read that chameleon at the Poetry Center. (I hope I do show some trace of Ezra Pound's condensed manner.)" Additionally, she writes: "I like that term 'amateur as a student'. I certainly do not 'cease to be a student'. Am I anything else?" and singles out as "A valuable—very original—saying" one of Duncan's remarks that, in her slight rewording, becomes: "The art of the poem is to establish the pattern even in departing from it."[9]

A few days later, on October 10, and as part of what may have been a larger tour through California, Moore delivered her Poetry Center reading at the San Francisco Museum of Art, a recording of which is available online through the Poetry Center Digital Archive.[10] Writing to Donald Allen about the event, Duncan shared that "Miss Moore's performance here was magnificent; I cannot imagine a more thorough entertainment, she removed us from any effort of appreciation into the full diversion of her charms and humors."[11] She also gave another Poetry Center sponsored reading eight days later at UC Berkeley, which is also online. In this reading Moore remembers to read "To a Chameleon," which she had promised Duncan she'd do in the earlier reading, and thanks him by name for having "restored [her] confidence in" the poem.[12]

The other noteworthy exchange that Duncan had with Moore is connected to the first and begins with a letter she had sent to his friend and fellow poet Jack Spicer. Apparently, Spicer sat in the front row during one of Moore's readings in California, and afterward sent her a copy of "Radar," which, as the concluding poem in his book *After Lorca*, appears as "*A Postscript for Marianne Moore.*" In response, she wrote him a postcard with the statement "The cure for loneliness is solitude," taken from "If I Were Sixteen Today," her essay offering advice to teenagers.[13] This line resonated with Duncan, although in later years he would misremember it as "Solitude is the only cure for loneliness," and he used it as the provocation for his own poem "Solitude" that he then presumably mailed to Moore (although no such letter survives).[14] On February 21, 1958, she sent him a postcard correcting one of his words and stating, "You are right about loneliness, Mr. Duncan. It is not exhilarating. // Isn't it 'philander*er*'? in your poem? Don't psyche me too carefully; am submerged in peripheral matters and do not do justice to very careful thinking!"[15]

Moore's last extant letter to Duncan is dated August 26, 1959, and reads in part: "That you feel that work of mine has done you good, encourages me greatly. I am incredulous, that what I have done so willfully, could bear some aid to others."[16] However, Duncan's enthusiasm for her writing seems to have waned shortly thereafter. In his essay, "Ideas of the Meaning of Form," written early in 1961, he contradicts his early notes on her poetics and refers to her verse as being of a "conventional persuasion." "Her splendid achievement," he writes, "is to excite our admiration of her performance, her risky equilibriums, and her resistance to deeper thought and feeling where personality is lost."[17] And in *The H.D. Book*, her poetry and poetics are judged to be less compelling than other modernists such as H.D. and Williams.

On Reading Marianne Moore

Robert Duncan

> a poem: a moment of balance, regaining
> one's sense of the language
> in time to display the animal grace
> of mind, a cat
> leaping about an imaginary figure
> sketchd on the ground.
> One's hair stands on edge to think
> of a witchcraft everywhere.
> Even the sea's energies
> designing caves or stones
> scarcely to be distinguishd from Arp's
> own sublime stones
> "shaped by human hands."
> St. Francis, who the Church denies
> talkd to birds and fish
> as if to save their souls, calld
> even fire brother.
> He was her worthy predecessor
> A mystic. Or a sorceress

like Joan to whom Spirits appeard
in the fairy grove: her avid
sense of the quality of things
defeats hierarchies without
breeding anarchy. A natural
magic, maybe. Easy
anyway and hard to get out of one's head,
as a jingle. Higgletee piggletee
my fat hen or Gertrude Stein's
insistent verbal designs. Poetry
for our ears she makes
contagious as Meade Lux Lewis
with a figured base.

Is beauty a cheat if it is so easy?
That even the wind may achieve it
mindless over time
working at cliff-face at
any resistant thing.[18]

Teaching and Learning
in the Digital Archive

CHAPTER ELEVEN

The Marianne Moore Digital Archive
Teaching and Research

Claire Nashar

Established in 2015 at the University at Buffalo, the Marianne Moore Digital Archive (MMDA) hosts digital reproductions and transcriptions of Marianne Moore's notebooks. The original (physical) notebooks are housed in the Rosenbach Museum and Library in Philadelphia, and the major work of the MMDA is to make these essential source materials easily and freely accessible to scholarly, classroom, and non-academic readers for the first time. To date, the MMDA has fully published four of Moore's notebooks, with eight more in various stages of transcription and editing, and others to come in the future. The digital editions of the notebooks are supported by a growing collection of related materials, such as a glossary, an interactive timeline of Moore's life and publications, searchable reproductions of the now hard-to-find *Marianne Moore Newsletter*, and (under development) integrated text and image search tools.

This chapter articulates some of the uses of the MMDA for scholars, teachers, and students of Moore's life, her poetry, and modernist culture, giving examples of how the various functionalities of the digital platform both facilitate new contributions to Moore studies and enliven scholarly and pedagogical connections to literature and to cultural history. The observations I make here are drawn from my experiences as both a developer and user of the archive. I have been a part of the MMDA team since 2015, first as a graduate editorial assistant and more recently as the archive's Project Manager and the co-editor of notebook 07.01.04[1] (a reading notebook from the year 1923). Through my involvement with the archive, I have started to incorporate the MMDA into both my scholarship (work on Moore and indexicality) and my teaching (in particular as it relates to creative practice and modernist culture).

The notebooks themselves are optimum objects for digital analysis and presentation. They are rich and complex sources that include "multiple genres, images (Moore frequently sketched objects that interested her), genetic layers of text (evidence of Moore's later editing of and additions to earlier notes, sometimes with different writing implements), and references to decades' worth of popular and academic source materials."[2] The MMDA presents each facsimile notebook page (or double-spread of pages) *face-à-face*, with a diplomatic transcription of the textual content of each page—"diplomatic"[3] because our transcriptions do not identify the "genetic" order in which Moore made marks on the page. We leave it to readers to compare between the transcription and the facsimile, and interpret the chronology of Moore's thinking and revising for themselves. Assisting this process, each line of digital transcription is also connected to the corresponding section of facsimile through an image–text linking feature so that hovering the cursor over one section of text (either facsimile or transcription) will highlight the appropriate section of the other. This is particularly useful in Moore's poetry-drafting notebooks in which some pages are so dense with writing and emendations that individual lines are difficult to identify and parse in relation to others.

Other digital features of the MMDA that aid interpretation of the notebooks include in-transcription representations of both the writing implement Moore uses and the genre in which she writes at any given point, both factors which can fluctuate within a given line of text. Moore's writing-implements are signaled by corresponding colors of type in the transcription and are captured by TEI XML encoding (more on the functionality of this below). As might be expected, her writing-tools sometimes change day by day, successively through the notebooks, but at other times a change of writing implement can be more suggestive. For instance, when returning to revise a section of composition or to add to a section of note-taking, Moore will sometimes use a different color or shift between pencil and ink. By recording these changes, the digital transcriptions facilitate without dictating genetic analysis of the notebooks, which in turn enables inquiry into Moore's processes of composition, citation, and so on.

Representations of Moore's shifts between genres of writing are also useful to analyses of her creative process. The MMDA uses highlighting in the left margin of transcription pages to indicate the genres of text contained in each line of transcription (aqua for conversation notes, orange for reading notes, green for prose composition, pink for verse, and so on). By mapping her transitions between reading notes, poetry composition, notes on conversations, and so on, this element of the MMDA transcriptions helps visualize a full and multi-generic picture of Moore's poetic practice. This picture corroborates existing scholarly analyses of the importance of reading and broader cultural consumption to Moore's writing (as manifested by citation and quotation in finished poems), but also furnishes excellent examples of modernist creative practice for classroom exploration (more on this below, too).

The genre, color, and type of writing implement that Moore uses in her notebooks are part of the TEI XML encoding schema of the MMDA, along with other elements that denote foreign language, quotation, italics, underline, blank space within a line, drawn elements, and more.[4] The MMDA TEI schema has been elaborated from the general guidelines of the Text Encoding Initiative, a consortium "which collectively develops and maintains a standard for the representation of texts in digital form."[5] The Text Encoding Initiative's guidelines set out encoding methods for machine-readable texts, chiefly in the humanities, social sciences, and linguistics, and are "widely used by libraries, museums, publishers, and individual scholars to present texts for online research, teaching, and preservation." The MMDA's TEI XML encoding, which is mostly inserted by editors at the time of transcription, is both what (where relevant) produces the visual representations of the element in the transcription (e.g., causes a word to be presented as italicized, underlined, colored, etc.), and what makes each notebook machine-readable, and consequently also searchable by encoded attribute.

While not currently available to the public, the ability to search Moore's notebooks by TEI XML element has the potential to be highly generative for scholarship in the future. Unlike a plain text search, which produces exact textual matches for a given word or phrase (like a concordance), searching by TEI XML attribute draws results from the established network of elements produced and curated by the MMDA's editors (like an index). This is the difference, for instance, between text searching for the phrase "foreign language" in a work, which will yield every instance of the phrase "foreign language," and searching TEI XML for all "foreign language" elements, which will result in all instances of foreign language use, without the searcher needing to know any phrases of exact text ahead of searching.

The uses of this kind of search are many and applicable across different aspects of Moore studies. For example, the MMDA's TEI XML will allow users to call up every instance in the notebooks in which Moore drafts toward a particular poem or work, since these have all been encoded in advance by editors. This is not only hugely labor saving for researchers and students, but also improves ordinary text search results by capturing smaller fragments and subtle phrases that might otherwise be overlooked. Search results like these are also useful for plotting compositional timelines, since they highlight the set of dates that Moore drafted the work and collect them in a list; perhaps all the drafting toward one poem is confined to the early part of a 1923 notebook, or alternatively, perhaps another poem is drafted over a series of notebooks, spanning years and perhaps even notebook genres.

Combining text searches and TEI XML searches can produce excellent results as well. While completing a text search for "Shakespeare" would pull up every exact text match to "Shakespeare," results would be more comprehensive if the TEI XML encoded "source" element is also queried, adding to the list of results all instances when editors have identified Shakespeare as the source author of a snippet of quotation in Moore's notes. Editorial annotations might also be added to the search, calling up all other peripheral Shakespearean connections that editors have noted.

Another case study that illustrates the usefulness of combined text and TEI XML searching is an exploration of Moore's interest in prosody and experimentation with poetic meter. Throughout the notebooks, Moore uses various prosody marks, either when drafting her own work or when reading someone else's, and usually writes prosodic annotation in the line above the language she scans, over time using a variety of marks to denote unstress and stress. The MMDA standardizes representations of those prosody marks as a hyphen (-) for unstressed and accent aigu (´) for stress. Consequently, prosody markings are consistently searchable (most effectively in combination; say, an iamb "- ´") across the MMDA, despite the slight variations in Moore's orthography over time. Expanding this line of inquiry to the MMDA's TEI XML elements with the appropriate search words ("meter," "rhythm," "prosody," etc.) would yield further layers of information: sources cited by Moore that contain one of these words in their title or their mention in editorial annotations (see below) and quotations. This same combined search strategy could easily be applied with great impact to other search parameters: locations or regions, people in her life, publication titles and press names, among others.

While the MMDA's search functions are still under development, the MMDA currently provides a number of other aids to research and teaching created or curated by the archive's editors. In addition to the introductions that accompany each published notebook, notebook transcriptions are supported by editorial annotations that contextualize Moore's writing and life, including giving citations for the original source texts that Moore quotes or invokes in the process of her notetaking and connecting sections of draft or note taking to published poems, essays, and other works. Where relevant, editorial annotations link directly to the MMDA's "Glossary" page, which provides descriptions of significant points of reference (be they people, publications, places, etc.) in Moore's life, as well as to "Moore's Sources," a page that collects saved digital copies of Moore's primary source materials—from museum catalogues and news articles to advertising film reels. This last page is a continuous work in progress, with new sources added regularly, but overall provides unique access (free of paywalls) to many primary sources that today can be difficult or expensive to locate.

Under the site headings "Scholarship" and "Education," the MMDA also hosts a series of broader resources for scholars, teachers, and students of Moore's work. Under the "Education" heading can be found: an interactive timeline of Moore's life and works that plots life events and poem publications along a scrollable axis; an "About the Poet" page, which gives a brief biography of Moore and description of her significance in twentieth-century literature; an "About the Poems" page, a growing library of excerpts of critical commentary about individual Moore poems, organized by poem; a "Context and History" page, which contains short articles that link Moore (her life and her poetry) to her context (for example, "Marianne Moore, Muhammad Ali, and Late Night Talk Radio" by Linda Leavell with Elizabeth Gregory); a "Syllabuses and Lesson Plans" page, which houses syllabuses and lesson plans for graduate and undergraduate courses focused in-full or in-part on Moore; a "For Students by Students" page, which publishes examples of polished, high quality writing by high school, undergraduate, and early-stage graduate students, with the dual goals of recognizing excellence in student writing about Moore, and providing a forum for students to engage the work of their peers; and, lastly, a page entitled "Poems To or About Moore," which (as its name suggests) collects poems written to or about Moore and her work. Each of these pages accepts submissions from the wider Moore community through a "Submit" button. Submissions are reviewed by MMDA editors as they are received.

In addition to the "Glossary" mentioned earlier, the "Scholarship" section of the MMDA contains other helpful resources, too: a "Bibliography" page, which lists "Standard and Useful Editions" of Moore's works, as well as a searchable critical bibliography of writing on or about Moore (with 174 discrete entries), and a list of other published Moore bibliographies; a digitized archive of the *Marianne Moore Newsletter* (1977–83); a library of "Hard to Find Essays" on Moore, including special journal editions dedicated to her work; and a list of further "Useful Sites" for Moore scholars. Submissions are also accepted for these pages and are vetted by editors as they are sent in.

While each of these pages is of course useful on their own, perhaps the most exciting advantage of the MMDA being a *digital* archive is its hypertextual nature—that these ancillary resources link back and forth to the notebooks themselves, as well as to other primary and secondary sources. Following the architecture of links that the MMDA provides, users can make fantastic connections between Moore's note taking, her poetry, and her broader cultural context. In particular, the hyper-textuality of the edition annotations, and the connection between these and many of Moore's primary sources are highly adaptable to pedagogical exercises and to the classroom experience more generally, where they not only bring a sense of poetry's dynamic relationship to life, history, and other media, but also prompt important questions for students about the very nature and purpose of poetry.

One example of the MMDA's hypertextual connections that I have enjoyed using in the classroom (in my instance, an introduction to creative writing) is the connections it facilitates between, first, Moore's description in her miscellaneous Notebook 07.03.11 (1929–1940) of aquatic acrobats (or "aquabats," as they were called) in an aquatic spectacular held at a grand hotel in Coral Gables Florida in 1932; second, a copy of the film footage (of the aquabats) that Moore's notetaking responds to (located in "Moore's Sources"); and, third, Moore's poem, "The Frigate Pelican" (first published July 1934), the drafting of which seems likely to have been informed by Moore's observations about the Coral Gables aquabats. The relevant notes start of page 21-recto of 07.03.11 and pick up again briefly two pages later on page 22-recto:

>   Dec 10 32
>   The Aquabats at Coral Gables
> Col. _____ 150 dive. and
> "I wonder what he's thinking about when he's
> the greased flagpole with 3 little
>   to pluck before diving
> flags at the end. Some sidle out
> and finally lose their balance and
> flounder off ~~into~~ in a dive. One comes
> out with a whizz, and not a
> tremor of the body to nearly the
> end of the pole on the momentum
> of ~~his~~ the running start and with
>   forward
> arms raised, curves over
>   ease
> and down with the smoothness of
> the frigate bird—left leg slowly
> rising like the ~~wheel~~ rim of the
>   ball of the
> gyroscope, the ^ right foot adhering

> to the curve of the pole for
> > palm of the treetoad
> a second ~~like the as it rolls~~
> ~~slide in the slide forward~~
> ~~like the palm of the tree toad~~
> before it slid off
> "What an aquabat!" (page 21-recto)
>
> Several quivered & trembled along
> the pole before giving themselves up for lost
> tadpoles
> (one came out w a whizz to within almost
> the end of the pole, and raising
> both arms slowly & gracefully let
> himself fall forward w the ease of
> the frigate-bird— (page 22-recto)[6]

Reading these notes alongside the video of the Coral Cables aquabats, students develop avenues for critical inquiry. They observe how Moore's description both clearly maps onto the choreography of the aquabats, but also diverges and becomes embroidered: humans become treetoads and frigate-birds through the quality of their actions. Then, with those images in mind, the word "flagpole" homophonically conjures the word "tadpoles" in the left margin, and so on. Brainstorming their observations and questions in small groups (or, if the class is small, as a whole class), my students have come up with such questions as: What were aquatic spectaculars, and why were luxury hotels holding them in the 1930s? What was it about the movements of these performers that connected them in Moore's imagination to animals? What is the relationship between birds and toads, and how has Moore made us rethink it? What does that relationship in turn tell us about human creativity and artistry?

Adding the third layer of Moore's "The Frigate Pelican" only deepens and complicates their investigations, leading students to explore ideas about influence and the connections between creativity, art, and the material world. In an introductory course to creative writing, populated largely by freshmen, the exercise is often also my students' first encounter with archival sources, and is consequently intended to give a model for how such sources can enrich and test our textual analyses of primary literary texts.

It goes without saying that this kind of comparative research does not require digital hyperlinks, but the linked nature of the MMDA nevertheless provides an initial architecture for students to learn to connect sources and put the images and ideas that they identify into constellation with one another. It lends itself exceedingly well to self-directed learning exercises, where students explore notebooks and find their own clusters of connected sources to analyze and write about.

When I first presented a shorter version of these reflections on the MMDA and its usefulness at a roundtable on archives at the "Marianne Moore and The Archives" Conference," some members of the Moore community expressed understandable anxiety about the way these digital tools might affect the way we read, study, and teach Moore's poetry. In particular, concern was expressed that these tools might foreclose the range of interpretations possible for each of her poems (say, by authoritative or exhaustive annotation or citation) and preclude the excitement of searching ourselves for an elusive reference or connection. This is an argument I have thought about often during my years working on the MMDA, especially when I have often been the one discovering and encoding connective links between the notebooks, primary sources, and published poems: would this flatten the experience of reading for others?

It is true that the MMDA furnishes its users with many citational and annotational aids, but these are far from exhaustive, and, more to the point, are usually not highly interpretive in nature. That is to say, they point users in a certain bibliographic direction, but do not overdetermine the results of inquiry. In the same way that the relationship traced between the aquabat film and Moore's "The Frigate Pelican" resists the simple one-to-one analysis of the physical forms of diving bodies, I see the citations and annotations provided by MMDA editors to be calls to exploration. For scholars as for students, they open up fields of inquiry, pointing to the deep cultural genesis of Moore's writing, but ultimately leaving the work of exploration, description, and interpretation to the user.

Origins of the Archive

CHAPTER TWELVE

An Interview with Patricia C. Willis

Karin Roffman

Patricia Willis (b. 1938) served as the first curator of the Marianne Moore archive at the Rosenbach Library from 1975 to 1987, and then as the Elizabeth Wakeman Dwight Curator of the Collection of American Literature at the Beinecke Library at Yale from 1987 to 2008. In addition to her monumental work as editor of *The Complete Prose of Marianne Moore* (1986) and curator of the traveling exhibition, *Marianne Moore: Vision into Verse* (1987), Willis has published crucial essays on "An Octopus" and "Marriage," including: "The Road to Paradise: First Notes on Marianne Moore's 'An Octopus,'"[1] *Marianne Moore and the Pipes of Pan: Mt. Rainier and Mt. Olympus*,[2] and "A Modernist Epithalamium: Marianne Moore's 'Marriage,'"[3] among others. She also inaugurated the *Marianne Moore Newsletter* at the Rosenbach (which can be viewed at the Marianne Moore Digital Archive), is featured in the Annenberg Learner podcast, *Voices & Visions: Marianne Moore*,[4] and currently writes a blog on Moore.[5] During a long weekend in September 2022, Karin Roffman talked with Willis at her home in Sequim, Washington, about her life and work as a Marianne Moore scholar and curator, her immersion in the Moore archives at the Rosenbach in the years before the papers were cataloged, and the ways that she has sustained and deepened her thinking about this iconic modernist for sixty years.

Karin Roffman: How did you end up writing a dissertation on Marianne Moore?

Patricia Willis: I took a few years. I was back at University of Chicago for the PhD in the fall of 1968. This degree was a separate enterprise, with new matriculation after the MA, and I was in a class with James Miller, who was an Americanist, in the first semester. This course was on the archive of *Poetry* magazine, which is held at the university. Jim Miller was interested in developing a book of letters from authors who wrote to Harriet Monroe, the editor of *Poetry*. He gave us a list of poets represented in the archive by most letters and some letters, etc. He said if any one of you wants to claim one of these poets on the "most" list as a dissertation topic, let us know so we don't crowd you or take over what you need to look at. My hand went up, and I said I'll take Marianne Moore. I was just as surprised at myself as anything. I headed to the *Poetry* archive and spent the rest of my research time for that course there and wrote a paper.

Karin Roffman: What was it about?

Patricia Willis: What got me interested was the archive itself. The most important thing I remember about it was that Moore wrote to Harriet Monroe in 1918 and said, "*Poetry*'s approach to art is very different from my own … . I'm glad that I'm not ipso facto an alien." I noticed that at the same moment, Monroe was hearing from Williams and Pound, particularly, with the same sort of response, not as clear as Moore's, but the same kind of thing. All of them stopped submitting poetry to Monroe in 1918. They returned in the 1930s, that is, after the *Dial* magazine expired in 1929. Of course, they appeared in lots of other magazines too, but the *Dial* was central to their publishing during the 1920s. I was interested in what that dynamic was, and I think that's what I explored in my paper and what Moore was saying to Monroe. I worked in the archive and used lots of quotations from the papers in my essay.

Karin Roffman: Was that your first deep dive into an archive?

Patricia Willis: Yes. First ever. Never met one before.

Karin Roffman: And you loved it right away?

Patricia Willis: I did. I was fascinated.

Karin Roffman: What was the archive for you?

Patricia Willis: It was the original material. I had no way of knowing for sure, but it seemed like this material had not been explored. It wasn't in print anywhere. It was new. As you know, if you're a scholar, you are looking for the new and the unreported. And there it was.

Karin Roffman: How old were you? Where were you in life at that point?

Patricia Willis: Let's see, 1968. I'd just turned 30.

Karin Roffman: You were in graduate school, and you were also in the order at the same time. Is that right?

Patricia Willis: Right. Religious of the Sacred Heart.

Karin Roffman: Was the order putting you through grad school?

Patricia Willis: Well, yes and no. They were sending me to grad school, but I was also teaching two courses at their college in Lake Forest, Illinois, north of Chicago.

Karin Roffman: This is Barat College?

Patricia Willis: Yes, where I had also gone to college.

Karin Roffman: Somehow, I thought you had gone to college in Boston and not Chicago.

Patricia Willis: I began at Newton College of the Sacred Heart in Boston, but then my mother became ill while I was a freshman.

	She had breast cancer, and I came home to take care of her. After she died, I transferred to Barat.
Karin Roffman:	What was her name? I think I remember you mentioning that she was a musician—was she a singer?
Patricia Willis:	Blanche Reardon Cannon. She was a graduate of the University of Chicago. She had a teaching degree from what is now the University of Wisconsin at River Falls and taught high school for a few years. Then she went to Chicago for a "PhB," their version of the BA. She also studied music at the Chicago Musical College, Chicago's Juilliard, and during the Depression, she and her sister supported themselves by performing musical skits for schools and women's clubs in the Midwest.
Karin Roffman:	What did your father do?
Patricia Willis:	He was an intellectual property trial lawyer in private practice in Chicago and New York.
Karin Roffman:	When did you graduate Barat College? When you went back to teach, I imagine you were instructing students who were very much like you?
Patricia Willis:	My graduation year is 1960, but by then I was in the order. I left college after my junior year and then went back for one summer to graduate. When I started teaching, some of the students were like me but it was also a moment when older women were going back to school, and these students were very satisfying—they brought life experience with them.
Karin Roffman:	What classes were you teaching?
Patricia Willis:	They were American Lit courses of some kind. They needed teachers and administrators, which they were hoping I would become. They had nine colleges in the United States at that point.

Karin Roffman: Where does the archive fit into this? Because it seems like, at this moment, you were on multiple paths … a path to teaching and to university administration. And then, your love of the archive sent you onto a new path to curatorship.

Patricia Willis: That's a good question. There were several steps between finding the archive and curatorship. After that first year of PhD studies, I decided I needed to find some grants for a dissertation. I had a university fellowship for the first two years of PhD studies. I needed some outside money, and I had to have something unique enough to appeal to a donor like AAUW—a dissertation topic a little different from the ordinary. The summer after that year with the course in the *Poetry* magazine archive, I went east looking for library resources on Moore. I went to the New York Public Library, BPL, Houghton, Beinecke.

Karin Roffman: The Beinecke was a pretty new reading room in 1969. It had just opened in 1963.

Patricia Willis: I guess. I didn't think about that. It was exciting because they were nicely organized. And they had, of course, the *Dial* papers, for which Moore was editor from 1925 to 1929, its last years. I met Donald Gallup. He had to inspect me before I was allowed in the reading room. I spent some days there, and it was a delight to read through the *Dial* papers.

Karin Roffman: Was that also the summer you met Bob Willis, your future husband?

Patricia Willis: Yes, in New York in August.

Karin Roffman: In the midst of all these library trips?

Patricia Willis: Exactly. Bob had been in La Jolla, California studying with Carl Rogers, the well-known psychologist. A woman with whom I was teaching at Barat, named Bessie Chambers, who was also a religious, met Bob when they taught at Seattle University in the summer of 1969. They started a new program in religious education together. Bessie said to me, sometime in April, "What are you doing in August?" And I said, "I'll be in New York." And she said, "I'll see you then." I came back to my folks' apartment where I was staying one afternoon, and she was sitting there on the couch. She said, "Oh, by the way, I have a friend I met while in Seattle this summer, and he's in upstate New York right now evaluating the therapy at an institution for recovering heroin addicts. I know he'd love to get out of there for a weekend if we could invite him down to the city." Which we did. Bob came down, and the two of them talked all weekend. We may have gone to a show, but it was mostly sitting in the living room talking.

* * *

[Karin Roffman: Where did you go next?]

Patricia Willis: I went home to Chicago, but I made a telephone call. This is in the fall of 1969. I reached the director at the Rosenbach and asked him about the archive. I asked: "Do you have this and this?" and the answer was: "All of it." On the basis of that call, I wrote a grant proposal. I knew it was extensive and extraordinary, and no one had ever looked at it except the Rosenbach director, Clive Driver. When I went to the Rosenbach a year later, I realized that the huge collection had not been sorted except for the poetry manuscripts and some of the correspondence they thought really important, such as the letters from T. S. Eliot, from Ezra Pound, and from William Carlos Williams. The rest was just this gorgeous chaos.

Karin Roffman: You were living in Philadelphia starting in fall 1970 to be able to do this intensive, original research at the Rosenbach?

Patricia Willis: Actually, I was in Boston for the year. I'd been asked by the order to work there with the new people coming into the order. I went partly because I wanted to be on the East Coast where the archive was. It just so happened that the Jesuits asked Bob to go to Boston and work with them, so he was living there too. We had some time together then.

Karin Roffman: Was that the first time you had seen each other since you met a year earlier?

Patricia Willis: No. In the spring of 1970, Bessie had asked Bob to come to our college and work with the faculty on inter-personal development, which was hot then, and also to work with the order, which was getting ready for what they called the general counsel, meaning a thorough examination of the administration of the order, internationally. Why was I involved? Because I had a car. And I knew Bob. I could pick him up at the airport and do that sort of thing. I was his host.

Karin Roffman: So for the year 1970–71 you lived in Boston. It's not that close from Boston to Philadelphia.

Patricia Willis: It's closer than Chicago to Philadelphia.

Karin Roffman: True! Were you going often to the Rosenbach? Then was not like now, where you can go to most libraries with your iPhone and take a thousand pictures and then return home and figure out what you have just seen. You had to be there.

Patricia Willis: I was going often. I can't remember all the details, but in the summer of 1970, I had a place to stay, not too far from the Rosenbach, down on Fourth Street with a religious group. I've forgotten what order they were, but they were willing to let out a room. Fourth Street to 21st is a bit far to walk, but I think I did walk or take the bus to the Rosenbach every day.

Karin Roffman: It is extremely helpful to be able to go multiple times in a row until one understands how an archive feels and functions.

Patricia Willis: It made all the difference. When I first got to the archive, of course, I was treated like any stranger. They put me up in the library at the partners' desk, you will remember.

Karin Roffman: Who is "They?" Is it Clive …

Patricia Willis: "They" was Clive Driver, who was the director. Moore was still alive then, and he was to become her literary executor too. Richard Talbot was Clive's companion and a worker at the library. They set me up at that desk with Moore's little notebooks, her very first reading notebooks. It was a set of five of them. Then they asked me if I'd like lunch, and I said, "Well, sure," and so they brought lunch up to the library. I was horrified. Within a day or two, I got myself down to the kitchen to have lunch with the staff because I didn't think there ought to be lunch up there with the Moore manuscripts.

Karin Roffman: Were there any other researchers with you or were you the only one then?

Patricia Willis: I was the only one. When I was first there, of course, I was like any visitor. After I was there lots of times, they gave me things to sort and look through. I was learning about the archive, hands on, since there was no catalog at all. Every time I was there, they would bring a box of papers for me to look through to see if it was useful. Eventually, they let me into the collection itself. I was still a graduate student. I wasn't the curator, but I was doing what a curator might have to do if she showed up there in this chaos.

Karin Roffman: That's remarkable. Was that progression from the partners' desk to the collection itself an act of generosity on Clive Driver's part? Was it a desire to have help? Did he recognize a fellow traveler?

Patricia Willis: I think, first, he knew that I wouldn't hurt the material. He knew that if I organized it, the order would be rational because that was in my interest as well as the archive's. If anybody was ever going to look at things, it had to have some order. But so far, I was the only one asking.

Karin Roffman: How long was it until there were other scholars clamoring to look at the papers?

Patricia Willis: It was about four or five years.

Karin Roffman: That's exciting to have that kind of time to get to know the papers so deeply. Did Moore herself come to the library?

Patricia Willis: No, never. The papers came down there in 1969. And by that time, I think she'd had a stroke. I don't think she was ambulatory after that, and I know she was never there.

Karin Roffman: But you met her?

Patricia Willis: I did. Clive and Richard took me to see her. She was living on West Ninth Street. She was sitting up in bed and bright. She had lost the ability to speak easily, given the strokes. This would've been, I can't remember, maybe 1971. She died in February 1972. She tried to make herself understood, gesturing to one of her books that included her poem "Novices." I later realized that Clive Driver must have told her that I was a member of a religious order, and she knew that Novices was the name of the first stage of joining. The other thing I remember about the meeting was that we all sang songs to her. She really had a hard time communicating. It was like visiting a shrine.

Karin Roffman: What was Clive Driver like?

Patricia Willis: New England. Taciturn, quiet, deeply interested in Moore, and had been for years and years. He was especially welcoming to me because he had convinced the trustees of the Rosenbach to buy Moore's papers for a substantial sum. I've forgotten what the figure was. Whatever it was, it was a huge stretch for that little place. He was very encouraging to scholars who wanted to use the archive, and I was very welcomed.

Karin Roffman: Did that money go to her care for those last couple years?

Patricia Willis: I'm sure some of it did. Some came from Bryher, who put money in her bank. She was able to have care at home the entire time. Gladys Berry had been with her for years and years, and near the end, Moore had round-the-clock care.

Karin Roffman: You finished your dissertation in 1972. I imagine the Moore papers were central to it. What did you end up arguing?

Patricia Willis: It was about her poetics, arguing that she had one. That first thing I mentioned earlier—that her attitude towards poetry was different from Harriet Monroe's—that was an opening. I had first asked: what was her attitude towards poetry and what was Harriet Monroe's? It set me off thinking about the whole modernist enterprise. That was the core. Things that contributed to answering that question were what interested me. What was an American modernist? Finding that answer in Moore, in her poems and papers, was what the dissertation was about.

Karin Roffman: What did you end up thinking about her in relation to other modernists?

Patricia Willis: She knew all of them. She knew their work. She knew some of them personally. She managed to make herself different and have no criteria for what she put out except herself, her own ideas. She didn't copy anybody. I don't think she bowed to anybody. Eliot, for example, in his introduction to her *Selected Poems* in 1934, talked about her uniqueness. Part of it was her subject matter, which was not friends and family, except maybe covertly. And the fact that her poetry was layered was important. There was that complex exterior and then underneath the hardness, the shell, there were personal relationships. That was always intriguing about Moore. Her poetry is totally intellectual and yet in it, there is connection with a real person, her person.

Karin Roffman: I remember going to the Moore archive and feeling amazed by the voluminous family correspondence, which Linda Leavell has made such sense of in her biography. In those first couple of years, did you deal with those? ... There's an astonishing number of family letters. Or did you think the answers to the questions that you were asking were primarily in the poetry?

Patricia Willis: The poetry, the drafts, the reading notebooks, especially. And her correspondence with other modernists. I didn't pay much attention to the family. I suppose I sorted it later, but it would take a Linda Leavell, or you, to make sense of it.

Karin Roffman: I didn't have the patience for Moore family correspondence—all those nicknames to make sense of, to keep track of. I was grateful that Linda was doing it.

Patricia Willis: Yes. Exactly. An enormous undertaking.

Karin Roffman: How did you go from turning in your dissertation to becoming the curator at the Rosenbach? You were in Boston from 1970–71, and then what happened next?

Patricia Willis: In 1971–72 I was back in Illinois to finish my dissertation. I was living in Hyde Park in the order, and I was commuting to teach two courses again at Barat College.

Karin Roffman: That's a lot while finishing a dissertation. Was your advisor James Miller? Did you have a defense?

Patricia Willis: Yes. I don't remember the process exactly, but I was told to come to a certain room at a certain time. I walked in, and there were 12 people there—I couldn't believe it—including Elder Olson, the last of the Chicago New Critics, from whom I had taken Modernist poetry as an MA student. Jim Miller led the discussion. They asked me questions about Moore and the archive. They didn't care about my dissertation. They were interested in Moore's archive.

Karin Roffman: Because you were the only one who had seen it?

Patricia Willis: Right. Jim went around the circle of people, letting them ask questions. He reached position number nine, Elder Olson, but time was up and, to my relief, Elder didn't get to ask a question. Then they sent me out for a minute while they had a discussion and finally brought me back and told me I'd passed. That was the end of that.

Karin Roffman: Did you go to graduation? Was it shortly after, that you and Bob both left the order and got married?

Patricia Willis: My graduation was during the first week in June, and I actually went to it, which was unusual at the time. Then we were married on the 4th of July.

Karin Roffman: In Chicago?

Patricia Willis: No, in La Jolla. I went out there and stayed in Bob's empty apartment because he and his roommate were up in Seattle in the third year of the course I mentioned. I spent time with an old friend, Abbe Salomon, who lived in town. Abbe was a law professor at Western California School of Law and a member of the San Diego City Council. Abbe invited herself to my wedding. Then she took me to the hospital to see her father, my father's friend, who was suffering from a heart condition. There in his hospital bed, Irving said, "I want to come to your wedding." I said, "That's wonderful." I told my father that, and my father said, "If Irving's going, I'm coming." They were all there at my wedding, which took place at the home of Bill and Audrey McGaw, friends of Bob's.

Karin Roffman: Can I ask what you wore?

Patricia Willis: I made a bright yellow dress with a long skirt and a miniature dress of the same for a friend's daughter, who was going to be the flower girl.

Karin Roffman: Did you leave the order right before the wedding? What exactly does it mean to leave the order?

Patricia Willis: Well, it meant I had to explain to the provincial that I was leaving, and she would have to say, "Okay." Then I had to write a letter to the Pope and then I received a form back from the Vatican when I was in La Jolla. It was all in Latin of course. There was one sentence in the letter that I could not make out. Bob didn't have a Latin dictionary at his apartment because he didn't need one. After Bob and I got married, and we were on our honeymoon somewhere in Oregon at the Pat Boone Motel, I said "Oh, I need your help." I took the letter out of my suitcase, and he translated the sentence. I signed and sent it back to Rome and that was the end.

Karin Roffman: Did it feel okay by that point?

Patricia Willis: Yes, things were pretty casual at the moment. It wasn't like ten years earlier, which would've been very cloak and dagger: when somebody left an order, they disappeared in the middle of the night. There were three members of my order at our wedding. There were four Jews, three Catholic nuns, a Jesuit priest, my dad, a couple of cousins and several Protestant friends.

Karin Roffman: And Bob left the Jesuit order at the same time?

Patricia Willis: They didn't want to let him go, so he wasn't officially out for a year and a half. They held back permission hoping he would change his mind or to punish him for doing it.

Karin Roffman: I guess it must have helped that you were doing this together.

Patricia Willis: You bet. It would have been harder not to do it together.

Karin Roffman: Before we return to the Rosenbach and how the curatorship of the Moore collection came about in 1975, I have one more question about this early period. Is there an intellectual link, do you think, between being part of the order and your work on Moore? I know that when I asked you how your work on Moore started, you began your response with graduate school, Elder Olson, and modernism, but is there an earlier point intellectually for you?

Patricia Willis: I don't know if I can connect it. When I was getting ready to go for the PhD, a friend of mine was at Harvard and she kept saying, "You should try to come to Harvard; it's wonderful." And I thought, "Well maybe," so I poked around, and I realized that Harvard would make me a very good generalist. I'd get to spend a semester studying Beowulf and the Elizabethans, but I had had enough of that during my MA. I wanted to be a specialist in Modern American Poetry. At Chicago, I could choose modernism at the beginning because all that general work, the Beowulf, etc., was behind me. As I said, my first teaching experience was American literature, but a college professor at Barat, Agnes Donohue, made me try to slant my English major in that direction. She shared her excitement for Eliot, Williams, and Stevens, and I was intrigued by the puzzle that was modernism, the seemingly impersonal intellectualism so far from newspaper verse and popular, uncomplicated poetry.

Karin Roffman: I am imagining an experience like the one you have described Moore had in Georgiana Goddard King's "Imitative Writing" class in her senior year at Bryn Mawr—when she realized her own "principles of style," a sense of writing and thinking that she had always felt instinctively but now could connect to a literary tradition, in her case, one that extended back to the great seventeenth-century stylists. It's also interesting that the order was French and ...

Patricia Willis: Yes, it was French from 1800—not 1920s Paris with Gertrude Stein and Ezra Pound at *Les Deux Magots*.

Karin Roffman: Then in the late summer of 1972 after your wedding you left Chicago permanently. Was it difficult to leave the city? What part of the city had you lived in growing up?

Patricia Willis: We lived in South Shore until 1947, when my parents bought a house in Wilmette, north of the city. It had been built for "The Century of Progress" at the 1933–34 World's Fair by the Libby Glass and the Stran Steel company. It reflected Bauhaus architecture with art deco interior design. Outside porcelain-plaited steel. Dull not shiny. Inside so much glass: a blue mirrored ceiling in the dining room—great if you know and are playing cards. The fireplace had a floor-to-ceiling mirrored wall with an art deco scene of archers. It was recently torn down.

Karin Roffman: I just looked up photos—your address was 2105 Chestnut Avenue. It was initially part of the "Homes of Tomorrow" exhibition at the World's Fair. What a cool house to live in—did you like it there?

Patricia Willis: I loved living there. I liked the fact that it was odd. But I was ready to leave Chicago. By the time Bob and I moved away right after our wedding, I hadn't lived in that house for a long time. My father had remarried, and I lived near the university.

Karin Roffman: Then you moved east?

Patricia Willis: Bob got a job teaching at La Salle College in Philadelphia, starting in the fall, and I spent some time trying to turn my dissertation into a book.

Karin Roffman: I read that you had a National Endowment of the Humanities fellowship.

Patricia Willis: I did, and I worked at it, but I ultimately decided that a New Critical approach to Moore, which is what I had written in my dissertation, ignored the depth of the author's vision, the author's life, what I was beginning to understand from the archive. The next year Bob was teaching at Rider College, and we moved to Ewing, New Jersey. I said to the English department, "If you need somebody, I'm handy." I taught composition. Meanwhile, I spent some time at the Rosenbach just as a researcher. By the spring of 1975, they had decided that the Moore collection needed a curator because there was beginning to be scholarly interest, and they asked me if I would like to do it.

Karin Roffman: Clive Driver asked you to do what he was doing or the kind of ordering work that you had already started to do in the collection?

Patricia Willis: The second. He was director of the institution, and he didn't have any time to organize the Moore papers. They were just sitting there unless somebody was brought in to deal with them. It was becoming mandatory now because people were regularly asking to see the collection. He asked me if I'd be interested, and of course it was way better than composition, which I did not enjoy teaching, so I said yes. They hired me to begin the summer of 1975. As a side note, the Rosenbach asked me to help with their James Joyce project before beginning with Moore. They were publishing a facsimile of the *Ulysses* manuscript with a reprint of the first edition annotated for variants from the MS. I spent the summer with the manuscript of *Ulysses* in one hand, and I'm sorry to say an ink pen in the other. We finished in September and then I went to the Moore archive.

Karin Roffman: What an immersion! How did it work then when visitors came to see the Moore papers before there was a catalog?

Patricia Willis: I remember that a new researcher would come in and want to see the Moore archive, and we would sit together and talk to figure out what she—it was usually she—needed and then I would try to find it. There wasn't any catalog until at least 1987 or 1988, shortly after I left.

Karin Roffman: How did you find things?

Patricia Willis: Well, of course the first thing I did was to explore the many boxes, which seemed like they had been packed in a hurry. I must have made files and lists of poems and correspondents.

Karin Roffman: Given all that on-the-job training, how did your thinking about archives evolve?

Patricia Willis: I only knew archives as an end user. I had no training of any kind. The Rosenbach had a fabulous rare book collection with significant manuscripts rather than any archives. It had a Chaucer manuscript, a Bay Psalm book, one hundred George Washington letters, manuscripts by Wordsworth, Shelley, Keats, the manuscript of *Dracula*, the art of Maurice Sendak, and on and on. In those days, while a *Dial* archive at Yale would receive full cataloging, a small library would not have such resources, and I was on my own. My sense of how to organize the archive was based on what people wanted to see, which was first the poetry manuscripts and then correspondence with other poets. Then I suppose maybe prose manuscripts and correspondence with other people and finally family correspondence. I went to visit the Buffalo archives. When Charles Abbott was in charge around the late 1930s, he told writers like Williams to give him everything that was in his desk drawer and not to throw anything out. "Everything in his wastebasket," I think that was his phrase. It was a collection of artifacts as well as papers and so on, which was very interesting. As you of all people know, that material is now understood to have value in the hands of an enlightened teacher. The Moore archive included her entire living room, recreated in an uncannily similar Rosenbach space, as well as dressers and cabinets full of books, China, mementos like the mechanical bird that inspired "My Crow Pluto"— a Charles Abbott dream.

Karin Roffman: My very first graduate school essay (in Professor Langdon Hammer's "Modern Poetry" class in fall 1998) was on some of the little things in that marvelous room at the Rosenbach in relation to her poems. I remember visiting the library several times to do research, meeting Linda Leavell there, and then one day Evelyn Feldman let me wander around and choose the things that I most wanted to write about. I loved that I could study papers *and* things, both of which were clearly important to Moore, and were saved and cared for at the library. By the way, speaking of Charles Abbott, I recently read Alison Fraser's terrific essay on his writers' "trash" project: "Creating the Twentieth-Century Literary Archives: A Short History of the Poetry Collection at the University at Buffalo" (2020).[6] Did your thinking about archives evolve as you organized Moore's archive after so many years as a researcher?

Patricia Willis: I went to some archival meetings, but in those days, archives were considered primarily historical, such as those of towns and counties. Those meetings were interesting, but there wasn't much help overall about literary archives. My thoughts about literary archives were simply who needs to use them and how should they be organized for that reason. Years later, I learned from the archivists at Yale what should happen to literary archives!

Karin Roffman: How an archive can be made more accessible to those who want to use it is already a meaningful way to think about writers' papers and things. You also started a newsletter while you were at Rosenbach. How did it come about? Was it your project or a group enterprise?

Patricia Willis: Mine entirely. I got to do some research and on work time for heaven's sakes. That was fun. The *Marianne Moore Newsletter* was a Rosenbach publication that appeared twice a year. The idea was just to share original Moore materials and interest people in her work. As you know from experience, it was hardly an academic-looking publication.

Karin Roffman: I've found it extremely useful and fascinating. Did your first essay on "An Octopus" (*Twentieth-Century Literature*, 1984) emerge from similar research?

Patricia Willis: That essay started percolating about a decade before I published it. I met Washington State on my honeymoon as we went there to visit Bob's family. He was from Yakima. If you arrive on a cloudy day in Seattle, all you see is a city on a hill under a gray sky. If the next day is sunny, you awaken to see this enormous mountain over that hill, right in your face. Moore spent two summer vacations with Mt. Rainier in view. There are pictures of the family at "Paradise," an inn with access to the glaciers. Moore began to write the poem on the train trip home in 1923. On another trip, Bob and I stayed at the same inn at "Paradise" and clearly something rubbed off!

Karin Roffman: Did you stay there because Moore did? Or did you later realize the connection?

Patricia Willis: I knew the connection, I think, but that was also the only place to stay. And once you get up there, it's nice to stay the night. It was very special to experience it.

Karin Roffman: "An Octopus" essay was part of a surge of scholarly writing on Moore. As the Moore papers became increasingly well-visited, did you hire other curators or assistants?

Patricia Willis: Clive Driver retired, and the trustees hired Ellen Dunlap to be director. By about 1985, increased use of the Moore collection made its formal processing necessary. The new Curator of Literature, Leslie Morris [now the Gore Vidal Curator of Modern Books and Manuscripts at the Houghton Library], took it on.

Karin Roffman: Was *Complete Prose* in 1986 the first big Moore book that you did?

Patricia Willis: Yes. I put the papers together first because they needed to be ready for anyone who wanted to read them. I wasn't about to do an edition of the poems. At that moment, the estate was in high dudgeon about publishing Moore, but they didn't have a problem with the prose.

Karin Roffman: Why?

Patricia Willis: I think they rightly figured the prose wouldn't bring them any income and the poetry might. There was no objection to publishing prose.

Karin Roffman: How long did it take you? The *Complete Prose* is revelatory and enormous.

Patricia Willis: I would have begun organizing it, I suppose, around 1984. I bought a word processor. This is before the IBM PC was available, about a year before. I bought a Tele-Video word processor in 1984, and that's when I started.

Karin Roffman: I imagine that you had to type up everything in the book. That in itself is a massive project.

Patricia Willis: And in those days, for word processing, you could type a sentence in an ordinary way, but to type punctuation, you had about three keystrokes per punctuation. One could not just type an exclamation point or a period. I can't remember exactly how it worked, but it was very complicated.

Karin Roffman: Did you come to know the prose, the rhythms of Moore's work, more intimately through that effort? Did that project change your sense of the poetry too?

Patricia Willis: I'm sure I became aware of her critical sense. Why did she make those choices? Why did she review what she did? Just looking at her mini reviews for the *Dial*, her choices of what to review were unusual.

Karin Roffman: And did you take a leave to do the prose book?

Patricia Willis: No, I kept working.

Karin Roffman: How did you have time even with your long commute? Although I think you told me once that you liked your commute.

Patricia Willis: I did like it. We lived at the end of one of the commuter lines from Philadelphia. I had about an hour each way to read quietly, and I could never overrun my stop, so I could really concentrate on reading. It was wonderful.

Karin Roffman: Did Bob's job as a counselor change your sense of what you read and of the world in general?

Patricia Willis: Oh, I'm sure it did. You don't live with a psychologist who is articulate without knowing more about how people behave, and it certainly made me more tolerant than I would've been.

Karin Roffman: You knew each other's work well?

Patricia Willis: No piece of writing went out of the house that wasn't proofread by the other person. If you catch anything in the first five pages, it's a great motivation to keep going. A few times there has been something really significant in the first pages. Something like a misspelling of someone's name that's important or some kind of problem with a title that would be a glaring error one might feel humiliated by or then feel like the whole rest of the book—its integrity—was called into question. That is very motivating to get you through the next 200 pages.

Karin Roffman: Shortly after you published *Complete Prose* you created a Moore exhibition—the exhibition catalog *Marianne Moore: Vision into Verse* is beautifully written, and the images are marvelous. It's one of my most beloved Moore books.

Patricia Willis: That was my last exhibition at the Rosenbach. Moore's centenary was in 1987 and celebrations were in order. The Rosenbach planned a major traveling exhibition: to Regenstein Library at the University of Chicago, the Folger Shakespeare Library in Washington, DC, and the Grolier Club in New York City. I gave a lecture at each of the shows and another at the Chicago Public Library with Richard Howard and an evening at the 92nd Street Y in New York. We were determined to make a big splash. In August, there was to be the first ever Moore Conference at the University of Maine, and it was my job to hire scholars for it. I want to mention that I mounted the shows in Philadelphia, Chicago, and New York, and Leslie Morris did the one in DC because I was in the process of moving to Yale.

Karin Roffman: I was just about to ask about that. It was the same year, 1987, that you left the Rosenbach to become Curator of American Literature at the Beinecke. Around that time there was also a big brouhaha about the *Dial* papers at the Beinecke. What happened with the *Dial* papers and how did your new curatorial job come about? Were they related?

Patricia Willis: Not related, but they were happening at the same time. In the summer of 1986 while I was still working at the Rosenbach Library, beloved Louis Silverstein and I were at the H.D. conference at University of Maine; 1986 was her centenary. Louis was a cataloger at the Beinecke. He knew everything about the poets who interested him. At the conference, Louis said to me, by the way, the Beinecke American Literature job is open; David Schoonover is leaving, and I think you should apply for it. I said immediately, no, thank you. I have no interest in leaving Philadelphia. Then sometime in late fall or early winter Ralph Franklin, who was the director of the Beinecke at that time, came down to the Rosenbach Library to check out the Emily Dickinson holdings because he was in the middle of editing her letters. I can remember we were up in the library. He said the Beinecke job is open, and I think you should put your hat in the ring. I said I can't apply for that. My husband Bob has a therapy practice in New Jersey. I told this to Bob one evening, and he said, well, you have never applied for a job, and I think it would be good for you. That's a true psychologist at work. I said, well, okay, I will apply.

Karin Roffman: The *Dial* papers drama unfolded at the Beinecke in the winter of 1987, and the story became quite public. What was going on?

Patricia Willis: To answer that I need to start in 1929 when the *Dial* folded. Scofield Thayer, who owned the papers, was still alive then. He was active until sometime in the mid-1930s when he was declared incompetent. In the 1940s, his papers were put on deposit at Yale, meaning that they were stored there but not owned by the university. Ordinarily, the holding library would not process them. At that time, though, Yale cataloged them completely, almost as if they owned them. In 1982, Scofield Thayer died, and by then none of the people who were named in his will were alive anymore, and it took several years before somebody realized that the *Dial* papers at the Beinecke actually belonged to the estate and were worth something. The estate notified Beinecke that they were going to sell them at Sotheby's.

Karin Roffman: On March 12, 1987, the *New York Times* published an article: "*Dial* Literary Collection to be Sold," which included the following quotation: "'To break up this irreplaceable archive,' said Patricia Willis, the curator of literature at the Rosenbach Museum and Library in Philadelphia, 'is like taking a national monument and slicing it in little pieces.'"

Patricia Willis: Yes. I don't know exactly how the author of that article, Edwin McDowell, found out about the sale, but Christa Sammons published a wonderful almost moment-by-moment recounting of the *Dial* drama in an article called, "The 'Dial' File," published in the *Yale Library Gazette* (1987).[7] Once it was all over and the *Dial* archive had been purchased by the Beinecke and was back in use by researchers, she recounted just how near the archive came to being broken up.

Karin Roffman: What do you remember from the time?

Patricia Willis: I remember hearing that Barbara Robinson, who was the wife of John Beinecke Robinson, a trustee, read McDowell's article and told her husband to spring into action, so that funding was made available; the Beinecke Library was able to buy the papers, and they were returned to the library.

Karin Roffman: I'm amazed at how close the Beinecke came to losing that archive, and how close scholars came to no longer having a cohesive archive to consult. Your quotation from that article suggests the danger that the archive was in—how perilously near to being sold in pieces.

Patricia Willis: Right, that's what we assumed would have happened to the archive at auction: they sell off the major manuscripts and letters—Eliot, Pound, Williams, Moore—likely to various collectors—and the archive loses its core. Those of us who cared about Moore, who had edited the *Dial* magazine during its last five years, were on the edge of our seats. The integrity of the archive mattered so much, and this sort of monetizing parts of an historically important archive and destroying research value was increasingly rare.

Karin Roffman: You started at the Beinecke in August of 1987, and you arrived just around the time the *Dial* papers were returned from Sotheby's. How did you end up taking the job?

Patricia Willis: I went up to New Haven in late winter for an interview. What I remember about it is that all day long people asked me: What would you collect? What would you collect? You have to know that at the Rosenbach there was no collecting. There was just a little bit of money that I could use to buy the odd Moore book that came on the market, so collecting was not what I was thinking about most. At the end of the interview day, I was sitting with the head of the libraries, Penny Abell. Penny asks: what would you collect? I respond by saying, doesn't anybody want to hear what I know about conservation and restoration and preservation? She responded quite sweetly: we think we know where we're going in those areas—what would you collect?

Karin Roffman: I imagine after you had that meeting with Penny Abell, you understood the job completely. Did you want the job? What happened between the interview and your start date?

Patricia Willis: Well, what happened was that I went home, and I told Bob about this visit. He encouraged me and said if you think you can do the job or want to do it, I think we ought to do it. He told me later that when I went for the interview, he applied for his psychologist's license in Connecticut. He seemed to know it was going to happen.

Karin Roffman: That's marvelously supportive.

Patricia Willis: He didn't have a job in Connecticut, but he got one before we ended up there. So that helped. We both had jobs.

Karin Roffman: Was the Beinecke job very different from the Rosenbach?

Patricia Willis: First, Beinecke was an academic library, part of the university library system. I had come from a staff that could sit around the lunch table. I began in August with two other new curators: Vincent Giroud in Modern European Literature and Bob Babcock in Classical and Medieval.

Karin Roffman: Were there women curators, or was it …

Patricia Willis: There were two: Christa Sammons, who was curator of the German collection, and Marjorie Wynn, who was sort of general curator at the time.

Karin Roffman: Given the question that you kept getting asked in your interview about collecting, is there something you were especially proud of bringing in to the Beinecke once you were settled into that role?

Patricia Willis: I was glad to bring in the papers of Monroe Wheeler and Glenway Westcott, Moore's friends since 1921. Wheeler became director of exhibitions at the Museum of Modern

Art, and Wescott was a novelist well connected to the New York literary scene. When I moved to the Beinecke, I knew I would be working with the papers of about sixty of Moore's friends—some like William Rose Benét from childhood, some like Pound from the beginning of her career. I was especially pleased later to adopt the papers of Barbara Guest, a poet and the biographer of H.D.—the important early fellow modernist. I was also glad to collect the papers of several Native American writers like Leslie Marmon Silko and James Welch, as well as the Violet Quill group of gay writers such as Edmund White and Andrew Holleran.

Karin Roffman: Before we stop, I wanted to ask you about your work on Moore during the last fifteen years since your retirement. I recently read one of Bob's fascinating autobiographies, *Breaking the Chains: A Catholic Memoir* (2005),[8] which he published about six years before he died, and in it he discusses quite beautifully your shared enterprise of writing and thinking, though you were always studying different things. After you moved together from Hamden, Connecticut, to Sequim, Washington, how have you continued to research, write, and think about Moore?

Patricia Willis: I started my blog when I retired from Yale in 2008. Over the years, I've kept a file on each of Moore's poems, including the unpublished. As time went on, as I learned something about a poem, I just tucked a note in the file. Some of them are virtually empty except for a copy of the poem, and some of them are quite thick with things related to either her footnotes or other things I've stumbled upon. I decided I wanted to share them and that's what began the blog.

Karin Roffman: And how often do you put new things on it?

Patricia Willis: Well, I did one recently ...

Karin Roffman: I read the new one on "Poetry" with great interest.

Patricia Willis: Yes, and another one on Monroe Wheeler. The Internet compensates for not having library access, living as I do at the far northwestern corner of the country. Happily, Moore found inspiration in printed matter, much of it now online. If you need a picture of an angwantibo ...

Karin Roffman: Is there something that you still most want to know or learn about Moore?

Patricia Willis: Finding sources is always entertaining and reading new scholarly work that illuminates the poems—like recent work on the late poems—brings real satisfaction. I am hugely indebted to Moore scholars and their careful work on editions or intriguing, thoughtful criticism. But what I still want to learn about, I think, is Moore's tolerance. There is something uncanny about her exoticism, her choices of illustrative material, which suggest to me a world view far from confined by ordinary prejudices of time and place, of religion or education. Where did that come from? How is it expressed? There is no doubt writing on the subject that I have missed.

Karin Roffman: I love that answer, and it already makes me think differently about her mode of expression, what you were saying earlier about the hard shell of her poems—the complex exterior and yet deeply human, warm interior of thought in the poems. Maybe your statement will be a provocation for a future Moore conference or even many conversations before it. Thank you so much for talking with me. I hope that we can plan a Part II soon.

Patricia Willis: I will look forward to that.

Notes

Introduction *Jeff Westover*

1. Wei Liu, "Dis/Appearance for Appeal: On Marianne Moore's 'Performing Archive,'" *Style* 56, no. 3 (2022): 290.
2. Peter Howarth, "Marianne Moore's Performances," *ELH* 87, no. 2 (summer 2020): 553–79.
3. Lauren Frey makes a similar point about Moore's handwritten revisions in her personal copies of *Poems* (1921) and *Observations* (1924) archived at the Rosenbach. She argues that "the revisions she wrote on these printed copies … destabilize the 'Ideal' published text and reveal an undated and ultimately *undatable* site of authorial play." Lauren Frey, "Marianne Moore's Ghost Revisions: *Poems* (1921), *Observations* (1924, 1925), and *Selected Poems* (1935)," *Textual Cultures* 14, no. 1 (spring 2021): 175.
4. Sally Bushnell, *Text as Process: Creative Composition in Wordsworth, Tennyson, and Dickinson* (Charlottesville: University Press of Virginia, 2009), 1.
5. Alison Fraser, "Mass Print, Clipping Bureaus, and the Pre-Digital Database: Reexamining Marianne Moore's Collage Poetics through the Archives," *Journal of Modern Literature* 43, no. 1 (fall 2019): 19–33. https://doi.org/10.2979/jmodelite.43.1.02.
6. Cristanne Miller, "The *Marianne Moore Digital Archive* and Feminist Modernist Digital Humanities," *Feminist Modernist Studies* 1, no. 3 (2018): 257. https://doi.org/10.1080/24692921.2018.1504421.
7. Miller, "The *Marianne Moore Digital Archive*," 258.
8. Claire Battershill, Helen Southworth, Alice Staveley, Michael Widner, Elizabeth Willson Gordon, and Nicola Wilson, *Scholarly Adventures in*

Digital Humanities: Making the Modernist Archives Publishing Project (New York: Palgrave Macmillan, 2017). https://doi.org/10.1007/978-3-319-47211-9. Amy Earhart describes the development of earlier online projects, including the Rosetti Archive and the Walt Whitman Archive. Amy E. Earhart, *Traces of the Old, Uses of the New: The Emergence of Digital Literary Studies* (Ann Arbor: University of Michigan Press, 2015). https://doi.org/10.2307/j.ctv65swvf.

9   Lisa Spiro singles this out as a value worth defending in "'This is Why We Fight': Defining the Values of the Digital Humanities," in *Debates in the Digital Humanities*, ed. Matthew K. Gold (Minneapolis: University of Minnesota Press, 2012), 17.

10 Stephen J. Mexal, "Material Knowledge: Democracy and the Digital Archive," *English Language Notes* 45, no. 1 (spring/summer 2007): 125.

11 Amy Gore and Glenn Koelling have discussed this kind of interaction in their description of the ways they have engaged undergraduates with physical archives. Amy Gore and Glenn Koelling, "Embodied Learning in a Digital Age: Collaborative Undergraduate Instruction in Material Archives and Special Collections," *Pedagogy* 20, no. 3 (October 2010): 453–72.

12 Miller, "The *Marianne Moore Digital Archive*," 259–60. Michael Hancher points out the virtue of keyword searches for enhancing interpretation in "Re: Search and Close Reading," in *Debates in the Digital Humanities 2016*, ed. Matthew K. Gold and Lauren F. Klein (Minneapolis: University of Minnesota Press, 2016), 114–38.

13 Bartholomew Brinkman, *Poetic Modernism in the Culture of Mass Print* (Baltimore, MD: Johns Hopkins University Press, 2017).

14 As David Berry et al. observe, "one complaint about the digital humanities is that, too often, making [digital projects] is seen as a substitution for hermeneutics." David M. Berry, M. Beatrice Fazi, Ben Roberts, and Alban Webb, "No Signal without Symbol: Decoding the Digital Humanities," *Debates in the Digital Humanities 2019* (Minneapolis: University of Minnesota Press, 2019), unpag. https://dhdebates.gc.cuny.edu/projects/debates-in-the-digital-humanities-2019.

15 Alan Liu, "Where is the Cultural Criticism in the Digital Humanities?" Gold, *Debates in the Digital Humanities*, 490–509. See also Gary Hall, "Has Critical Theory Run Out of Time for Data-Driven Scholarship?" Gold, *Debates in the Digital Humanities*, 127–32. According to Amy Earhart, New Historicism is a major influence on the development of the digital humanities. Details of this argument appear in "The Era of the Archive," chapter 2 of *Traces of the Old, Uses of the New*, 38–61.

16 Lisa Stead, "Introduction," *The Boundaries of the Literary Archive: Reclamation and Representation*, ed. Carrie Smith and Lisa Stead (Farnham: Ashgate, 2013), 4.

17 To distinguish transcribed items on the Marianne Moore Digital Archive from the original physical copies held at the Rosenbach Museum and Library, Arabic numerals and periods are used. By contrast, the original physical archives are designated by a Roman numeral followed by colons and Arabic numerals. See Miller, "The *Marianne Moore Digital Archive*," 267, n. 11.
18 Linda Anderson, Mark Byers, and Ahren Warner, eds., *The Contemporary Poetry Archive: Essays and Interventions* (Edinburgh: Edinburgh University Press, 2019), 9.
19 Fraser, "Mass Print, Clipping Bureaus, and the Pre-Digital Database," 30.
20 Stephen Brier, "Where's the Pedagogy? The Role of Teaching and Learning in the Digital Humanities," Gold, *Debates in the Digital Humanities*, 390–401.
21 Mary Chapman, "Digging in the Archive, Harvesting on the Web," *American Periodicals* 17, no. 1 (2007): 115–17.
22 Madeline B. Gangnes, "Togetherness with the Past: Literary Pedagogy and the Digital Archive," *disClosure: A Journal of Social Theory* 27 (July 2018): 113.
23 Jacques Derrida, "Archive Fever," *Diacritics* 25, no. 2 (1995): 27.

Chapter One: Postmarks and Watermarks: Reading through Marianne Moore's Letters Aurore Clavier

1 Marianne Moore, "Walking-Sticks and Paperweights and Watermarks" [1936], in *New Collected Poems*, ed. Heather Cass White (New York: Farrar, Straus and Giroux, 2017), 126.
2 Mary Ruefle, "Remarks on Letters," in *Madness, Rack, and Honey: Collected Lectures* (New York: Wave Books, 2012), 204, quoted in *Letter Writing among Poets, from William Wordsworth to Elizabeth Bishop*, ed. Jonathan Ellis (Edinburgh: Edinburgh University Press, 2015), 2. In this, and subsequent quotations, bracketed ellipses indicate my deletions, as opposed to the authors' own, marked by ellipses alone.
3 Ellis, *Letter Writing among Poets*, 3. Ellis's work on twentieth-century letter writing is presented as a response to such assumptions as those of Frank Kermode and Anita Kermode, who state that "[t]he great age of letter-writing was, roughly, 1700–1918," and that despite the existence of "many good letters after that … by the time of the Second World War there were a lot of those telephones about, admittedly less handy than they are now; and the postal service had begun to shrink and slow down." Frank Kermode and Anita Kermode, *The Oxford Book of Letters* (Oxford: Oxford University Press, 1995), xxiii, quoted in Ellis, *Letter Writing among Poets*, 3.

4   Bonnie Costello, "Introduction," in *Selected Letters of Marianne Moore*, ed. Bonnie Costello, Celeste Goodridge, and Cristanne Miller (New York: Knopf, 1997), xix.
5   Susan Howe, *Spontaneous Particulars: The Telepathy of Archives* (New York: New Directions, 2020 [2014]). Howe's work was initially conceived as "a collaged swan song to the old ways" of archival research in the face of increasing digitalization. Although not immune to the paradoxes of photographic reproduction, the various letters, envelopes, drafts, scribbles, and other scraps assembled by her own text celebrate the material accidents which unite material composition and archeological reading "by mystic documentary telepathy": "Each collected object or manuscript is a pre-articulate empty theatre where a thought may surprise itself at the instant of seeing. Where a thought may hear itself see." Howe, *Spontaneous Particulars*, 9, 18, 24.
6   "Moore seems from very early on to have conceived of her poetry in the related form of appreciative (if also, at times, contentious) and nonhierarchical exchange—between poet and tradition, poet and subject, poet and reader. Poetry, in this sense, resembles letter writing." Cristanne Miller, *Marianne Moore: Questions of Authority* (Cambridge, MA: Harvard University Press, 1995), 167.
7   The 25 cents postage stamp bearing Moore's effigy and issued by the U.S. Postal Service in 1990 serves as a starting point to Elizabeth Gregory's reflection on the authority and currency of the poet's public persona and later production. See "Stamps, Money, Pop Culture and Marianne Moore," *Discourse* 17, no. 1 (fall 1994): 123–46.
8   Luke Carson and Heather Cass White, "Difficult Ground: Poetic Renunciation in Marianne Moore's 'Walking-Sticks and Paperweights and Watermarks,'" *Twentieth Century Literature* 56, no. 3 (2010): 362.
9   "A poem such as 'Marriage' is an anthology of transit. It is a pleasure that can be held firm only by moving rapidly from one thing to the next. It gives the impression of a passage through. There is a distaste for lingering, as in Emily Dickinson." William Carlos Williams, "Marianne Moore" [1925], reprinted in the *Critical Response to Marianne Moore*, ed. Elizabeth Gregory (Westport, CT: Praeger, 2003), 69.
10 Bonnie Costello's analysis of the poem provides an accurate synthesis of the poem as an "invisible fabric of inconsistency." Progressing through its dazzling yet somewhat "too cluttered and digressive" associations of items, and noting the "reciprocity of thought and form" they display, she writes: "[the objects] are analogous to writing ... in that while they have turned something fluid into something solid and stable, they nevertheless reveal a flux and a vitality within their forms." See Bonnie Costello, *Marianne Moore: Imaginary Possessions* (Cambridge, MA: Harvard University Press, 1981), 105–7.

11 "Walking-Sticks and Paperweights and Watermarks" [1936], *New Collected Poems*, 125–26.
12 Building on ancient and medieval science, Renaissance thinkers such as Paracelsus refined an epistemic regime based on the intricate resemblances uniting all objects in God's creation, from seeds and plants to man's anatomy. In order for the divine pattern to remain intelligible, it was believed that these correspondences were signaled by various marks imprinted on nature. The purpose of knowledge was to decipher the signatures manifested in these signs, thus bridging the gap between the visible and the invisible, the material and the spiritual. See Michel Foucault, *The Order of Things* [1970], trans. Anon. (London: Routledge Classics, 2002), 28–33 and Giorgio Agamben, *The Signature of All Things: On Method*, trans. Luca D'Isanto, with Kevin Attell (New York: Zone Books, 2009), 33–80.
13 Sunday, September 23, 1923 entry, Reading Notebook 1930–1943 (RML VII:02:02).
14 James Jiang, "Curious Self-Evidence: Graphology and Gusto in Moore's Critical Prose," *Modernism/modernity* 26, no. 2 (April 2019): 375–98.
15 The word was originally derived, by way of Late Latin, from the Greek *symbolon*. In its most literal sense, the term designated a "token of identity verified by comparing its other half, from *symballein* to throw together." *Merriam Webster Dictionary*, s.v. "Symbol." www.merriam-webster.com/dictionary/symbol.
16 Ellis, *Letter Writing among Poets*, 7.
17 The term was initially used to describe Emily Dickinson's idiosyncratic usage of correspondence as a means to encase and circulate her poems, but also as an aesthetic model for the poems themselves: "Given [the] 'occasional,' event-specific or addressee-specific readings of some of Dickinson's poems, there arises a crucial problem which Margaret Dickie has referred to as 'reprivatisation' of the writer's poetry, and which Cristanne Miller has forcefully highlighted by concluding that 'if the poems and letters must be seen as inseparable elements of the same intergeneric form (letter-poem, poem-as-letter), then historical context,—if not biography outright—becomes the primary point of entry into the poem.'" Marietta Messmer, *A Vice for Voices: Reading Emily Dickinson's Correspondence* (Amherst: University of Massachusetts Press, 2001), 45.
18 Responding to the half-veiled dedication to their mother which Moore had included in her *Selected Poems*, Warner wrote: "'The 'Postscript' [to the volume] is the supreme touch to me. It is a beautiful thing from any point of view; and a poem in itself; but from the point of view of our family knowledge it is like the intimate fire of a diamond. It lights the present moment with divine fire, and at the same time, speaks of our entire history, or our Life hid in each other. In it there is the witness

to our origin, to our period of growth, to what we ever shall be." John Warner Moore, letter to Marianne Moore (April 16, 1935), quoted in "1935–1941: New Friends, New Forms," *Selected Letters of Marianne Moore*, 335.

19 "Walking-Sticks and Paperweights and Watermarks" [1936], *New Collected Poems*, 126.

20 Carson and White, "Difficult Ground," 342 *et passim*.

21 On Moore's troubled relationship to counting, see Fiona Green, "Moore's Numbers," in *Twenty-First Century Marianne Moore: Essays from a Critical Renaissance*, ed. Elizabeth Gregory and Stacy Carson Hubbard (New York: Palgrave Macmillan, 2017), 49–55.

22 "Postmark behests are clearer than / the watermarks beneath," the revised poem affirms, before listing the "ox, swan, / crane, or dolphin," and "eastern, open, jewelled, Spanish, Umbrian / crown" as less explicit "symbols of endurance." Moore, "Walking-Sticks and Paperweights and Watermarks" [1941], *New Collected Poems*, 388. By contrast, the original 1936 version evoked the same figures as mutually reinforcing emblems, inscribed in equally strong surfaces, such as "bark, silverer than the swan, / esparto grass," or "so-called Titan / parchment tougher / than Hercules' lion-skin." See *New Collected Poems*, 126. On the context of war correspondence and the revisions Moore felt compelled to make, see in particular Robin G. Schulze, "How Not to Edit: The Case of Marianne Moore," *Textual Cultures: Texts, Contexts, Interpretation* 2, no.1 (spring 2007): 128–31.

23 On several of Moore's numerous drafts of the poem, this work of recombination is marked off by red numbers or letters attached to the successive stanzas in order to signal their permutations. See Poem Drafts, RML I:05:05.

24 As Moore's notes to the poem make clear, the final stanzas are constructed around complementary musical references: "The fugue's reiterated chain: exposition, development, conclusion," and "The Twelve Presents," whose structuring first line, "One the first day of Christmas," she quotes from "*Christmas: Legends, Carols, Stories* collected by Eleanor Graham (Dutton)." See *New Collected Poems*, 313.

25 "Walking-Sticks and Paperweights and Watermarks" [1941], *New Collected Poems*, 388.

26 Marianne Moore, letter to Bryher (January 18, 1936), *Selected Letters of Marianne Moore*, 360. On the Christian symbolism in the poem, see Carson and White, "Difficult Ground," 357–60 and Schulze, "How Not to Edit," 129–31.

27 Green, "Moore's Numbers," 52.

28 "Wide letters, such as M & W, are difficult to cast, and take much time, therefore I do not make more casts of them than I actually need," Thursday,

October 1923 entry, Reading Notebook 1930–1943 (RML VII:02:02). The copied lines are from Paul Koch's essay, "The Making of Printing Types," published in the first issue of *The Dolphin: A Journal of the Making of Books* (1933).

29   A most representative example is given in the "The Wood-Weasel," whose upside-down acrostic pattern reveals the name of Moore's close friend Hildegarde Watson. Indulging in the playful hide-and-seek shared by the poem, its tutelary animal and the black-and-white designs of the Chilcat blanket which inspired the composition, readers may note that the wood-weasel—Hildegarde's animal persona, the only one who "shall associate" with the poet—also bears the reverse initials of Marianne Moore herself. See *New Collected Poems*, 163 and Patricia C. Willis, *Marianne Moore: Vision into Verse* (Philadelphia, PA: Rosenbach Museum and Library, 1987), 57–59.

30   Moore, "Marriage," *New Collected Poems*, 68.

31   Linda Leavell, *Holding On Upside Down; The Life and Work of Marianne Moore* (New York: Farrar, Straus and Giroux, 2013), 52–56, 113–14, 173–77, 330–31.

32   In a poem-shaped letter dated March 26, 1953, Marianne Moore responded to the publication of Wallace Stevens's *Selected Poems*, by addressing him a typical assortment of her favorite lines in the book, also acknowledging the tribute paid to friends as "a few verbal pineapples / such as you see fit to share with certain friends / of whom I hope I am one." TMS (typed manuscript), RML V:63:22.

33   Roland Barthes, *A Lover's Discourse: Fragments*, trans. Richard Howard (New York: Hill & Wang/Farrar, Straus and Giroux, 1978), 5.

34   Marianne Moore, letter to Bryher (July 7, 1921), *Selected Letters of Marianne Moore*, 164–65; emphasis mine.

35   In the early 1920s, "Moore expressed both an intense interest in self-promotion and an equally fierce modesty," a tension made most salient when letters to modernist promoters such as Eliot or Pound are read side to side with family letters, some of which reveal "she had been considering, at least as early as 1915, the publication of a book of her work." *Selected Letters of Marianne Moore*, 118, 120.

36   *The Letters of Robert Browning and Elizabeth Barrett, 1845–1846* (New York: Harper & Brothers, 1899), quoted in Robin G. Schulze, ed., *Becoming Marianne Moore: The Early Poems, 1907–1924* (Berkeley: University of California Press, 2002), 175.

37   Moore, "Injudicious Gardening," *New Collected Poems*, 10.

38   Marianne Moore, "Comment," *Dial* 80 (April 1927): 359–60, reprinted in *The Complete Prose of Marianne Moore*, ed. Patricia C. Willis (London: Faber & Faber, 1987), 180–82.

39   Marianne Moore, "Bowls," *New Collected Poems*, 60.

40 Moore, "The Dial: A Retrospect," in *Life and Letters To-Day* 27 (December 1940): 175–83 and 28 (January 1941): 3–9; reprinted in *Complete Prose of Marianne Moore*, 357–64.
41 Marianne Moore, "Emily Dickinson," *Poetry* 41 (January 1933): 219–26; reprinted in *Complete Prose of Marianne Moore*, 290–93.
42 Moore, "Emily Dickinson," *Complete Prose of Marianne Moore*, 290–91.
43 For a sample of the many recurrent comparisons made between the two poets during Moore's lifetime, see Gregory, *Critical Response*, 37, 53, 65, 69, 151, 203. Although some of these comments highlighted literary resemblances, others relied on the more superficial and erroneous image of the reclusive spinster. For a more specific analysis of Moore's and Dickinson's poetical affinities, see Cynthia Hogue, "'The Plucked String': Emily Dickinson, Marianne Moore, and the Poetics of Select Defects," *Emily Dickinson Journal* 7, no. 1 (spring 1998): 89–109.
44 Moore, "Emily Dickinson," *Complete Prose of Marianne Moore*, 293.
45 On Dickinson's private system of publication, see Cristanne Miller, "Whose Dickinson," *American Literary History* 12, no. 1/2 (spring–summer 2000): 230–53; Marietta Messmer, *A Vice for Voices: Reading Emily Dickinson's Correspondence* (Amherst: University of Massachusetts Press, 2001); Jane Donahue Eberwein and Cindy MacKenzie, eds., *Reading Emily Dickinson's Letters: Critical Essays* (Amherst: University of Massachusetts Press, 2009).
46 The clipping, cut from *Town and Country*, included a list of celebrities who could "hold their own with either intellectuals or Bohemians," and placed Moore in the first category. Elizabeth Bishop was equally amused: "Louise Crane sent me this page torn from *Town & Country*. I hope you don't mind if I send it on to you. The red pencil is hers, and I think it is rather funny. I hope you aren't being besieged with too many dinner invitations!" Letter to Marianne Moore (February 25, 1937), in *One Art: Letters*, ed. Robert Giroux (New York: Farrar, Straus and Giroux, 1994), 59.
47 Marianne Moore, letter to Louise Crane (February 21, 1937), *Selected Letters of Marianne Moore*, 381.
48 Marianne Moore, "The Paper Nautilus," *New Collected Poems*, 158.
49 Elizabeth Gregory highlights the financial language underlying the exchange, Crane having offered the paper nautilus "as a form of 'interest'" for her 'casualness in returning [Moore's] shell-books'" (February 20, 1937, RML V:05:01), while Moore "added value to her epistolary exchanges—the pun in her name (more!) marking this pattern of supplement." Gregory, *Apparition of Splendor: Marianne Moore Performing Democracy through Celebrity, 1952–1970* (Newark: University of Delaware Press, 2021), 127, 225.

50 Marianne Moore, letter to Hildegarde Watson (August 19, 1957), quoted in Leavell, *Holding On*, 363.
51 Letter to Richard Avedon (October 17, 1959), quoted in Leavell, *Holding On*, 363.
52 Leavell, *Holding On*, 284.
53 Leavell, *Holding On*, 359–60.
54 For a consistent sampling of such letters, see, for example, Eileen G. Moran, "Selected Letters of Marianne Moore to Hildegarde Watson," PhD dissertation, Bryn Mawr, 1985.
55 Gregory, *Apparition of Splendor*, 134.
56 Gregory, *Apparition of Splendor*, 125–37; Elizabeth Wilson, "El Greco's Daughter: Necessary Deflection in Marianne Moore's 'For February 14th' and 'Saint Valentine,'" in *Critics and Poets on Marianne Moore: "A Right Good Salvo of Barks,"* ed. Linda Leavell, Cristanne Miller, and Robin G. Schulze (Lewisburg, PA: Bucknell University Press, 2005), 192–207.
57 "For February 14th" was initially rejected by the *New Yorker*, under the title of "Overture." Moore then changed its title for publication in the *New York Herald Tribune* on February 13, 1959.
58 Katharine S. White, letter to Marianne Moore (January 2, 1960), RML V:45:02.
59 Marianne Moore, "Saint Valentine," *New Collected Poems*, 258.
60 Among many homages, the poet inspired a curious "Valentine for Marianne Moore" published in 1958 (one year before "For February 14th") by Elder James Olson, a leading figure of the Chicago School of criticism. Through a peculiar blend of conventional compliments and formalist analyses supported by references to Plato, Aristotle, and Wagner, the poem celebrates Moore's vision, truthfulness, grace, and perfection, as crystallized in the closing stanza:
> True beauty is most truly praised
> By the glass which is most true.
> Madam, this glass is mine,
> The loveliness within is you.
> Accept this for your valentine.
> It has my heart's shape, and no more;
> I scorn to dress it with the common lace;
> Let it have no grace but your grace.

Elder James Olson, "A Valentine for Marianne Moore," *Poetry* 91, no. 6 (March 1958), 348–49.
61 Elizabeth Bishop, *Prose: The Centenary Edition* (London: Chatto & Windus, 2011), 140.
62 Barthes, *A Lover's Discourse*, 5.

Chapter Two: The *Literary Digest*, Moore's Scrapbooks, and the Archive of Mass Print *Bartholomew Brinkman*

1. Patricia C. Willis recounts her experiences with Moore's Rosenbach materials in "Archiving Marianne Moore," in *Twenty-First Century Marianne Moore: Essays from a Critical Renaissance*, ed. Elizabeth Gregory and Stacy Carson Hubbard (New York: Palgrave Macmillan, 2018), 255–60. The Marianne Moore Digital Archive can be found at https://moorearchive.org.
2. Alison Fraser, "Mass Print, Clipping Bureaus, and the Pre-Digital Database: Reexamining Marianne Moore's Collage Poetics through the Archives," *Journal of Modern Literature* 43, no. 1 (fall 2019): 23.
3. Lesley Wheeler and Chris Gavaler, "Imposters and Chameleons: Marianne Moore and the Carlisle Indian School," *Paideuma: Modern and Contemporary Poetry and Poetics* 33, no. 2/3 (fall/winter 2004): 53–82.
4. Linda Leavell, *Holding On Upside Down: The Life and Work of Marianne Moore* (New York: Farrar, Straus and Giroux, 2015), 120.
5. These scrapbooks are housed at the Rosenbach Museum and Library. I initially encountered them in summer 2007 and obtained high-resolution photographs of scrapbook pages at the time, including scrapbook pages referred to here. More on the scrapbooks can be found in Bartholomew Brinkman, "Scrapping Modernism: Marianne Moore and the Making of the Modern Collage Poem," *Modernism/modernity* 18, no. 1 (2011): 43–66; revised and expanded as Chapter 3 of *Poetic Modernism in the Culture of Mass Print* (Baltimore, MD: Johns Hopkins University Press, 2017), 105–40. Leavell also briefly touches on scrapbooks in *Holding On Upside Down*, noting the ways in which they reveal engagement with key literary and artistic figures and movements of the time.
6. Ellen Gruber Garvey, *Writing with Scissors: American Scrapbooks from the Civil War to the Harlem Renaissance* (Oxford: Oxford University Press, 2013).
7. Nikolaus Wasmoen, "Composure and Composition: Marianne Moore's Serial Imagination," *Journal of Modern Periodical Studies* 9, no. 1 (2018): 57.
8. Victoria Bazin, *Modernism Edited: Marianne Moore and the* Dial *Magazine* (Edinburgh: Edinburgh University Press, 2019), 7.
9. I downloaded PDFs of *The Literary Digest* [LD], volume 45 (July–December 1912), volume 46 (January–June 1913), and volume 48 (January–June 1914) from the Internet Archive in December 2021. I downloaded Volume 47 (July–December 1913), which was not available through the Internet Archive, from HathiTrust in December 2021. I applied Optical Character Recognition (OCR) to all PDF files using

ABBYY 15, producing searchable PDFs and plain text files. I then used PDFs to locate clippings in *Digest* pages and queried plain text files for term frequencies. I uploaded these files to R for further processing, including word vectorization, noted below.

10 *The Literary Digest*'s paucity of critical attention might be attributed to modernist studies' longstanding emphasis on little magazines, often at the expense of their bigger cousins. In recent years, however, scholarly attention has more clearly shifted to the "big magazines," as evidenced by Donal Harris's *On Company Time: American Modernism in the Big Magazines* (New York: Columbia University Press, 2019); a special issue of the *JMPS: Journal of Modern Periodical Studies* 11, no. 1 (2020) devoted to "Investigating Big Magazines," guest edited by Anne Reynès-Delobel, Benoît Tadié, and Cécile Cottenet; and the Circulating American Magazines: Visualization Tools for U.S. Magazine History website, available at https://sites.lib.jmu.edu/circulating/titles-included.

11 Marianne Moore, "Leaves of a Magazine," in *The Poems of Marianne Moore*, ed. Grace Schulman (New York: Penguin, 2003), 23. I discuss this poem in *Poetic Modernism*, 111.

12 *Poems of Marianne Moore*, 71.

13 As *Britannica* notes, "The *Literary Digest*, in particular, with a circulation of more than 1,000,000 in the early 1920s, was something of an American institution. Its famous straw votes successfully predicted the result of the presidential elections after 1920, and its highly publicized wrong prediction of the outcome of the 1936 election played a decisive part in its collapse." *Encyclopædia Britannica Online*, s.v. "*Time* magazine." www.britannica.com/topic/publishing/Time-magazine. Accessed February 4, 2022.

14 There are 5,600,474 total words with a vocabulary size of 35,910.

15 I trained a skip-gram word2vec model in R with 300 vectors at 30 iterations, a window size of 6, and 10 negative samples. I initially explored the model through unsupervised k-means clustering, with 150 cluster centers and 40 iterations, returning the 15 most central terms (many of which are noted below). I am grateful for the summer 2021 advanced digital humanities institute, "Word Vectors for the Thoughtful Humanist," sponsored by the National Endowment for the Humanities and the Women Writers Project, where I was able to refine my understanding of these methods.

16 Politics: state, president, party, Wilson, republican, board, committee, governor, secretary, members, democratic, Roosevelt, administration, progressive, campaign. Government: government, law, bill, congress, act, federal, commission, commerce, tariff, laws, authority, legislation, authorities, rights, supreme. State politics: senator, California, Virginia, Illinois, Colorado, Texas, Florida, Missouri, chairman, Massachusetts,

Carolina, Oklahoma, Wisconsin, root, Indiana. Asian imperialism: chief, king, Japanese, republic, minister, lord, cabinet, Chinese, prince, count, von, emperor, parliament, imperial, ambassador. American imperialism: Panama, canal, Cuba, indies, Porto, Jamaica, Rico, Nicaragua, Colombia, Bermuda, costa, Rica, Santo, Haiti, Juan. Mexican revolution: Mexico, army, military, Mexican, battle, huerta, officers, forces, navy, killed, fighting, revolution, soldiers, command, villa. World War: war, Germany, France, peace, Russia, European, Japan, China, powers, Turkey, nations, Russian, Balkan, Turkish, empire.

17 Cities and states: Orleans, Atlanta, Columbus, Houston, Syracuse, Ga, Charleston, Jacksonville, Akron, Fla, Birmingham, Colo, Savannah, Ala, Augusta. City streets: st, Chicago, street, Philadelphia, bldg, Cleveland, pa, Cincinnati, Michigan, Pittsburgh, Minn, Adams, Madison, chestnut, sts. Indian territory: country, America, land, south, west, east, near, western, countries, India, eastern, territory, lands, Indian, middle. Canada: Canadian, Toronto, Montreal, ltd, Winnipeg, Ont, Johns, Vancouver, Quebec, Halifax, Ontario, distributors, Manville, Ottawa, Scotia. Countries: Australia, Brazil, Argentina, Rio, Grande, Zealand, Chile, Buenos, Argentine, Aires, Peru, Hongkong, Bolivia, Janeiro, Kobe. Europe: Italy, Mediterranean, Spain, Switzerland, Norway, Holland, cape, Naples, Scotland, Sweden, Riviera, isles, Portugal, Adriatic, Belgium. World cities: London, German, Paris, Berlin, organ, Tokyo, dispatches, Petersburg, Vienna, Westminster, des, Shanghai, Hague, Manchester, pall.

18 Historic England: via, historic, Eng, Liverpool, wales, Plymouth, Bristol, Shakespeare's, Chester, Stratford, Avon, connects, Cornwall, Warwick, Fishguard. Travel: Greece, Egypt, holy, Nile, Palestine, camping, yacht, Cairo, cataract, Hawaii, Java, Allah, Ceylon, Tahiti, Athena. Cruises and shipping: line, weekly, ships, tons, steamers, steamship, Hamburg, port, cruises, steamer, ports, cruise, fleet, sailings, Victoria. Railroad: miles, north, lines, pacific, southern, railway, central, grand, river, lake, trip, northern, island, coast, route. Car and train: car, motor, cars, road, built, automobile, equipment, roads, truck, operation, horse, freight, manufacturers, gasoline, train.

19 Capitalism: labor, trade, control, methods, railroads, rates, sale, loss, industry, protection, failure, competition, transportation, increasing, profits. Investments: interest, railroad, stock, bonds, capital, paid, bank, companies, market, trust, investment, issue, property, income, banks. Building: building, construction, wood, walls, concrete, roof, windows, roofing, brick, lumber, Hy, Barrett, plaster, fireproof, shingles. Buildings: house, room, cities, private, town, houses, places, buildings, stores, offices, homes, rooms, streets, sections, factories. Farm: food, farm, products, animals, cotton, corn, soil, farmers, meat, farms, crops, crop, farmer, cattle, acre.

20 Court: court, judge, police, justice, district, charges, strike, investigation, officials, prison, crime, attorney, murder, criminal, charged. Medicine: cases, treatment, disease, cure, eases, diseases, accidents, tuberculosis, patients, decay, fever, germs, insects, cured, poison.
Physics: length, experiments, motion, contact, objects, structure, medium, wave, rays, produces, processes, waves, ray, radium, parallel. Religion: church, union, Christian, religious, religion, catholic, churches, Sunday, bible, services, bodies, mission, Christ, Jewish, protestant. College: school, study, college, schools, university, education, scientific, science, medical, association, training, students, expert, domestic, teachers. Ivy League: principal, girls, hall, founded, academy, institute, dean, Harvard, opens, superintendent, Yale, Connecticut, Cambridge, Princeton, seminary. Baseball: club, game, won, manager, league, ball, team, baseball, playing, played, hit, players, prize, games, Murphy. Horticulture: plant, garden, plants, trees, grown, sweet, grow, flowers, seeds, varieties, flower, seed, lawn, hardy, roses. Food: milk, fresh, sugar, pound, bottle, coffee, drink, cup, bread, brand, gallon, tea, pan, drinking, wine. Cooking: bouillon, chicken, pea, mutton, mock, pepper, turtle, clam, celery, broth, okra, chowder, asparagus, gumbo, julienne. Art: English, art, history, French, century, Italian, born, ancient, Spanish, Irish, Rome, artists, painting, ages, learning. Photography: pictures, colored, instrument, plates, camera, instruments, screen, film, Kodak, daylight, photographic, films, illumination, slides, optical. Stage: play, music, stage, theater, opera, plays, musical, drama, performance, songs, piano, metropolitan, actors, speakers, Wagner.

21 Watch and jewelry: model, watch, models, Howard, clock, watches, jeweler, jewelry, buttons, vest, sterling, Elgin, jewelers, Mazda, dial. Razor: safety, edge, razor, shaving, gem, blades, blade, edges, strop, shave, Hoder, pike, barber, shaves, autostrop. Clothes: suit, silk, clothes, wool, shoes, dress, fabric, fancy, holeproof, men's, women's, pairs, suits, oxford, underwear. Tires: tires, tire, rubber, rim, tread, mileage, inner, repair, repairs, cuts, cushion, motorists, skid, pneumatic, treads. Cigars: box, smoke, tobacco, pipe, cigar, tuxedo, cigars, Havana, smoking, plug, leaf, handy, mild, packed, packages. Cereal: taste, wheat, cream, flavor, wholesome, delicious, foods, rice, grains, nuts, nut, meal, breakfast, oats, puffed. Food: fruits, beans, baked, butter, vegetables, vegetable, Heinz, apples, tomato, preserves, soup, potatoes, apple, pork, sliced. Medicine: acid, throat, lithia, stomach, ills, rheumatism, congestion, poisons, uric, liver, colds, constipation, gout, chronic, kidney. Cleaning products: floor, furniture, interior, floors, fixtures, kitchen, polish, cleaning, wax, rugs, tips, finishing, bathroom, carpet, noiseless. Mail-order catalog: free, book, send, write, full, sent, booklet, address, illustrated, today, information, list, catalog, request, valuable.

22 Books: books, following, subject, recent, written, author, facts, volume, literature, report, writing, published, account, article, works. Publisher: pp, sons, 8vo, Houghton, Macmillan, Mifflin, Scribner's, Harper, Lippincott, Stokes, Holt, Doran, Putnam's, vols, reviewed. Writing instruments: pencil, pencils, longest, copying, Venus, smoothest, cleanest, outlasts, indelible, Mephisto, erase, bb, Koh, Blaisdell, crayon. Typewriter: easy, machine, easily, typewriter, costs, quickly, saving, machines, adding, economical, visible, operate, priced, rent, saves. Printing: paper, etc., letters, sales, card, monthly, printing, lists, print, cards, prints, file, stationery, checks, sheets. Proper language: words, word, correct, language, sentence, dictionary, meaning, kindly, phrase, conversation, spoken, pronounced, sentences, correctly, verb. Literature: story, interesting, manner, poetry, stories, reader, delightful, verse, rare, brilliant, poems, novel, pleasant, fiction, dramatic. Literature: sir, Shakespeare, Scott, Oliver, biography, Lawrence, Herbert, Whitman, Irving, Lodge, Morris, autobiography, Emerson, Stevenson, Reynolds. Poem: song, poem, Alfred, shorter, Phillips, smart, Noyes, Harper's, Stephen, exile, Byron, gale, Lippincott's, ghost, rime.

23 Isabelle Parkinson, "*Useful Knowledge* Beyond the Beinecke: Gertrude Stein Reading Discourses of Democracy and Nationalism in *Life Magazine* and *The Literary Digest*," in *Historicizing Modernists: Approaches to "Archivalism*," ed. Matthew Feldman, Anna Svendsen, and Erik Tonning (London: Bloomsbury Publishing, 2021), 99–115.

24 Parkinson, "*Useful Knowledge*," 110.

25 *LD*, September 13, 1913, 438–39. Dates are typically derived from pencil notes on the clippings themselves (presumably in Moore's hand). Page numbers are then found in the magazine issue itself. A few clippings are not labeled and most have been traced to issues from the same general time period.

26 Word count is in itself a crude indicator of attention or impact, and it is often the case that a relatively small number of texts might include a term multiple times, potentially skewing results. Such counts do provide a quick snapshot of term frequency, however, and provide a basis for some of the other methods I employ throughout this chapter.

27 *LD*, September 6, 1913, 391.

28 As Laura O'Connor has observed, "Although she seems an unlikely poet with which to explore the gendered discourse of Celticism and the long history of colonization in Ireland, Moore's poetry engages these subjects in ways that suggest an abiding identification with her ethnic homeland." *Haunted English: The Celtic Fringe, The British Empire, and De-Anglicization* (Baltimore, MD: Johns Hopkins University Press, 2006), 152.

29 *LD*, September 20, 1913, 504.

30 *LD*, September 27, 1913, 547.

31 The September 6, 1913, issue, from which "O Drimin Dhe Deelish" derives, contains five additional poems: Seamus MacManus's "The House with the Green Door," Dorothy Margaret Stuart's "Edmund Shakespeare," Phil J. Fisher's "Make Me Music," Herman Scheffauer's "The Sea Widower," and D. F. W. Bourdillon's "The Bird and the Beacon." The September 13, 1913, issue, from which "The Wanderer" derives, contains two other poems: Dorothy Margaret Stuart's "A Song of St. Nicholas' Clerks" and James B. Dollard's "Song of the Little Villages."

The September 27, 1913, issue, from which "Night-Errantry" derives, contains six additional poems: Thomas Walsh's "Coelo et in Terra," Edith Wyatt's "Niagara," John Masefield's "London Town," W. N. Hodgson's "The Hills," Katharine Tynan's "Lambs," and Madison Cawein's "The Twilight Witch."

32 Rachel Trousdale, *Humor, Empathy, & Community in Twentieth-Century American Poetry* (Oxford: Oxford University Press, 2021), 67.

33 Victor S. Navasky, *The Art of Controversy: Political Cartoons and their Enduring Power* (New York: Alfred A. Knopf, 2013), xxi–xxii.

34 LD, May 24, 1913, 1179–80.

35 LD, May 17, 1913, 1119.

36 Since the Kaiser was referred to as both William and Wilhelm, and since these names might indicate other figures, the term "Kaiser," which appears 116 times in the issues I am examining here, is a good indicator of the attention given to Kaiser Wilhelm II.

37 LD, May 17, 1913, 1110. Reprinted from Evans in the Baltimore *American*.

38 LD, May 17, 1913, 1110–11.

39 Including the use of the possessive, "Woodrow Wilson" appears 101 times, "President Wilson" appears 549 times, "Governor Wilson" appears 120 times, and "President-elect Wilson" appears 16 times. Wilson is most closely associated with presidents Theodore Roosevelt and William Howard Taft, and Wilson's Secretary of State, William Jennings Bryan.

40 LD, May 17, 1913, 1109.

41 LD, May 17, 1913, 1116.

42 LD, June 7, 1913, 1260.

43 LD, November 30, 1912, 1015.

44 *Poems of Marianne Moore*, 69.

45 Shaw appears 166 times and Rodin appears 54 times during this period.

46 November 15, 1912. Publication uncertain.

47 I've not been able to identify the exact date and place of publication, though the image itself includes a note of "Copyright 1910, Patriot Pub. Co."

48 LD, November 30, 1912, 1033.

49 LD, February 28, 1914, 433–34. Bernhardt is mentioned forty-four times in the issues I am considering.

50 *LD*, March 7, 1914, 479. The cartoon is presumably referencing a toll exemption for crossing the Panama Canal. In the magazine issue, the cartoon is juxtaposed against another from [Charles Lewis] Bartholomew, reprinted from the *Minneapolis Journal*, depicting Wilson beckoning a donkey for a ride. The donkey has a saddle labeled "1916" and a placard with "One Good Term Deserves Another." The caption is "All Aboard!"

51 I have not been able to identify the source of this clipping, but it is clearly from a newspaper—a fact made obvious in the lower-quality newsprint that calls attention to the scrapbook's material basis. There is a signature: "All."

52 *LD*, February 21, 1914, 394.

53 *LD*, February 28, 1914, 449. The poem would later be renamed "Spectres that Grieve."

54 There has been some attention to this fact. Rachel Blau DuPlessis has identified a "Prose Tradition" that fueled the "programmatic use (by Pound and Eliot as well) of such sources of modern poetry as the novelists and writers Henry James, Joseph Conrad, G. B. Shaw, Thomas Hardy, and Ford Madox Ford." Of course, there are gender implications of such a tradition as DuPlessis goes on to suggest. Rachel Blau DuPlessis, "No Moore of the Same: The Feminist Poetics of Marianne Moore," *William Carlos Williams Review* 14, no. 1 (spring 1998): 7.

55 *Poems of Marianne Moore*, 47.

56 *LD*, February 21, 1914, 410.

Chapter Three: The Poet's Room as Archive Robert Volpicelli

1 I have gathered the information in this paragraph about the opening of this exhibit from Donald Janson's news article, "Marianne Moore Room Set Up at Museum," *New York Times*, November 14, 1972, 36.

2 This was the apartment in which Moore had resided from 1965 until her death in 1972. Linda Leavell, *Holding On Upside Down: The Life and Work of Marianne Moore* (New York: Farrar, Straus and Giroux, 2013), 382–83.

3 Patricia Willis, "Archiving Marianne Moore," in *Twenty-First Century Marianne Moore: Essays from a Critical Renaissance*, ed. Elizabeth Gregory and Stacy Carson Hubbard (New York: Palgrave Macmillan, 2017), 257.

4 Collection Summary, The Marianne Moore Collection, Rosenbach Museum and Library, Philadelphia, 2; my emphasis. Such an appeal is appropriate because, as Catherine Paul argues, Moore's poems operate similar to the habitat dioramas of natural history. See Paul, *Poetry in the Museums of Modernism: Yeats, Pound, Moore, Stein* (Ann Arbor: University of Michigan Press, 2003), 141–94.

5   For more information about the Dickinson Homestead, see "Our Story," *Emily Dickinson Museum*. www.emilydickinsonmuseum.org/.
6   "Ralph Waldo Emerson's Study," *Concord Museum*. https://concordmuseum.org/collection/ralph-waldo-emersons-study/.
7   Nicola J. Watson, *The Author's Effects: On Writer's House Museums* (Oxford: Oxford University Press, 2020), 4.
8   Watson, *The Author's Effects*, 14.
9   The Marianne Moore Collection Summary includes an abbreviated list of the objects found in the Moore Room.
10 The room originates through a codicil to Moore's will that was signed in 1969 and filed in 1972.
11 Here, I am borrowing from Jacques Derrida, who coins the phrase "archive drive," playing off Freud's concept of the death drive. See Derrida, *Archive Fever: A Freudian Impression*, trans. Eric Prenowitz (Chicago: University of Chicago Press, 1996), 19. I return to Derrida's analysis of the archive in the next section of this essay.
12 For Moore's correspondence with Abbott, see Marianne Moore, letters to Charles D. Abbott (ALs and TLs), 1926–1955, Box 710, Folder 6-21, Contemporary Manuscripts Collection. The Poetry Collection of the University Libraries, University at Buffalo, The State University of New York at Buffalo.
13 Alison Fraser, "Creating the Twentieth-Century Literary Archives: A Short History of the Poetry Collection at the University at Buffalo," *Information & Culture* 55, no. 3 (summer 2020): 252–70. Fraser describes how Abbott's idea of assembling a broad collection of drafts revolutionized the "literary archival collection" and offered a blueprint for other institutions to follow, like Yale University and the University of Texas at Austin (253). For more on the context of Abbott's work, see Linda Anderson, Mark Byers, and Ahern Warner, eds., *The Contemporary Poetry Archive* (Edinburgh: Edinburgh University Press, 2019), 1–24.
14 Jeremy Braddock, *Collecting as Modernist Practice* (Baltimore, MD: Johns Hopkins University Press, 2013), 216.
15 See Bartholomew Brinkman, *Poetic Modernism in the Culture of Mass Print* (Baltimore, MD: Johns Hopkins University Press, 2017), 186.
16 Moore ultimately gave Abbott a fair copy of "See in the Midst of Fair Leaves" and typescripts of "The Frigate Pelican" and "The Pangolin." In the 1950s, she also donated a typescript of "Then the Ermine." See Marianne Moore, Box 290, Folder 2-5, Contemporary Manuscripts Collection. The Poetry Collection of the University Libraries, University at Buffalo, The State University of New York at Buffalo.
17 William Carlos Williams had already sent significant amounts of material to Buffalo by the early 1940s; see Fraser, "Creating the Twentieth-Century Literary Archives," 263. However, Moore's collection preceded that of

Ezra Pound, whose papers were sold to Yale in 1973, after his death; see Yale Collection of American Literature, Beinecke Rare Book and Manuscript Library. https://archives.yale.edu/repositories/11/resources/1584. In this respect, Moore was also ahead of Wallace Stevens, whose papers went to the Huntington between 1974 and 1977. See Wallace Stevens Papers, The Huntington Library, Manuscripts Department. https://oac.cdlib.org/findaid/ark:/13030/tf3489n60h/admin/#did-1.2.1.

18 On the midcentury rise of institutional collecting and its consequences for the value of literary papers, see Stephen Enniss, "'Casting and Gathering': Libraries, Archives, and the Modern Writer," in *The Meaning of the Library: A Cultural History*, ed. Alice Crawford (Princeton, NJ: Princeton University Press, 2015): 223–25. See also Jean-Christophe Cloutier's analysis of how the market for literary papers valued the work of white and Black writers differently, in *Shadow Archives: The Lifecycles of African American Literature* (New York: Columbia University Press, 2019), especially 56–65.

19 Leavell, *Holding On Upside Down*, 383. Leavell also notes that Moore's alma mater, Bryn Mawr College, was the original destination for her collection, but the space restrictions there made the move impossible.

20 Leavell, *Holding On Upside Down*, 383. Driver also appealed to Moore's love of animals by bringing a lamb from his family farm to the negotiations.

21 "Mission & History," Rosenbach Museum and Library. https://rosenbach.org/about/mission-history/.

22 Walter Benjamin, "Unpacking My Library: A Talk about Book Collecting," in *Illuminations*, trans. Harry Zohn (New York: Mariner Books, 2019), 1.

23 A. S. W. Rosenbach, *Books and Bidders: The Adventures of a Bibliophile* (Boston: Little, Brown, and Co., 1927), 4.

24 Rosenbach, *Books and Bidder*, 18.

25 For more on how research libraries began to specialize in the twentieth century in conjunction with academic disciplines more generally, see William Joyce, "The Evolution of the Concept of Special Collections in American Research Libraries," in *Rare Books and Manuscripts Libraries* 3, no. 1 (1988): especially 26–27.

26 "Mission & History," Rosenbach Museum and Library. For a snapshot of Rosenbach's collection in the late 1930s, see *The World of Yesterday: Rare Books, Manuscripts and Autograph Letters* (Philadelphia, PA: Rosenbach Co., 1939).

27 See A.S.W. Rosenbach's obituary in *Proceedings of the American Antiquarian Society* (October 1952), 117. As a museum and library, the Rosenbach can be classified as what Joan Oleck calls a "hybrid institution." Joan Oleck, *Trends in Rare Book and Documents Special Collections Management* (New York: Primary Research Group, 2011), 31. The

Morgan Library & Museum in New York is another example of this type of institution. For more on the history of the Morgan, see Paul Spencer Byard, Cynthia Davidson, Charles E. Piece, Jr., and Brian Regan, *The Making of the Morgan: From Charles McKim to Renzo Piano* (New York: W.W. Norton, 2008), 2–31.
28 Leavell, *Holding On Upside Down*, 383.
29 Anderson, Byers, and Warner, *Contemporary Poetry Archive*, 3.
30 Brinkman, *Poetic Modernism*, 169.
31 The Collection Summary for the Marianne Moore Collection states that the "collection is remarkable for its inclusiveness." More specifically, the scope of the collection includes the periodicals in which Moore's poems first appeared; drafts and "setting copies" of most of her poems; unpublished work; "working materials" like the famous notebooks into which Moore copied the quotations she would mine for her poems; and "clippings on hundreds of subjects, another history of her reading, are arranged in vertical files" (2). The collection also contains Moore's correspondence with over 3,000 different individuals as well as "other notable material" like address books and even some sketches (2–3).
32 Some poetry archives, like Buffalo's Poetry Collection, already made a practice of collecting realia, or everyday objects, alongside manuscripts and literary papers. See Fraser, "Creating the Twentieth-Century Literary Archives," 258. Yet, as a collection of objects held within a literary archive, the Rosenbach's Marianne Moore Room is still extraordinary for its depth and scale.
33 Derrida, *Archive Fever*, 2.
34 Derrida, *Archive Fever*, 1.
35 Derrida, *Archive Fever*, 2.
36 Derrida, *Archive Fever*, 2.
37 For more information on the history of the Freud Museum, see "About Us," *Freud Museum London*. www.freud.org.uk/about-us/.
38 Derrida, *Archive Fever*, 20.
39 Derrida, *Archive Fever*, 19; emphases original. Freud's original essay, "A Note upon the 'Mystic Writing-Pad,'" can be found in *The Standard Edition of the Complete Psychological Works of Sigmund Freud*, vol. 19, trans. James Strachey (London: Hogarth Press, 1961), 226–32.
40 Though Freud is never explicit on this matter, in his reading of Jensen's novel he repeatedly hints at the connection between the relief as a material object and the psychological process of registering unconscious impressions. The following passage is exemplary: "The *mark* of the repressed material is that, in spite of its intensity, it cannot break through into consciousness. In Hanold's case, therefore, it was a matter, at the appearance of the bas-relief on his horizon, of a repressed unconscious, in short of a repression." Sigmund Freud, *Delusion and Dream in Wilhelm Jensen's*

Gradiva, trans. Helen M. Downey (Copenhagen: Green Integer, 2003), 159; my emphasis.

41 To take just one relevant example, Moore was almost incapacitated by homesickness during her first two years at Bryn Mawr. "If anyone was ever homesick," Moore later wrote, "*I* was in college. It was very painful. I was at sea two years." Quoted in Leavell, *Holding On Upside Down*, 64; emphasis original.

42 I have written on this subject in another essay. See Robert Volpicelli, "Against Things: The At-Home Objects of Marianne Moore," *Twentieth-Century Literature* 58, no. 4 (winter 2012): 640–62. Also related to this domestic aesthetic is Moore's interest in Chinese antiques. See Zhaoming Qian, *The Modernist Response to Chinese Art: Pound, Moore, Stevens* (Charlottesville: University Press of Virginia, 2003), 111–22. For more on modernism's anti-domestic prejudices, see Elisabeth Oliver, "Aestheticism's Afterlife: Wallace Stevens as Interior Decorator and Disruptor," *Modernism/modernity* 15, no. 3 (2008): 527–45.

43 Linda Leavell, *Marianne Moore and the Visual Arts: Prismatic Color* (Baton Rouge: Louisiana State University Press, 1995), 132.

44 See Janson, "Marianne Moore Room," 36.

45 For a facsimile of this poem and an image of Warner's horn, see *Marianne Moore Newsletter* 5, no. 2 (fall 1981), 2. https://moorearchive.org/aboutus/contact/2:uncategorised/106:marianne-moore-newsletter-volume-5-number-2-fall-1981-2.

46 I seek here to add a layer to the existing scholarship on Moore's deployment of ekphrasis. See, for example, Elizabeth Bergmann Loizeaux, "Women Looking: The Feminist Ekphrasis of Marianne Moore and Adrianne Rich," in *In the Frame: Ekphrastic Poetry from Marianne Moore to Susan Wheeler*, ed. Jane Hedley, Nick Halpern, and Willard Spiegelman (Newark: University of Delaware Press, 2009), 121–44.

47 Sarah Berry, "Marianne Moore's Cabinets of Curiosity," *Journal of Modern Literature* 41, no. 3 (2018): 18–19.

48 Berry, "Marianne Moore's Cabinets of Curiosity," 21.

49 Marianne Moore, "When I Buy Pictures," in *New Collected Poems*, ed. Heather Cass White (New York: Farrar, Straus and Giroux, 2017), 51.

50 Moore, "When I Buy Pictures," *New Collected Poems*, 51.

51 "Black Earth" was first published in *The Egoist* in 1918; Moore then included it in *Observations* (1924). See Robin G. Schulze, ed., *Becoming Marianne Moore: The Early Poems, 1907–1924* (Berkeley: University of California Press, 2002), 87–89, 237–39.

52 Cristanne Miller, *Marianne Moore: Questions of Authority* (Cambridge, MA: Harvard University Press, 1995), 145.

53 Miller, *Marianne Moore: Questions of Authority*, 146–47. Other critics, who also read this as an animal poem, have followed on this point. See

Sabine Sielke, *Fashioning the Female Subject: The Intertextual Networking of Dickinson, Moore, and Rich* (Ann Arbor: University of Michigan Press, 1997), 70–79 and Kristin Hotelling Zona, *Marianne Moore, Elizabeth Bishop, and May Swenson: The Feminist Poetics of Self-Restraint* (Ann Arbor: University of Michigan Press, 2002), 31–37.

54 Marianne Moore to Ezra Pound, January 9, 1919, in *Selected Letters of Marianne Moore*, ed. Bonnie Costello, Celeste Goodridge, and Cristanne Miller (New York: Knopf, 1997), 122. The Rosenbach's Moore Room features a small menagerie of such elephant figurines above the fireplace (Figure 3.2), although it is not readily apparent which of these the poet had named "Melanchthon."

55 See, for example, Fiona Green, "'Black Obsidian Diana': Moore, Pound, and the Curation of Race," *Yearbook of English Studies* 50 (2020): 61–80.

56 Marianne Moore, "Black Earth," *New Collected Poems*, 41.

57 Moore, "Black Earth," *New Collected Poems*, 41.

58 Marianne Moore, "People's Surroundings," *New Collected Poems*, 56.

59 Moore, "People's Surroundings," *New Collected Poems*, 56.

60 Michel Foucault, *The Archeology of Knowledge*, trans. A. M. Sheridan Smith (New York: Routledge, 2002), 145, 146.

61 Collection Summary, The Marianne Moore Collection, 4.

62 Cloutier notes that, although there is a practice of archiving literary papers in their "original order" (meaning their order at time of acquisition), this order is often influenced by an author's pre-organizing of their materials with their later archiving in mind. In many cases, archivists also eventually intervene in this order, most often for the sake of functionality. See Cloutier, *Shadow Archives*, 76–86.

63 Vogel uses this term in his examination of what critics have left out of the "official" account of the Harlem Renaissance. See Shane Vogel, *The Scene of Harlem Cabaret: Race, Sexuality, Performance* (Chicago: University of Chicago Press, 2009), 130.

64 Susan Howe, *Spontaneous Particulars: The Telepathy of Archives* (New York: New Directions, 2014), 43.

65 For more information on the inclusion of poets' libraries within the literary archive, see Mary Catherine Kinniburgh, "The Postwar American Poet's Library: An Archival Consideration with Charles Olson and the Maud/Olson Library," *Journal of the Early Book Society* 23 (2020): 206–36.

66 Collection Summary, The Marianne Moore Collection, 14.

67 For more on the relationship between archives and exclusion, see David Greetham, "'Who's in, who's out': The Cultural Poetics of Archival Exclusion," *Studies in the Literary Imagination* 31, no. 1 (spring 1999): 1–28.

68 Marianne Moore, *Complete Poems* (New York: Penguin, 1981), unpag.

Chapter Four: Out-Casts and Stay-at-Homes: Marianne Moore, Arthur Mitchell, and LGBTQ Migration in NYC   Elizabeth Gregory

1. Mitchell recorded interviews in The History Makers Digital Archive (www.thehistorymakers.org/biography/arthur-mitchell) and the National Visionary Leadership Project (NVLP) (www.loc.gov/item/2021687926/). As with many personal retrospectives, some details are modified in these accounts.
2. Garafola is the author of several books about dance and the curator of the exhibition *Arthur Mitchell: Harlem's Ballet Trailblazer* at the Wallach Art Gallery at Columbia University, where Mitchell's papers reside. The biography is forthcoming from Yale University Press's Black Lives series.
3. Leavell, *Holding On Upside Down: The Life and Work of Marianne Moore* (New York: Farrar, Straus and Giroux, 2013), 17.
4. See Leavell, *Holding On*, for a lot more detail.
5. Leavell, *Holding On*, 30.
6. This is a dense history. Moore did not leave records directly describing her view of or role in the school's closure. She did not appear at the federal hearing that led to its shutdown for "cruel neglect and abuse," apparently at the advice of her brother, to avoid scandal. She was accused by the superintendent of spurring sedition amongst the students in her business contracts class, whom she respected. Those students included the school's stellar football backfield, among them the preeminent Olympian Jim Thorpe (winner of the pentathlon and the decathlon in 1912, while Moore's student) and Gus Welch, who initiated the petition that led to the closure. She relayed her response to the superintendent in a letter to her brother: "'You mustn't hold me responsible for my pupils' stubbornness. I crush out disrespect and rancor whenever I see it, and I give the students as thorough a training in political honor as I can'—He accepted the explanation very pleasantly" (January 15, 1914). As Leslie Wheeler and Chris Gavaler note, "Moore's understanding of disrespect, rancor and honor, of course, may have been very different from [the superintendent's]; her statement deftly leaves this issue ambiguous." "Impostors and Chameleons: Marianne Moore and the Carlisle Indian School," *Paideuma* 33, no. 2/3 (2004): 65. See also, Siobhan Phillips, "The Students of Marianne Moore: Reading the Ugly History of the Carlisle Indian Industrial School, Where the Poet Taught," *Poetry Foundation* (March 14, 2017) www.poetryfoundation.org/articles/92768/the-students-of-marianne-moore; Leavell, *Holding On Upside Down*, 116–19; and Gregory, *Apparition of Splendor: Marianne Moore Performing Democracy through Celebrity, 1952–1970* (Newark: University of Delaware Press, 2021), 52–53.

7   George Chauncey, *Gay New York: Gender, Urban Culture and the Making of the Gay Male World, 1890–1940* (New York: Basic Books, 2019 [2008; 1994]), 229.
8   Burke, in *Voices and Visions: Marianne Moore* (New York: NY Center for Visual History, Annenberg Media, Video, 1986), 38:20.
9   Leavell, *Holding On Upside Down*, 186.
10 Ryan, *When Brooklyn Was Queer: A History* (New York: St. Martin's Press, 2019), 144–54.
11 Cited in Joseph X. Dever, "'If She Were Here Tonight, She'd Be Right at Home,'" *Philadelphia Evening Bulletin*, November 17, 1972, 8B.
12 See discussion in Gregory, *Apparition of Splendor*, 19–26 et passim.
13 Mitchell says 113th Street in an interview, but Garafola confirms the address was 17 W. 112th Street. In that interview, Mitchell shares a family story that when he was born feet first, the midwife declared "This child will be a dancer!" "Growing Up in Harlem," NVLP.
14 Mitchell interview, History Makers Digital Archive.
15 Mitchell interview, "The Fallacy of Blacks and Ballet," NVLP. www.youtube.com/watch?v=VLoPWiXrmHM.
16 See Jennifer Homans, *Mr. B: George Balanchine's 20th Century* (New York: Random House, 2022), loc. 5510, Kindle.
17 Police and prosecution documents in Mitchell's file in the NYC Municipal Archives, shared by Lynn Garafola.
18 African American dancer Arthur Bell also performed with the company in the late 1940s. Jim Yardley, "Through Sad Haze, A Glimpse of Beauty; Homeless Man's Past Emerges: A Black Pioneer in the Ballet," *New York Times*, March 25, 1998, B1.
19 Homans, *Mr. B*, loc. 5510, Kindle.
20 Alastair Macaulay, "50 Years Ago, Modernism Was Given a Name: 'Agon,'" *New York Times*, November 25, 2007, 229.
21 In 1966, New York local PBS channel, WNET, broadcast sections of *Agon*, with Mitchell partnered with Suzanne Farrell for the pas de deux, but it was not shown nationally. In 1969, Mitchell and Farrell were invited to perform another piece, *Slaughter on Tenth Avenue*, on the *Tonight Show*, but once the crew realized it involved interracial touching, they displayed the dance only in silhouette (email message to author from Lynn Garafola).
22 In the initial version of the poem, the last three lines did not trail, so that was an evolution of the poem not linked to direct description.

> Slim dragon-fly
> too rapid for the eye
>   to cage,
> contagious gem of virtuosity,
> make visible, mentality,
> your jewels of mobility
> reveal and veil a peacock-tail.

23 See Gregory, *Apparition of Splendor* for more in-depth analysis of "Blue Bug" and "Arthur Mitchell."
24 In his History Maker interview, Mitchell describes living in a loft on 23rd Street with Shook, and Martha Graham star dancer Mary Hinkson refers to Shook and Mitchell sharing a loft in her oral history.
25 Moore to Albert Gelpi, May 26, 1964, Rosenbach Museum and Library (RML) V:21:40. Cited in Patricia Willis, "Letter to Albert Gelpi," *Marianne Moore Newsletter* 3, no. 1 (spring 1979): 11.
26 Painter Loren MacIver (1909–98); her husband, poet, and critic Lloyd Frankenberg (1907–75); Flynn (1909–96) was a theatre, film, and TV character actress; Miller (1916–71) was a MoMA curator and friend of Moore, MacIver, and Frankenberg, as well as Elizabeth Bishop's college roommate at Vassar, who lost her right forearm in an accident while traveling by car in France with Bishop and their mutual friend Louise Crane in 1937.
27 The Berkshire School, in Sheffield, Massachusetts.
28 Lynes complemented his commercial career with an extensive portfolio of erotic male nudes that were not for sale and which he bequeathed to the Kinsey Institute.
29 Mitchell, cited in the *Lexington Herald-Leader*, June 25, 1989. Cited in Judy Tyrus and Paul Novosel, *Dance Theatre of Harlem* (New York: Dafina, 2021).
30 Chauncey, *Gay New York*: 172–73, 356.
31 Kirstein to Moore, January 6, 1962. RML V:34:13. Ellipses in original.

Chapter Five: "His Shield": Prester John, Amphibiousness, and Black Fugitivity in Marianne Moore's Haile Selassie Poems
Ryan Tracy

1 Marianne Moore, *New Collected Poems*, ed. Heather Cass White (New York: Farrar, Straus and Giroux, 2017), 171. Cristanne Miller has pointed out that the draft lines of "In Distrust of Merits" indicate that Haile Selassie is the referent for "black imperial lion of the Lord." See Miller, "Distrusting: Marianne Moore on Feeling and War in the 1940s," *American Literature* 80, no. 2 (2008): 353–79.
2 Moore, *New Collected Poems*, 227. For a recent discussion of this poem, see Elizabeth Gregory, *Apparition of Splendor: Marianne Moore Performing Democracy through Celebrity, 1952–1970* (Newark: University of Delaware Press, 2021), 109–12.
3 Moore, *New Collected Poems*, 228.
4 Michael E. Brooks, "Visual Representations of Prester John and His Kingdom," *Quiditas* 35 (2014): 168–69.

5 According to Nadia Nurhussein, the Solomonic Dynasty used the fourteenth-century religious text *Kebra Nagast* to justify its imperial consolidation of power and support its claim to be descended from a romantic liaison between King Solomon and the Queen of Sheba. See Nadia Nurhussein, *Black Land: Imperial Ethiopianism and African America* (Princeton, NJ: Princeton University Press, 2019), 7.
6 "Haile Selassie Rejects Proposal of Mussolini," *Afro-American Courier*, 10, no. 2 (March 1938).
7 See John Cullen Gruesser, *Black on Black: Twentieth-Century African-American Writing about Africa.* (Lexington: University Press of Kentucky, 2015); William R. Scott, "Black Nationalism and the Italo-Ethiopian Conflict 1934–1936," *Journal of Negro History* 63, no. 2 (1978): 118–34; Ivy Wilson, "'Are You Man Enough?': Imagining Ethiopia and Transnational Black Masculinity" *Callaloo* 33, no. 1 (2010): 265–77; Robert Alexander Findlay, "Emperors in America: Haile Selassie and Hirohito on Tour," Master's thesis, Portland State University, 2011.
8 For more on *Ethiopiansim*, see Nurhussein, *Black Land* and Wilson J. Moses, "The Poetics of Ethiopianism: W. E. B. Du Bois and Literary Black Nationalism," *American Literature* 47, no. 3 (1975): 411–26. Psalm 68:31 is the most-cited biblical reference for African American identification with Ethiopia: "Princes shall come out of Egypt; Ethiopia shall soon stretch out her hands unto God" (in Wilson, "'Are You Man Enough?'" 266).
9 Robert A. Hill. "*Ethiopian Stories*: George S. Schuyler and Literary Pan-Africanism in the 1930s," *South Asia Bulletin* 14, no. 2 (1994): 67. Spike Lee's 2008 film *Miracle at Santa Ana*, which narrates aspects of the second Italo-Abyssinian conflict (including a racist Italian folk song meant to foment support for the colonization of Ethiopia), demonstrates the longevity of the war's impact on African American expressive culture.
10 Nurhussein, *Black Land*, 145.
11 Jennifer Wilson, "A Forgotten Novel Reveals a Forgotten Harlem," *Atlantic*, 9 March 2017, www.theatlantic.com/entertainment/archive/2017/03/a-forgotten-novel-reveals-a-forgotten-harlem/518364 (accessed October 17, 2022).
12 Nurhussein, *Black Land*, 144.
13 Langston Hughes, "Emperor Haile Selassie," *The Complete Poems of Langston Hughes*, ed. Arnold Rampersad (New York: Vintage Books, 1994), 192.
14 Hughes, "Emperor Haile Selassie," 551.
15 Nurhussein, *Black Land*, 148–49.
16 Findlay, "Emperors in America," 52–53.
17 Findlay, "Emperors in America," 35, 36.
18 Findlay, "Emperors in America," 38–39.

19 See Richard Bruce Nugent, "Pope Pius the Only," in *Gay Rebel of Harlem: Selections from the Work of Richard Bruce Nugent* (Durham, NC: Duke University Press, 2002), 244–48; George Schuyler, *Ethiopian Stories*, ed Robert A. Hill (Boston: Northeastern University Press, 1994); Claude McKay, *Amiable with Big Teeth* (New York: Penguin Books, 2017).
20 See Bernard F. Engel, "A Disjointed Distrust: Marianne Moore's World War II," *Contemporary Literature* 30, no. 3 (1989): 434–43.
21 Engel, "A Disjointed Distrust," 440. Moore, *New Collected Poems*, 172.
22 Engel, "A Disjointed Distrust," 440.
23 Engel, "A Disjointed Distrust," 440.
24 See Robert F. Reid-Pharr's discussion of the Abraham Lincoln Brigade and the Spanish Civil War in *Archives of Flesh: African-America, Spain, and Post-Humanist Critique* (New York: New York University Press, 2016): "Those black militants who traveled to Spain to fight as part of the international brigades ... particularly the all-American Abraham Lincoln Battalion, were quick to narrate the war as an extension of the generations of struggle against slavery and white supremacy of which they were intimately familiar" (43–44).
25 Moore, *New Collected Poems*, 171.
26 Linda Leavell, *Holding On Upside Down: The Life and Work of Marianne Moore* (New York: Faber & Faber, 2013), 369.
27 Harry Belafonte, *My Song: A Memoir*, with Michael Schnayerson (New York: Knopf, 2011), 47 and 385. For more on the significance of Belafonte's week of hosting *The Tonight Show*, see Henry Louis Gates, Jr., "Harry Belafonte's Balancing Act," *New Yorker*, August 18, 1996, and Elia Gasull Balada, Yoruba Richen, and Valerie Thomas, *The Sit-In: Harry Belafonte Hosts* The Tonight Show, documentary directed by Yoruba Richen, starring Harry Belafonte and Whoopie Goldberg. For details about Moore's acquaintance with Belafonte and her appearance on *The Tonight Show*, see Leavell, *Holding On Upside Down*, 370–71.
28 Importantly, Harry Belafonte regarded his discussions about the Italian invasion of Italy with other Black soldiers during World War II as a pivotal moment in his turn to activism. See Dennis McDougal, "Belafonte: A New Role as Diplomat," *Los Angeles Times*, June 23, 1985.
29 Rosenbach Museum and Library (RML) XIVb:01:18.
30 John Underwood, "The Number Two Lion in the Land of Sheba," *Sports Illustrated* 22, no. 15 (April 1965): 86.965. It feels worth noting that Abebe Bikila is misidentified in Patricia C. Willis's *Vision into Verse* as "*Haile Selassie*." Such misidentification demonstrates the need for continued research in the African and African American cultural contexts with which Moore was in conversation. See Patricia C. Willis, *Marianne Moore: Vision into Verse* (Philadelphia, PA: Rosenbach Museum and Library, 1987), 84.

31 Leavell, *Holding On Upside Down*, 368–69. See also Elizabeth Gregory, "Marianne Moore's 'Blue Bug': A Dialogic Ode on Celebrity, Race, Gender, and Age," *Modernism/modernity* 22, no. 4 (2015): 759–86. For a discussion of Moore's relationship with Native American athletes, such as the professional American football player Jim Thorpe, see Lesley Wheeler and Chris Gavaler, "Impostors and Chameleons: Marianne Moore and the Carlisle Indian School," *Paideuma: Modern and Contemporary Poetry and Poetics* 33, no. 2/3 (2004): 53–82.

32 RML XIVb:02:03 (vertical file); Marianne Moore Library 1505 (Asfa Yilma's book). Hannah Holland was the mixed-race daughter of a Swiss missionary and an Ethiopian princess. Married twice to British men, she was bestowed the title "Asfa Yilma" by Haile Selassie, a "distant relative." See www.npg.org.uk/collections/search/person/mp89599/hannah-princess-asfa-yilma-mrs-algernon-holland.

33 RML XIVd:01:03.

34 Fiona Green, "Moore, Pound, Syllabics, and History," *Twentieth-Century Literature* 63, no. 4 (2017): 440.

35 Rajiv C. Krishnan, "Empire in *The Cantos* of Ezra Pound," *CIEFL Bulletin* 12, no. 1/2 NS (2002): 99–115.

36 The white journalist John Gunther once described Selassie as "a gnome," "exceptionally short," and looking like "a mushroom." See Findlay, "Emperors in America," 41.

37 Charles Janson, "Ethiopia's Experiment with Progress," *The Listener*, May 5, 1955, 778–80. RML XIVb:02:03.

38 Findlay, "Emperors in America," 39.

39 RML XIVb:02:03, "Selassie, in Year Since Revolt, Has Granted Moderate Reforms," *New York Times*, December 31, 1961.

40 For a discussion of Moore's use of "racial romanticism" in representing black figures, see Cristanne Miller, "Marianne Moore's Black Maternal Hero: A Study in Categorization," *American Literary History* 1, no. 4 (1989): 786–815.

41 Fred Moten, *In the Break: The Aesthetics of the Black Radical Tradition* (Minneapolis: University of Minnesota Press, 2003), 12.

42 Moten, *In the Break*, 12.

43 Moten, *In the Break*, 35, 202, 273n19, 289n48, 304n24. See also Stefano Harney and Fred Moten, *The Undercommons: Fugitive Planning and Black Study* (Wivenhoe: Minor Compositions, 2013), 50 and Fred Moten, "Blackness," in *Keywords for African American Studies* (New York: New York University Press, 2018), 27–29. Although he does not use the word "fugitivity" in his essay "Blackness," Moten nevertheless portrays blackness as a shape-shifting ontological inhabitation of freedom from subjection.

44 Moten, *In the Break*, 289n49.

45 *The Norton Anthology of African American Literature*, 3rd ed., vol. 1, ed. Henry Louis Gates, Jr. and Valerie Smith (New York: W.W. Norton, 2014): William Craft and Ellen Craft, "Running a Thousand Miles for Freedom," 431–44; Frederick Douglass, "The Narrative of the Life of Frederick Douglass, an American Slave, Written by Himself," 330–93; Harriet Jacobs, "Incidents in the Life of a Slave Girl," 224–61.

46 *Oxford English Dictionary*, s.v. "amphibian, adj. & n.," July 2023. https://doi.org/10.1093/OED/9576763413.

47 *Norton Anthology of African American Literature*, "All God's Chillen Had Wings," 1:57–58. Paul Laurence Dunbar, *The Collected Poetry of Paul Laurence Dunbar*, ed. Joanne M. Braxton (Charlottesville: University Press of Virginia, 1993), 102.

48 Marianne Moore, *The Poems of Marianne Moore*, ed. Grace Schulman (New York: Viking Press, 2003), 12.

49 Moore, *New Collected Poems*, 110.

50 *Oxford English Dictionary*, s.v. "basilisk, n.," September 2023. https://doi.org/10.1093/OED/3753835691.

51 Moore, *New Collected Poems*, 107.

52 Moore, *New Collected Poems*, 111.

53 I thus depart from Bonnie Costello's view that "His Shield" is a poem "about Presbyter John." See Bonnie Costello, "Marianne Moore's Wild Decorum," *American Poetry Review* 16, no. 2 (1987): 50.

54 Moore, *New Collected Poems*, 179.

55 Moore, *New Collected Poems*, 179. Draft lines for "His Shield" in Moore's poetry notebooks show that "permanent pig on the instep" refers to the practice of sailors tattooing images of pigs on their feet to superstitiously ward off death by drowning. See MMDA, 07.04.04, page 0137-verso. http://moorearchive.org/. This detail links the poem even more to the context of global war during which it was written. The image of tattoos also plays visually on the spots that salamanders often have on their water-resistant skin.

56 For literature on Prester John, see Bernard Hamilton, "The Lands of Prester John: Western Knowledge of Asia and Africa at the Time of the Crusades," *Haskins Society Journal* 15 (2004): 126–42. For more on the Prester John Legend, see Findlay, "Emperors in America," n. 8, as well as Jeff Bowersox, "A Letter from Prester John (ca. 1165–1170)," *Black Central Europe*. https://blackcentraleurope.com/sources/1000-1500/a-letter-from-prester-john-ca-1165-1170/; Karl F. Helleiner, "Prester John's Letter: A Mediaeval Utopia," *Phoenix* 13, no. 2 (1959): 47–57 and Kathleen Kemezis, "Prester John," BlackPast.org (2010); Nicholas Morton, *Speculum* 91, no. 4 (2016): 1076–77.

57 For more on Moore as a poet "fascinated with the animate nature of myth and legend," see Robin G. Schultze, "Marianne Moore's 'Imperious Ox,

Imperial Dish' and the Poetry of the Natural World," *Twentieth Century Literature* 44, no. 1 (1998): 1–33.
58 For the text of the Prester John letter that I am using, see *Black Central Europe*. https://blackcentraleurope.com/sources/1000-1500/a-letter-from-prester-john-ca-1165-1170/.
59 Nurhussein, *Black Land*, 154.
60 Moore, *New Collected Poems*, 179.
61 Marianne Moore Library 1505, 76. Moore underlines the phrase "That is his humility." Asfa Yilma, *Haile Selassie* (London: Sampson Low, 1935).
62 Marianne Moore, "Humility, Concentration, Gusto," *The Complete Prose of Marianne Moore*, ed. Patricia C. Willis (New York: Viking Press, 1986), 420.
63 *Poems of Marianne Moore*, 179.
64 Moore, *New Collected Poems*, 228. Yilma, *Haile Selassie*, 78.
65 Costello, "Marianne Moore's Wild Decorum," 50.
66 Yilma, *Haile Selassie*, 78.
67 See W. E. B. Du Bois, *The World and Africa* and *Color and Democracy*, ed. Henry Louis Gates, Jr. (Oxford: Oxford University Press, 2007), 93.
68 See Du Bois, *The World and Africa*, 75–76n63. Asfa Yilma's account of Ethiopia's indigenous ethnic groups is emblematic of the mental contortions Europeans (and European-identified Ethiopians, such as Asfa Yilma) would go through to portray Ethiopians as "not Negroes!" (Du Bois's phrase, 76). After accounting for a "third race" of Ethiopians "whose hair is woolly and intensely curly and whose lips are thick," Yilma immediately writes: "There are no negroes in Abyssinia except as slaves. Do not think of negroes" (*Haile Selassie*, 23). While Moore marks this passage and transcribes it in the back of her copy of Yilma's book (Moore writes: "23 There are no negroes"), my sense is that Moore disagrees with Yilma, ultimately representing Prester John/Selassie with racial markers that, in the American context, would have been read as "Negro." For Yilma's and Moore's annotations, see Marianne Moore Library 1505.
69 Costello, "Marianne Moore's Wild Decorum," 50.
70 Miller, "Marianne Moore's Black Maternal Hero," 807.
71 Leavell, *Holding On Upside Down*, 225.
72 Moore, *New Collected Poems*, 79.
73 MMDA, 07.04.04, page 0100-verso.
74 MMDA, 07.04.04, page 0106-verso.
75 MMDA, 07.04.04, page 0116-verso.
76 MMDA, 07.04.04, pages 0115-recto, 0139-verso.
77 For more on Ezra Pound's racial anxiety following his reading of "Black Earth," see Fiona Green, "'Black Obsidian Diana': Moore, Pound, and the Curation of Race," *Yearbook of English Studies* 50 (2020): 61–80.
78 MMDA, 07.04.04, page 0092-verso.

79 MMDA, 07.04.07, page 0040-verso.
80 Moore, *New Collected Poems*, 133–35.
81 See Cristanne Miller's discussion of "The Buffalo," in "The *Marianne Moore Digital Archive* and Feminist Modernist Digital Humanities," *Feminist Modernist Studies* 1, no. 3 (2018): 257–68.
82 Leavell, *Holding On Upside Down*, 287.
83 Moore, *New Collected Poems*, 383.
84 *Oxford English Dictionary*, s.v. "prudence, n.," July 2023. https://doi.org/10.1093/OED/6944178180.
85 The English word derives from the Latin *niger*, which means black, or jet. *Oxford English Dictionary*, s.v. "niger, n.,¹" September 2023. https://doi.org/10.1093/OED/3515738907.
86 Schultze's discussion of "The Buffalo" is relevant here. Though Schulzte does not explicitly connect Moore's juxtaposition of "black" and "white" in the poem to issues of race, her view that the poem represents Moore's condemnation of "the West" and its scientific desire to bring all living things under human control might support enquiries into how the *racialized* subjection of black Americans in America—and black Americans' resistance to subjection—might be informing Moore's poetics. See Schultze, "Marianne Moore's 'Imperious Ox, Imperial Dish,'" 24, 14–15.
87 MMDA, 07.04.04, page 0015-verso.
88 MMDA, 07.04.04, page 0016-verso.
89 MMDA, 07.04.04, page 0121-recto.
90 MMDA, 07.04.07, page 0031-recto.
91 Moore, *New Collected Poems*, 179.
92 Moore, *New Collected Poems*, 209.
93 Moore, *New Collected Poems*, 151. "He 'Digesteth Harde Yron'" was first published in the 1941 July–August issue of *The Partisan Review*. Selassie re-entered Addis Ababa on May 5 of that year, five years to the day after the Italian military had entered the Ethiopian capital. See Andrew Carlson, "Emperor Haile Selassie I Returns Triumphant to Ethiopia," *Origins: Current Events in Historical Perspective*, May, 2016. https://origins.osu.edu/milestones/may-2016-emperor-haile-selassie-i-returns-triumphant-ethiopia?language_content_entity=en (accessed December 4, 2022).
94 We might add, then, the ostrich of "He 'Digesteth Harde Yron'" to Cristanne Miller's list of Moore's "black maternal" heroes. See Miller, "The *Marianne Moore Digital Archive*," n. 41.
95 Moore, *New Collected Poems*, 152.
96 Moore, *New Collected Poems*, 152–53.
97 Moore, *New Collected Poems*, 151.
98 Beyoncé, "Ghost," *2013*, CD. Parkwood Entertainment.
99 Beyoncé, "Ghost."
100 Moore, *The Poems of Marianne Moore*, 12.

Chapter Six: Archives of Excess and "power over the poor": Marianne Moore's "The Jerboa" *Linda Kinnahan*

1. Elsewhere I have discussed other poems from this period in regard to ideas of labor, work, and economics. For a discussion of "The Pangolin," especially in relation to Thorstein Veblen's essays in *The Dial*, see "Marianne Moore and Modern Labor," in *Twenty-First Century Marianne Moore: Essays from a Critical Renaissance*, ed. Elizabeth Gregory and Stacy Carson Hubbard (New York: Palgrave Macmillan, 2017), 149–66. In relation to issues of labor and colonial history, see the discussion of "Virginia Britannia" in "Tourism and Taxonomy: Marianne Moore and Natasha Trethewey in Jefferson's Virginia." *Humanities* 18 (2019): 1–18.
2. Linda Leavell, *Holding On Upside Down: The Life and Work of Marianne Moore* (New York: Farrar, Straus and Giroux, 2014), 265. Leavell argues that "'Too Much' expresses her outrage over the irresponsible spending that she believed caused the country's economic collapse"; "'Abundance' presents the self-sufficient and graceful jerboa as an alternative to 'too much' wealth," which depends on "exploitation of slaves, dwarfs, 'the poor,' and of a wide variety of animals" (265).
3. See Odile Harter, "Marianne Moore's Depression Collectives," *American Literature* 85, no. 2 (2013): 333–61 and Luke Carson, "Republicanism and Leisure in Marianne Moore's Depression," *Modern Language Quarterly* 63, no. 3 (2002): 315–42.
4. *Selected Letters of Marianne Moore*, ed. Bonnie Costello, Celeste Goodridge, and Cristanne Miller (New York: Knopf, 1997), 369.
5. Leavell, *Holding On Upside Down*, 265.
6. *Selected Letters of Marianne Moore*, 298, 299.
7. Harter, "Marianne Moore's Depression Collectives," 336, 346.
8. Laura Engel, *Women, Performance and the Material of Memory: The Archival Tourist, 1780–1915* (New York: Palgrave Macmillan, 2019), 14, 9.
9. All quotations from the poem are taken from its first presentation in *Hound and Horn*, 1932, and reproduced in facsimile form in Marianne Moore, *A-Quiver with Significance, 1932–1936*, ed. Heather Cass White (Victoria: ELS Editions, 2008). https://archive.org/details/aquiverwithsigni0000moor/.
10. See Kinnahan, "Tourism and Taxonomy: Marianne Moore and Natasha Trethewey in Jefferson's Virginia," *Humanities* 18 (2019): 1–18.
11. Harter, "Marianne Moore's Depression Collectives," 336.
12. Sarah Berry, "Marianne Moore's Cabinets of Curiosity," *Journal of Modern Literature* 41, no. 3 (2018): 20, 21.
13. Victoria Bazin, *Marianne Moore and the Cultures of Modernity* (Burlington, VT: Ashgate, 2010), 153, 174.
14. Bazin, *Marianne Moore and the Cultures of Modernity*, 152.

15 Berry, "Marianne Moore's Cabinets of Curiosity," 19.
16 Berry, "Marianne Moore's Cabinets of Curiosity," 27.
17 Catherine Paul, *Poetry in the Museums of Modernism: Yeats, Pound, Moore, Stein* (Ann Arbor: University of Michigan Press, 2002), 143–44.
18 Paul, *Poetry in the Museums of Modernism*, 143.
19 Paul, *Poetry in the Museums of Modernism*, 153.
20 Paul, *Poetry in the Museums of Modernism*, 143.
21 Rodney G. S. Carter, "Of Things Said and Unsaid: Power, Archival Silences, and Power in Silence," *Archivaria: The Journal of the Association of Canadian Archivists* 61 (2006): 216. https://archivaria.ca/index.php/archivaria/article/view/12541. Cited by Irma McClaurin in Irma McClaurin and Emily Ruth Rutter, "Archival Interventions and Agency: Irma McClaurin in Conversation with Emily Ruth Rutter about the Irma McClaurin Black Feminist Archive," *Tulsa Studies in Women's Literature* 40, no. 1 (spring 2021): 125–26.
22 Laura Engel, in Laura Engel and Emily Rutter, "Women and Archives," *Tulsa Studies in Women's Literature* 40, no. 1 (spring 2021): 9.
23 See Laura Engel, *Women, Performance and the Material of Memory*, 14, 9.
24 Griselda Pollock, *Encounters in the Virtual Feminist Museum: Time, Space and the Archive* (London: Routledge, 2007), 12. Quoted in Laura Engel, *Women, Performance and the Material of Memory*, 12.
25 Thomas Osbourne, "The Ordinariness of the Archive," *History of the Human Sciences* 12, no. 2 (1999): 62.
26 Laura Engel, *Women, Performance and the Material of Memory*, 8.
27 Laura Engel, in Engel and Rutter, "Women and Archives," 7.
28 Julie Phillips Brown, "Archival Theater: Susan Howe's Tactile Elegies," *Tulsa Studies in Women's Literature* 40, no. 2 (spring 2021), 310.
29 Susan Howe, *Spontaneous Particulars: The Telepathy of Archives* (New York: New Directions, 2020 [2014]), 24.
30 Bazin, citing Patricia Willis, notes that "Moore saw a picture of the fountain in *The Periodical* 17 (February 1929)," which shows the peacock "dwarfed" by the pine cone. *Marianne Moore and the Cultures of Modernity*, 171.
31 Bazin, *Marianne Moore and the Cultures of Modernity*, 172.
32 Harold Loeb, "The Mysticism of Money," *Broom* 3, no. 2 (September 1922): 115.
33 While Moore's Republican support of Hoover and disappointment in FDR is clear in letters to friends, the context of national politics includes Hoover's own role in considering government's role in supporting communal need. As Harter reminds us, "Hoover had by 1932 signed into law unprecedented commitments on the part of the state to secure the welfare of its citizens … paving the way for Roosevelt's New Deal

government to expand its mandate even further." "Marianne Moore's Depression Collectives," 333.
34 Bazin, *Marianne Moore and the Cultures of Modernity*, 171.
35 Bazin, *Marianne Moore and the Cultures of Modernity*, 173.
36 Bazin, *Marianne Moore and the Cultures of Modernity*, 174.
37 Bazin, *Marianne Moore and the Cultures of Modernity*, 174.
38 Roland Barthes, *Camera Lucida: Reflections on Photography*, trans. Richard Howard (New York: Hill & Wang, 1981), 26.
39 Marianne Moore, *Observations*, ed. Linda Leavell (New York: Farrar, Straus and Giroux, 2016), 80.
40 Moore, *A-Quiver with Significance*, 18.
41 Marianne Moore, *Observations*, 44.
42 Paul, *Poetry in the Museums of Modernism*, 162.
43 Laura Engel, in Engel and Rutter, "Women and Archives," 7.
44 *Selected Letters of Marianne Moore*, 283.
45 *Selected Letters of Marianne Moore*, 282.
46 *Selected Letters of Marianne Moore*, 283.
47 *Selected Letters of Marianne Moore*, 281.
48 Chippendale attained a relative degree of fame after publishing the furniture making guide, *The Gentleman and Cabinet-Maker's Director*.
49 *Selected Letters of Marianne Moore*, 265; my emphasis.
50 Bazin, *Marianne Moore and the Cultures of Modernity*, 197.
51 Sidonie Smith and Julia Watson, "Alternative, Imaginary, and Affective Archives of the Self in Women's Life Writing," *Tulsa Studies in Women's Literature* 40, no. 1 (2021), 17, 19.

Chapter Seven: "Possible Meaning": Marianne Moore's Anagogical Reading of Rilke, Herbert, La Fontaine, and Hölderlin
Luke Carson

1 See *Selected Letters of Marianne Moore*, ed. Bonnie Costello, Celeste Goodridge, and Cristanne Miller (New York: Knopf, 1997), 399. Auden left no lecture notes from this talk. See *Complete Works of W. H. Auden*, ed. Edward Mendelson, *Prose*, vol. 3, *1949–1955* (Princeton, NJ: Princeton University Press, 2008), 614.
2 In her published critical work, she mentions it in "Humility, Concentration, and Gusto" and "E. McKnight Kauffer." *The Complete Prose of Marianne Moore*, ed. Patricia C. Willis (London: Faber & Faber, 1987), 422, 427. I will only address the first of these appearances.
3 Reading Notebook 1938–1942 (RML VII:02:03). On Moore's public speaking commitments in this period, see Linda Leavell, *Holding On Upside Down: The Life and Work of Marianne Moore* (New York: Farrar, Straus and Giroux, 2013), 311ff.

4   I provide a clearer sense of why I turn to the concept of anagogy in n. 23, below, on Henri de Lubac. Lubac's thorough historical analysis of the medieval concept is contemporary with the most important literary restoration of the medieval idea, which was undertaken by Northrop Frye in *Anatomy of Criticism* (1957), a treatment that later became important to Fredric Jameson in *The Political Unconscious* (1981). Frye was, like Moore, deeply committed to William Blake, but "anagogy" as a serious concept was not of course current in the critical world Moore was absorbed in while keeping her reading notebook. More immediately relevant to Moore, Peter Nicholls very helpfully demonstrates that Ezra Pound came to discover its usefulness as a literary concept in the 1950s. "Hilarious Commentary: Ezra Pound's Canto XCVIII," *Glossator* 10 [2018]: 73–77. While I do not explicitly use Frye's concept of anagogy in this essay, as relevant as I think it is to Moore, I will borrow from Paul Ricœur a formulation of Frye's idea that clarifies my use of it in this essay: "From an ... anagogic perspective ... all imagery is inadequate in relation to the apocalyptic imagery of fulfilment and yet at the same time in search of it." Paul Ricœur, "*Anatomy of Criticism* and the Order of Paradigms," in *Centre and Labyrinth: Essays in Honour of Northrop Frye*, ed. Eleanor Cook et al. (Toronto: University of Toronto Press, 1983), 10. While I appreciate Jennifer Leader's careful distinction between the medieval four levels of interpretation and the typological model she argues is more appropriate to Moore's historical, philosophical, and theological context, I think understanding Moore's comment on Matthiessen requires seeing her in relation to eschatological hope and vision. See Jennifer Leader, *Knowing, Seeing, Being: Jonathan Edwards, Emily Dickinson, Marianne Moore, and the American Typological Tradition* (Amherst: University of Massachusetts Press, 2017), 6–7.

5   The first readers of *American Renaissance*, such as Moore, may not have known that Matthiessen identified himself as a "Christian socialist," although it is conceivable that their mutual friend W. H. Auden may have told Moore of his religious identification. It was only in 1948 that Matthiessen stated that he had "been influenced by the same Protestant revival that has been voiced most forcefully in America by Reinhold Niebuhr." See F. O. Matthiessen, *The Heart of Europe* (New York: Oxford University Press, 1948), 153. When Moore was reading *American Renaissance*, Matthiessen and Auden had become friends, and given Moore's own friendship with Auden there is reason to think Moore was anecdotally aware that Matthiessen's criticism may have been informed by Christian principles.

6   F. O. Matthiessen, *American Renaissance* (New York: Oxford University Press, 1942), 369.

7   Reading Notebook 1938–1942 (RML VII:02:03), 184–85. Moore's comments on "special meaning" resume the observations of her 1936

review of Eliot's *Collected Poems* (*Complete Prose of Marianne Moore*, 334). The "special meaning" of triumph is quite explicitly defined by Thomas à Becket in *Murder in the Cathedral*: "triumph by fighting, by stratagem, or by resistance" is "the easier victory" in contrast with triumph "by suffering": "Now is the triumph of the cross," he says, and we can take "now" as also implying the "special meaning" Eliot proposes in "Burnt Norton," which derives from the drafts of *Murder in the Cathedral*.

8   *Complete Prose of Marianne Moore*, 184.
9   T. S. Eliot, "The Music of Poetry," in *The Complete Prose of T. S. Eliot: The Critical Edition; The War Years, 1940–1946*, ed. David E. Chinitz and Ronald Schuchard (Baltimore, MD: Johns Hopkins University Press, 2017), 316.
10   Although he doesn't use the word *verstehen*, Richards does briefly refer to the post-Kantian tradition associated with Dilthey and Schleiermacher, which developed the concept of *verstehen* as hermeneutic understanding: "other senses of 'understanding' can, of course, be constructed—a sense in which 'understanding' is contrasted with 'knowledge,' for example"; but his aim here is "to keep [his] treatment as simple and unspeculative as possible." I. A. Richards, *Practical Criticism* (New York: Harcourt, Brace, and Company: [1929] n.d.), 308n4.
11   Richards, *Practical Criticism*, 309.
12   Richards, *Practical Criticism*, 308 and 308n5.
13   Eliot, "The Music of Poetry," 316.
14   J. B. Leishman and Stephen Spender, "Introduction" to Rainer Maria Rilke, *Duino Elegies* (New York: W.W. Norton, 1939), 17.
15   Reading Notebook 1938–1942 (RML VII:02:03), 130.
16   Leishman and Spender, "Introduction," 16–17.
17   *Complete Prose of Marianne Moore*, 422.
18   Though I do not have space in this essay to treat this matter adequately, I would like to point out the importance to Moore of the idea of suffering. See especially her discussion of Eliot in this regard (*Complete Prose of Marianne Moore*, 335) and her related comments on Hölderlin (*Complete Prose of Marianne Moore*, 374).
19   William Empson, *Seven Types of Ambiguity* (London: Chatto & Windus, 1930), 151.
20   Marianne Moore, "The Hero," in *New Collected Poems*, ed. Heather Cass White (New York: Farrar, Straus and Giroux, 2017), 98.
21   Robin G. Schulze, ed., *Becoming Marianne Moore: The Early Poems, 1907–1924* (Berkeley: University of California Press, 2002), 57, 177.
22   Moore, *Complete Poems* (New York: Macmillan, 1967), 234.
23   Henri de Lubac argued that anagogy is the fulfillment of the medieval system of allegorical meaning: for the "mystery" that allegory signifies "to be fully itself, it must be brought to fulfillment in two ways. First it is

interiorized and produces its fruit in the spiritual life, which is treated by tropology; then this spiritual life has to blossom forth in the sun of the kingdom; in this [spiritual life consists] the end of time which constitutes the object of anagogy: for that which we realize now in Christ through deliberated will is the very same thing which, freed of every obstacle and all obscurity, will become the essence of eternal life." *Medieval Exegesis: The Four Senses of Scripture*, vol. 2, trans. E. M. Macierowski (Grand Rapids, MI: Eerdmans, 2000 [1959]), 201–2.

24 Moore, *New Collected Poems*, 136.
25 *Complete Prose of Marianne Moore*, 435.
26 *Complete Prose of Marianne Moore*, 435. The fable appears in *The Fables of La Fontaine*, trans. Marianne Moore (New York: Viking Press, 1964 [1954]), 155–56.
27 *Complete Prose of Marianne Moore*, 435.
28 *Complete Prose of Marianne Moore*, 435.
29 Jean de La Fontaine, *Fables* (Paris: Flammarion, 1997), 231.
30 *Complete Prose of Marianne Moore*, 435.
31 *Fables of La Fontaine*, trans. Moore, 78.
32 La Fontaine, *Fables*, 141.
33 *Fables of La Fontaine*, trans. Moore, 78.
34 *Fables of La Fontaine*, trans. Moore, 79.
35 *Fables of La Fontaine*, trans. Moore, 78.
36 La Fontaine, *Fables*, 140.
37 La Fontaine, *Fables*, 140.
38 *Complete Prose of Marianne Moore*, 184.
39 *Complete Prose of Marianne Moore*, 435.
40 *Complete Prose of Marianne Moore*, 184.
41 Moore's source for the quote from Varley is Arthur Symons, *William Blake* (London: Archibald Constable and Company, 1907), 354.
42 *Complete Prose of Marianne Moore*, 435.
43 *Oxford English Dictionary*, s.v., "keeping," noun, 9.a. (Oxford: Clarendon Press, 1989). Bridges uses the word in his essay "Poetic Diction," in *Collected Essays Papers &c.*, vol. 2 (London: Oxford University Press, 1928), 65–66.
44 G. K. Chesterton, *William Blake* (London: Duckworth & Co., 1910), 154, 153.
45 *Complete Prose of Marianne Moore*, 335.
46 *Complete Prose of Marianne Moore*, 184.
47 Religion Notebook 1914 (RML VII:08:03). Cited in Leader, *Knowing, Seeing, Being*, 152. In addition to Leader's important discussion of these Bible classes (146–58), see Cristanne Miller, *Cultures of Modernism: Marianne Moore, Mina Loy, and Else Lasker-Schüler* (Ann Arbor: University of Michigan Press, 2005), 150–54.

48 *Complete Prose of Marianne Moore*, 372.
49 *Complete Prose of Marianne Moore*, 373.
50 Frederic Prokosch, *Some Poems of Friedrich Hölderlin* (New York: New Directions, 1943), unpag.
51 The German text faces the English in Prokosch's collection.
52 *Complete Prose of Marianne Moore*, 372.
53 *Complete Prose of Marianne Moore*, 373.
54 Editors have narrowed down the likely date to between 1795 and 1798. See Friedrich Hölderlin, *Odes and Elegies*, ed. and trans. Nick Hoff (Middletown, CT: Wesleyan, 2008), 208.
55 John Dewey, "Moral Theory and Practice," *International Journal of Ethics* 1, no. 2 (1891): 203.
56 Moore, *New Collected Poems*, 27, 139, 188, 143.
57 Moore, *New Collected Poems*, 140.
58 Moore, *New Collected Poems*, 144.
59 Moore, *New Collected Poems*, 103.
60 Genesis 28:11–22 (King James Version).
61 *Complete Prose of Marianne Moore*, 373–74.
62 J. B. Leishman, *Rainer Maria Rilke: Later Poems* (London: Hogarth Press, 1938), 63. For Moore's transcription from this book, see RML VII:02:03, page 130. They are quite brief and do not include "To Hölderlin" or Leishman's discussion of Hölderlin (*Rilke: Later Poems*, 220–23), but she does transcribe passages from the commentary on Rilke's "Five Songs," poems which appear immediately after "To Hölderlin." The commentary she transcribes concerns Rilke's experience of World War I and his "heroic attempt to transmute what most of us would call evil into good" (*Rilke: Later Poems*, 227). The notebook is dated 1938–1942, but even though *Rilke: Later Poems* was published in 1938 it is likely that Moore was reading Rilke in 1942 as she prepared for her course at the Cummington School. Among the Rilke works she cites from before turning to Leishman is C. F. MacIntyre's *Rainer Maria Rilke: Fifty Selected Poems* (Berkeley: University of California Press), which was published in 1940, and soon after *Rilke: Later Poems* she begins extensive transcriptions from Matthiessen's *American Renaissance*, which was published by Oxford University Press in 1942. She had clearly read "To Hölderlin" and Leishman's commentary shortly before writing her review of Prokosch.
63 Leishman, *Rilke: Later Poems*, 220–21.
64 Moore, *New Collected Poems*, 103.
65 *Complete Prose of Marianne Moore*, 374.
66 *Complete Prose of Marianne Moore*, 374. Before this citation Moore identifies the biblical texts as "Acts 17:27, Rev. 1:15 and 17 and Isaiah 40:31."

Chapter Eight: Questioning Categories to Revitalize Words: Meaning and Mottoes in the Poetry of Marianne Moore
Jeff Westover

1. Michel Foucault, *The Order of Things* (New York: Vintage Books, 1994), xv.
2. Srikanth Reddy and Linda A. Kinnahan have addressed Moore's response to taxonomies. See Reddy, "'To Explain Grace Requires a Curious Hand': Marianne Moore's Interdisciplinary Transgressions," *American Literature* 77, no. 3 (September 2005): 451–81. https://doi.org/10.1215/00029831-77-3-451 and Linda A. Kinnahan, "Tourism and Taxonomy: Marianne Moore and Natasha Trethewey in Jefferson's Virginia," *Humanities* 8, no. 4 (2019): 180. https://doi.org/10.3390/h8040180. See also Ben Reizenstein, "Perspicuous Opacity: Marianne Moore and Truth in a Fallen World," *Cambridge Quarterly* 36, no. 4 (2007): 317–37. https://doi.org/10.1093/camqtly/bfm027. In his contribution to this volume, Robert Volpicelli points out that even Moore's material possessions at the Rosenbach raise questions about categories.
3. Marianne Moore, *New Collected Poems*, ed. Heather Cass White (New York: Farrar, Straus and Giroux, 2017), 95.
4. Aristotle, *Aristotle's Metaphysics*, ed. W. D. Ross. (Oxford: Clarendon Press, 1924). My translation.
5. MMDA, 07.02.02.(moorearchive.org).
6. Barry Ahearn, *Pound, Frost, Moore and Poetic Precision: Science and Modernist American Poetry* (New York: Palgrave Macmillan, 2020), 222.
7. Moore, *New Collected Poems*, 115. For an important discussion of the role of evolution in Moore's thinking, see Robin G. Schulze, "Marianne Moore's 'Imperious Ox, Imperial Dish' and the Poetry of the Natural World," *Twentieth Century Literature* 44, no. 1 (spring 1998): 1–33. For a discussion of grafting and hybridity in Moore's poetry, see Aurore Clavier, "Arts and Grafts: Marianne Moore's Poetry and the Culture of Exception," *Miranda* 23 (2021). https://doi.org/10.4000/miranda.42440.
8. Moore, *New Collected Poems*, 112–13.
9. Moore, *New Collected Poems*, 45. See Reizenstein, "Perspicuous Opacity," 323–25.
10. Moore, *New Collected Poems*, 110.
11. Moore, *New Collected Poems*, 121.
12. Moore, *New Collected Poems*, 139.
13. Marianne Moore, *The Poems of Marianne Moore*, ed. Grace Schulman (New York: Viking Press, 2003), 249.
14. Friedrich Nietzsche, *The Nietzsche Reader*, ed. Keith Ansell Pearson and Duncan Large (Malden, MA: Blackwell, 2006), 118.
15. Moore, *New Collected Poems*, 139 and 137.

16 Moore, *New Collected Poems*, 151 and 153.
17 MMDA, 07.02.02. I have found the first two, *platax orbicularis* (round batfish) and *chaetedon unimaculatus* (teardrop butterflyfish) in contemporary reference works. Moore's third item may be a misspelling of *holacanthus semicirculatus*, which is a kind of angelfish. The outdated name has been replaced by *Pomacanthus semicirculatus*. See the World Register of Marine Species (marinespecies.org).
18 *Selected Letters of Marianne Moore*, ed. Bonnie Costello, Celeste Goodridge, and Cristanne Miller (New York: Knopf, 1997), 311.
19 Moore, *New Collected Poems*, 98.
20 Robert Pinsky, "Marianne Moore's 'Poetry'": Why Did She Keep Revising It?" *Slate*, June 20, 2009. www.slate.com/articles/arts/poem/2009/06/marianne_moores_poetry.html.
21 Moore, *New Collected Poems*, 27.
22 Moore, *New Collected Poems*, 10.
23 Robin G. Schultze, "'Injudicious Gardening': Marianne Moore, Gender, and the Hazards of Domestication," in *Critics and Poets on Marianne Moore: "A Right Good Salvo of Barks,"* ed. Linda Leavell, Cristanne Miller, and Robin G. Schulze (Lewisburg, PA: Bucknell University Press, 2005), 78. For a helpful summation of critical views about this poem, see 88–89.
24 MMDA, 07.04.04. One must be careful in making claims about the contents of Moore's notebooks, for she "often takes notes on or quotes from sources with which she does not agree." Cristanne Miller, "The *Marianne Moore Digital Archive* and Feminist Modernist Digital Humanities," *Feminist Modernist Studies* 1, no. 3 (2018): 259. doi.org/10.1080/24692921.2018.1504421.
25 David Crystal, *The Cambridge Encyclopedia of Language* (New York: Cambridge University Press, 1987), 160.
26 Marianne Moore, *Complete Prose of Marianne Moore*, ed. Patricia C. Willis (New York: Vintage Books, 1986), 397.
27 Moore, *New Collected Poems*, 14. "Masks" is an earlier poem with phrases in common with "A Fool, A Foul Thing, A Distressful Lunatic." It appeared in *Contemporary Verse* in 1916 and is collected by Robin G. Schulze, ed., *Becoming Marianne Moore: The Early Poems, 1907–1924* (Berkeley: University of California Press, 2002), 363.
28 MMDA, 07.02.02.
29 Moore, *New Collected Poems*, 14.
30 Ahearn, *Pound, Frost, Moore and Poetic Precision*, 223.
31 Moore, *New Collected Poems*, 102.
32 "It / honors the sand by assuming its color." Moore, *New Collected Poems*, 104.
33 Moore, *New Collected Poems*, 195.

34 Margaret Holley pays sustained attention to mottoes, citing them in the list of sources Moore quotes. Margaret Holley, *The Poetry of Marianne Moore: A Study in Voice and Value* (Cambridge: Cambridge University Press, 1987), 15. Bonnie Costello points out the relevance of Renaissance emblem books to Moore's work, situating Moore's "emblematic imagination ... in the long tradition of the *impressa* in which image is juxtaposed to abstract idea in order to give the latter immediacy and concreteness." *Marianne Moore: Imaginary Possessions*, 202.

35 MMDA, 07.02.02. See pages 0049-recto; 0050-verso; 00115-recto; 00117-verso; 00122-verso; and 00203-recto. In the same notebook, Moore drew a picture of a heraldic shield on page 0029-verso.

36 Thank you to the annotators of the digitized version of the notebook for providing such information.

37 Moore, *New Collected Poems*, 276. A first version of the poem was published with different lineation as "Councell to a Bachelor" in 1913. See Schulze, *Becoming Marianne Moore*, 349.

38 Pamela White Hadas, *Marianne Moore: Poet of Affection* (Syracuse, NY: Syracuse University Press, 1977), 196.

39 In a blog posting of April 2, 2010, Jen Rajchel writes, "By introducing the concept of marriage into one [of] the Bryn Mawr literary magazines, Moore questions how marriage ... fits into the intellectual life that Bryn Mawr prepares students for. 'Councell to a Bachelor' challenges women to think about what choice they are going to make upon leaving the College." "Mooring Gaps: Marianne Moore's Bryn Mawr Poetry." https://mooreandpoetry.blogs.brynmawr.edu/the-lantern/.

40 No motto is borrowed or adapted in "Quoting an Also Private Thought," but Moore's study of blazonry would be worth exploring in relation to the poem's reference to a scutcheon. Heather Cass White includes the poem in Moore's *New Collected Poems*, 190.

41 Moore, *New Collected Poems*, 166.

42 Jonathan Culler, *Theory of the Lyric* (Cambridge, MA: Harvard University Press, 2015), 35–36.

43 Moore, *New Collected Poems*, 113.

44 Benjamin Franklin, *Writings* (New York: Library of America, 1987), 1197.

45 Franklin, *Writings*, 1201.

46 Franklin, *Writings*, 1369.

47 Moore, *New Collected Poems*, 113. Robin Schulze reads this line for its political ramifications, writing, "Only the watchful who question custom and rise with imaginative power beyond oppressive thoughts remain free." "The Frigate Pelican's Progress: Marianne Moore's Multiple Versions and Modernist Practice," in *Gendered Modernism*, ed. Margaret Dickie and Thomas Travisano (Philadelphia: University of Pennsylvania Press, 1996), 130.

48 Moore, *New Collected Poems*, 113.
49 Moore, *New Collected Poems*, 114.
50 Moore, *New Collected Poems*, 114.
51 MMDA, 07.02.02, page 00134-recto.
52 Moore, *New Collected Poems*, 114.
53 Holley, *The Poetry of Marianne Moore*, 105.
54 Moore, *New Collected Poems*, 114.
55 Moore, *New Collected Poems*, 131.
56 Moore, *The Complete Poems of Marianne Moore* (New York: Macmillan, 1982), 279. The note originally appears in Moore, *What are Years* (New York: Macmillan, 1941), 52. See Catherine E. Paul, *Poetry and the Museums of Modernism* (Ann Arbor: University of Michigan Press, 2002), 189.
57 Marianne Moore, *A-Quiver with Significance: Marianne Moore, 1932–1936*, ed. Heather Cass White (Victoria: ELS Editions, 2008), 128. https://archive.org/details/aquiverwithsigni0000moor/.
58 MMDA, 07.02.02, page 0093-verso.
59 MMDA, 07.02.02, pages 0093-recto and 0094-verso.
60 MMDA, 07.02.02, page 0094-recto.
61 Moore, *New Collected Poems*, 140.
62 Moore, *New Collected Poems*, 140. Heather Cass White reproduces the printer's mark with the motto in *A-Quiver with Significance*, 128 and in *Adversity and Grace: Marianne Moore, 1936–1941* (Victoria: ELS Editions, 2012), 100. The latter also includes Moore's drawing of the image from Rosenbach Museum and Library (RML) VII:02:02.
63 Holley, *The Poetry of Marianne Moore*, 105.
64 White calls attention to the subject of racial division in her discussion of George Plank's drawing for *The Pangolin and Other Verse*. See *A-Quiver with Significance*, 127–29.
65 As Holley points out, the poem first appeared in 1935, the same year Mussolini invaded Ethiopia. *The Poetry of Marianne Moore*, 106.
66 *Complete Prose of Marianne Moore*, 663.
67 MMDA, 07.02.02, page 00230-recto.
68 Moore, *New Collected Poems*, 197.
69 Moore, *New Collected Poems*, 197.
70 Moore, *New Collected Poems*, 170.
71 Hadas, *Marianne Moore: Poet of Affection*, 197.
72 Moore, *New Collected Poems*, 404.
73 Marianne Moore, *Like a Bulwark* (New York: Viking Press, 1957), 8–11.
74 The index appears in Linda Leavell's edition of Moore's *Observations* (New York: Farrar, Straus and Giroux, 2016), 111–19. Leavell discusses Moore's work as a teacher at the Carlise Indian School in *Holding On Upside Down: The Life and Work of Marianne Moore* (New York: Farrar,

Straus and Giroux, 2013), 116–20. Leavell describes her six-year stint as a part-time librarian on pages 167–68 and her job as the editor of the *Dial* on pages 229–47. Charles Molesworth provides an account of her editorship in *Marianne Moore: A Literary Life* (Boston: Northeastern University Press, 1991), 208–46.

75 Moore, *New Collected Poems*, 96.
76 MMDA, 07.02.02, page 0044-verso.
77 As James Maynard points out in his contribution to this volume, Robert Duncan characterized Moore herself as "an ever-ready student" in "Notes on the Poetics of Marianne Moore," which he included in a letter to her, dated October 1, 1957. In the letter she wrote back to him on October 4, 1957, she singles out his phrase "amateur as student," asking, "Am I anything else?"
78 Moore, *New Collected Poems*, 95.
79 Moore, *New Collected Poems*, 95. My translation. Thank you to Dr. Michael Faletra of Reed College for confirming my translation of the motto.
80 Paul, *Poetry and the Museums of Modernism*, 144.
81 Moore, *New Collected Poems*, 124.
82 Moore, *New Collected Poems*, 126.
83 MMDA, 07.02.02, page 0094-verso. Moore, *New Collected Poems*, 125.
84 Linda Leavell points out that Moore studied Horace for a year in Latin courses she took at Bryn Mawr. *Holding On Upside Down*, 67.
85 Moore, *New Collected Poems*, 125.
86 MMDA, 07.02.02, page 00183-verso. Abbreviations in the original. See Paul Koch, "The Making of Printing Types," *The Dolphin: A Journal of the Making of Books* 1 (1933): 24–57.
87 The seal belonged to Hildegarde Watson. White features a photo of it and of a triskelion from an advertisement in *Adversity and Grace*, 129, 138–39.
88 Moore, *New Collected Poems*, 127.
89 MMDA, 07.02.02, page 0075-verso. Underlining in the original.
90 Moore, *New Collected Poems*, 69.
91 Luke Carson and Heather Cass White, "'Difficult Ground': Poetic Renunciation in Marianne Moore's 'Walking-Sticks and Paperweights and Watermarks,'" *Twentieth Century Literature* 56, no. 3 (fall 2010): 341–70. Carson and White might not agree with my sense of the significance of the connections between "Walking-Sticks" and later poems, but I have benefited from their argument.

Chapter Nine: "This is how the mind works": Marianne Moore and the Aesthetics of Notebooks Roger Gilbert

1 MMDA 7.04.07, page 0016-verso.
2 MMDA 7.04.04, page 0002-verso.
3 For a highly curated selection of extracts from poets' notebooks, see *The Poet's Notebook: Excerpts from the Notebooks of 26 American Poets*, ed. Stephen Kuusisto, Deborah Tall, and David Weiss (New York: W.W. Norton, 1997).
4 Marianne Moore, *New Collected Poems*, ed. Heather Cass White (New York: Farrar, Straus and Giroux, 2017), 27.
5 Moore, *New Collected Poems*, 60.
6 Patricia Willis, "Road to Paradise: First Notes on Marianne Moore's 'An Octopus.'" *Twentieth Century Literature* 30, no. 2/3 (1984): 247ff.
7 MMDA 7.04.04, page 0006-verso.
8 Cristanne Miller, "Introduction to Poetry Notebook 7.04.04." MMDA. https://moorearchive.org/nb07-04-04-intro.
9 MMDA 7.04.04.
10 MMDA 7.04.04, page 0009-recto.
11 Cats were very much on Moore's mind after the departure of her neighbor's Peter, whose name appears on several early pages of the notebook (though the poem about him had already been written), followed a year later by the death of her beloved kitten Buffalo, chloroformed by her mother. See Linda Leavell, *Holding On Upside Down: The Life and Work of Marianne Moore* (New York: Farrar, Straus and Giroux, 2013), 206–7.
12 MMDA 7.04.07, page 31-recto.
13 MMDA 7.04.07, pages 31-recto and 32-verso.
14 MMDA 7.04.07, page 32-verso.
15 Moore, *New Collected Poems*, 93.

Chapter Ten: Robert Duncan, "On Reading Marianne Moore": An Introduction James Maynard

1 Robert Duncan, "Biographical Note," in *The New American Poetry*, ed. Donald Allen (New York: Grove Press, 1960; repr., Berkeley: University of California Press, 1999), 434–35.
2 Robert Duncan, "For a Muse Meant," in *Robert Duncan: The Collected Early Poems and Plays*, ed. Peter Quartermain (Berkeley: University of California Press, 2012), 642.
3 There are a total of six letters surviving from Moore to Duncan in the Poetry Collection and two letters from Duncan to Moore at the Rosenbach, which additionally holds three carbon copies of letters from Moore to Duncan (neither of the two dated June 22, 1957, is to be found in

Buffalo). The Duncan-related materials in the Marianne Moore Collection at the Rosenbach Museum and Library are included with Moore's correspondence with the San Francisco State College Poetry Center, Series V, General Correspondence: Section 5, V:49:18. My sincere thanks to Librarian Elizabeth Fuller for providing me with information regarding Duncan's correspondence with Moore.

4   Robert Duncan, "The Maiden," *The Collected Later Poems and Plays*, 24, 25.
5   Marianne Moore to Robert Duncan, July 28, 1947, Box 58, Folder 14A, PCMS-0110, Robert Duncan Collection, ca. 1900–1996. The Poetry Collection of the University Libraries, University at Buffalo, The State University of New York at Buffalo.
6   Robert Duncan, "Poetry, a Natural Thing," *The Collected Later Poems and Plays*, 44–45.
7   Marianne Moore to Robert Duncan, August 20, 1957, Box 58, Folder 14A, PCMS-0110, Robert Duncan Collection, State University of New York at Buffalo.
8   Robert Duncan, Introduction to Marianne Moore's Poetry Center Reading at the San Francisco Museum of Art, October 10, 1957, The Poetry Center at San Francisco State College, Box 12, Folder 8, PCMS-0079, Helen Adam Collection, 1890–2009 (bulk 1914–1985). The Poetry Collection of the University Libraries, University at Buffalo, The State University of New York. Duncan's introduction to this reading by Moore was subsequently published posthumously by Robert Bertholf as "Notes on the Poetics of Marianne Moore" in his edition of Robert Duncan, *A Selected Prose*, ed. Robert J. Bertholf (New York: New Directions, 1995), 94–96, and again in *Chicago Review* 45, no. 2 (1999): 104–6.
9   Marianne Moore to Robert Duncan, October 4, 1957, Box 58, Folder 14A, PCMS-0110, Robert Duncan Collection, State University of New York at Buffalo.
10 Marianne Moore: October 10, 1957, Poetry Center Digital Archive. https://diva.sfsu.edu/collections/poetrycenter/bundles/191206.
11 Robert Duncan to Donald Allen, October 12, 1957, quoted in Lisa Jarnot, *Robert Duncan: The Ambassador from Venus; A Biography* (Berkeley: University of California Press, 2010), 171.
12 Marianne Moore: October 18, 1957, Poetry Center Digital Archive. https://diva.sfsu.edu/collections/poetrycenter/bundles/191187.
13 This exchange between Spicer and Moore is recounted by Lewis Ellingham and Kevin Killian in *Poet Be Like God: Jack Spicer and the San Francisco Renaissance* (Hanover, NH: Wesleyan University Press/University Press of New England, 1998), 147.
14 Robert Duncan, "Solitude," *The Collected Later Poems and Plays*, 94–95.

15 Marianne Moore to Robert Duncan, February 21, 1958, Box 58, Folder 14A, PCMS-0110, Robert Duncan Collection, State University of New York at Buffalo.
16 Marianne Moore to Robert Duncan, August 26, 1959, Box 58, Folder 14A, PCMS-0110, Robert Duncan Collection, State University of New York at Buffalo.
17 Robert Duncan, "Ideas of the Meaning of Form," in *Robert Duncan: Collected Essays and Other Prose*, ed. James Maynard (Berkeley: University of California Press, 2014), 73, 76.
18 "On Reading Marianne Moore," by Robert Duncan, is copyright © the Jess Collins Trust and appears with permission. It appears undated in Notebook 12, ca. early to mid-1950s, Box 2, Folder 5, PCMS-0110, Robert Duncan Collection, State University of New York at Buffalo.

Chapter Eleven: The Marianne Moore Digital Archive: Teaching and Research   Claire Nashar

1 The MMDA's numbering convention is based on that of the Rosenbach's manuscripts. The only two differences are that, as we publish each notebook, we change the initial number to Arabic numerals and the separating colons to periods (e.g., 07.03.11) to distinguish it from the Rosenbach's manuscripts (VII:03:11).
2 https://moorearchive.org/about/archive.
3 For a more detailed explanation of diplomatic translation, see D. C. Greetham, *Textual Scholarship: An Introduction* (New York: Garland Publishing, 1994), 350.
4 See the archive's "Project Documentation" page for a full list. https://moorearchive.org/about/archive/project-documentation.
5 Text Encoding Initiative. https://tei-c.org/.
6 MMDA, 07.03.11, pages 0021-recto and 0022-recto.

Chapter Twelve: An Interview with Patricia C. Willis   Karin Roffman

1 Patricia Willis, "The Road to Paradise: First Notes on Marianne Moore's 'An Octopus,'" *Twentieth Century Literature* 30, no. 2/3 (1984): 242–66.
2 Patricia Willis, *Marianne Moore and the Pipes of Pan: Mt. Rainier and Mt. Olympus* (Athens: Attica Tradition Educational Foundation, 2001).
3 Patricia Willis, "A Modernist Epithalamium: Marianne Moore's 'Marriage,'" *Paideuma* 32, no. 1/3 (2003): 265–99.
4 *Voices & Visions: Marianne Moore* (New York Center for Visual History, 1988). www.learner.org/series/voices-visions/marianne-moore/.
5 Marianne Moore: Poetry. https://moore123.com.

6 Alison Fraser, "Creating the Twentieth-Century Literary Archives: A Short History of the Poetry Collection at the University at Buffalo," *Information & Culture* 55, no. 3 (summer 2020): 252–70.
7 Christa Sammons, "The 'Dial' File," *Yale Library Gazette* 62, no. 1/2 (October 1987): 12–18.
8 Robert J. Willis, *Breaking the Chains: A Catholic Memoir* (New York, iUniverse, 2005).

Contributors

Bartholomew Brinkman is Associate Professor of English at Framingham State University, where he is also founding director of the Center for Digital Humanities, director of the Modern American Poetry Site, and project director for a National Endowment for the Humanities, Humanities Initiatives grant focused on digital humanities and race. He has recently been named a Digital Ethnic Futures Consortium teaching fellow and a Rare Book School M. C. Lang Fellow in Book History, Bibliography, and Humanities Teaching with Historical Sources. He is the author of *Poetic Modernism in the Culture of Mass Print*, along with multiple articles and essays on modern poetry, print culture, periodical studies, and digital humanities that have appeared in such venues as *Modernism/modernity*, *Journal of Modern Literature*, *Journal of Modern Periodical Studies*, *African American Review*, and multiple book collections.

Luke Carson is Associate Professor and Chair of the English Department at the University of Victoria in British Columbia. He is the author of "Republicanism and Leisure in Marianne Moore's Depression" and co-author (with Heather Cass White) of "Difficult Ground: Poetic Renunciation in Marianne Moore's 'Walking-Sticks and Paperweights and Watermarks'" and "A Variety of Hero: Marianne Moore's Romance." As the General Editor of ELS Editions, he oversaw the publication of two facsimile editions of Moore's poems, both edited by Heather Cass White:

A-Quiver with Significance: Marianne Moore, 1932–1936 and *Adversity and Grace: Marianne Moore 1936–1941*. He is the Datebook Series Editor at the Marianne Moore Digital Archive.

Aurore Clavier is an Associate Professor of North American Literature at the Université Paris Cité and a member of the LARCA research unit. Her research bears on twentieth- and twenty-first-century poetry and the relationships between form, tradition, and the spatial and historical constructions of "America." She is the author of a French monograph entitled *Marianne Moore ou la Tradition Singulière: Réinventions Américaines* (forthcoming). Her various articles on Marianne Moore (one of which was awarded an essay prize by the Marianne Moore Society), William Carlos Williams, Wallace Stevens, and John Ashbery have appeared in essay collections (*Twenty-First Century Moore: Essays from a Critical Renaissance*, *The Suburbs: New Critical Perspectives*, and *Ashbery Hors Cadre*, among others) and in such reviews as *Transatlantica*, *Miranda*, *Études anglaises*, and *Wallace Stevens Journal*. She is currently co-editing a special issue of *Transatlantica* on the poetry book in multiple versions and the pedagogical issues they raise. She has recently started a research project on anthologies of Native American and Indigenous poetry, centering on former Poet Laureate Joy Harjo's signature project "Living Nations, Living Words."

Roger Gilbert teaches courses on American poetry, Shakespeare, and Toni Morrison at Cornell University. He is the author of *Walks in the World: Representation and Experience in Modern American Poetry* (1991) and co-editor of several anthologies, including *The Walker's Literary Companion* (2000, with Jeffrey Robinson and Anne Wallace) and *Considering the Radiance: Essays on the Poetry of A. R. Ammons* (2005, with David Burak). He has published essays and reviews on poetry, aesthetics, and popular culture in such journals as *Contemporary Literature*, *Epoch*, *Michigan Quarterly Review*, *Northwest Review*, *Parnassus*, *Salmagundi*, *Sagetrieb*, *Southwest Review*, and the *Wallace Stevens Journal*. His previous publication on Marianne Moore was "'These Things': Moore's Habits of Adduction," which appeared in *Twenty-First Century Marianne Moore*, edited by Elizabeth Gregory and

Stacey Hubbard (2017). His primary project for the last two decades has been a critical biography of A. R. Ammons. He has presented excerpts from this project in journals such as *Asheville Poetry Review*, *Chicago Review*, *Epoch*, *Genre*, and *Southern Review*, and at various conferences and symposia. He hopes to complete the book within a year and turn his attention to other endeavors. He recently published his first poem in the journal *Literary Imagination*.

Elizabeth Gregory is the Taylor Professor of Gender & Sexuality Studies and a Professor of English at the University of Houston, where she directs the Women's, Gender & Sexuality Studies Program and the Institute for Research on Women, Gender & Sexuality. A long-time Moore scholar, her most recent book, *Apparition of Splendor: Marianne Moore Performing Democracy through Celebrity, 1952–1970*, brings back into critical discussion the long-overlooked fifty+ poems Moore wrote and performed in her later life. Gregory's earlier books include *Ready: Why Women Are Embracing the New Later Motherhood* (2007/2012) and *Quotation and Modern American Poetry: "Imaginary Gardens with Real Toads"* (1996) on Eliot, Williams, and Moore, as well as two edited collections on Moore: *Twenty-First Century Marianne Moore* (2017, with Stacy Carson Hubbard) and *The Critical Response to Marianne Moore* (2003). She collaborates on the Marianne Moore Digital Archive and hosts the Moore Society listserv. In addition to poetry, her research explores the intersections of fertility, gendered work, and the economy.

Linda Kinnahan is Professor of English at Duquesne University. She is co-author of the website "Mina Loy: Navigating the Avant-Garde" and the digital book *Mina Loy: Scholarly Book for Digital Travelers* (2020), which received a 2022 MLA book prize and is forthcoming as a revised print monograph, *Travels with Mina Loy*. Her monographs include *Mina Loy, Photography, and Contemporary Women Poets* (2017); *Lyric Interventions: Feminist Experimental Poetry and Contemporary Social Discourse* (2004); and *Poetics of the Feminine: Literary Tradition and Authority in Williams, Loy, Levertov, and Fraser* (1994). She edited the *Cambridge History of 20th-Century American Women's Poetry* (2016). Her forthcoming book, *Feminist Modernism, Poetics, and the New Economy: Mina Loy, Lola Ridge,* *and Marianne Moore*, focuses on economics and modernist poetics in Marianne Moore, Mina Loy, and Lola Ridge.

James Maynard is Curator of the Poetry Collection, the library of record for twentieth- and twenty-first-century poetry in English, and Coordinator of the Rare and Special Books Collection at the University Libraries, University at Buffalo, The State University of New York. He has published widely on and edited a number of collections relating to the poet Robert Duncan, including *Ground Work: Before the War/In the Dark* (2006), *(Re:)Working the Ground: Essays on the Late Writings of Robert Duncan* (2011), *Robert Duncan and the Pragmatist Sublime* (2018), and *No Hierarchy of the Lovely: Ten Uncollected Essays and Other Prose, 1939–1981* (2020). His edition of *Robert Duncan: Collected Essays and Other Prose* (2014) received the Poetry Foundation's Pegasus Award for Poetry Criticism.

Claire Nashar recently earned her PhD in English from the State University of New York, Buffalo, supported by a Mellon/ACLS Dissertation Completion Fellowship. Winner of an Excellence in Teaching Award, she has published a book of poems, *Lake* (2016), and a number of interviews, translations, poems, and critical essays. She edited a special issue of *Formes Poétiques Contemporaines* and is at work on a book-length translation from the French. Nashar has served as curator of the online Australian Poetry Library and as Project Editor and Manager for the Marianne Moore Digital Archive.

Karin Roffman is currently Senior Lecturer in Humanities, English and American Studies and the Associate Director of Public Humanities at Yale University. She was previously an Associate Professor of English at West Point and a Visiting Professor of Literature at Bard College. She most recently published the first biography of John Ashbery, *The Songs We Know Best: John Ashbery's Early Life* (2017), which was named one of the one hundred notable books for 2017 by the *New York Times*. She is currently completing a full biography of John Ashbery. A biography of the American painter Jane Freilicher will follow. In 2019, in collaboration with the Yale University Digital Humanities Lab, she published *John*

Ashbery's Nest, a virtual tour and website on John Ashbery's Hudson house (http://vr.ashberyhouse.yale.edu/). Her research has been supported by two ACLS fellowships (2011–12, 2017–18), the Howard Foundation (2011–12), and an NEH summer stipend (2009), as well as grants from the Houghton Library, the Harry Ransom Center, and the American Philosophical Society. She has published articles on twentieth- and twenty-first-century writers, painters, and musicians in *Evergreen Review*, *Raritan*, *Modern Fiction Studies*, *Artforum*, *Rain Taxi*, *Yale Review*, *Chicago Review*, *Wallace Stevens Journal*, and others. Her first book, *From the Modernist Annex: American Women Writers in Museums and Libraries* (2010), on the poetry and prose of Edith Wharton, Marianne Moore, Nella Larsen, and Ruth Benedict, won the University of Alabama Press's American Literature Elizabeth Agee Manuscript Prize and subsequent publication.

Ryan Tracy holds a PhD in English from The CUNY Graduate Center. His scholarship traverses the intersections of literary modernism, African American literature, Queer theory, and deconstruction. His scholarly work has appeared in *Feminist Modernist Studies*, *Arizona Quarterly*, and *Derrida Today*, and his research on Gertrude Stein and global warming is forthcoming in *PMLA*. Ryan's first book of poems, *Tender Bottoms*, was published in 2022.

Robert Volpicelli is an Associate Professor of English at Randolph-Macon College, where his research and teaching primarily focus on modern and contemporary poetry, transnational modernisms, and disability studies. His first book, *Transatlantic Modernism and the US Lecture Tour*, examines how the popular U.S. lecture circuit shuttled international modernist writers both to and through a complex American social landscape. In 2022, the book was awarded the Modernist Studies Association First Book Prize. His articles on modernist literature and culture have appeared in such journals as *PMLA*, *NOVEL*, *Textual Practice*, *Paideuma*, and *Twentieth-Century Literature*, among others. He has recently edited a special essay cluster on the topic of turn-of-the-century disability for the journal *Cusp: Late 19th-/Early 20th-Century Cultures*. Since 2021, he has also served as an Associate Editor of the journal *College Literature*. His current book project, tentatively entitled *Bad Visions*, focuses on how impaired eyesight triggered the experimental forms we associate with modern art and literature. A new essay from this project, "Monet's Cataracts, Re-examined," was published on the *Modernism/modernity* Print Plus platform.

Jeff Westover is Professor of English at Boise State University, where he teaches literature and writing. He has also taught at Howard University and the University of Nevada, Reno. He transcribed most of Moore's Reading Notebook 1930–1943 for the Marianne Moore Digital Archive (MMDA 7.02.02) and he is the author of *The Colonial Moment: Discoveries and Settlements in Modern American Poetry*, which was selected as an outstanding academic title by *Choice*. The book analyzes colonialism and imperialism in the poetry of Marianne Moore, Robert Frost, William Carlos Williams, Langston Hughes, and Hart Crane. More recently, he has published articles about Elizabeth Bishop (*Elizabeth Bishop and the Literary Archive*), W. S. Merwin (*Genre*), and H.D. (*Classics in Modernist Translation*).

Index

Abbott, Charles D. 46, 226
Africa 61, 80–81, 86–87, 94, 96, 99, 101–4, 111, 121–22, 124
African Americans 66, 68–69, 80–84, 89–90, 94
Ahearn, Barry 155, 159
Ailey, Alvin 68–69, 76
Allen, Donald 191
anagogy 132
Anderson, Linda 6
Aquinas, Thomas 138
Archive xi, 1–7, 11–12, 26–27, 43, 46, 48–52, 55–58, 62, 68–69, 84–87, 98, 107–14, 119–27, 156, 175–77, 179, 185, 192, 197–98, 202, 205, 209–11, 213–20, 232–33, 224–27
   Dial papers 231
   Moore papers 225
Aristotle 154
Ashbery, John 177, 184
   The Vermont Notebook 177
Auden, W. H. 71, 74, 131, 135

Bailey, Pearl 69
Balanchine, George 67, 69–71
   Agon 69–71
Balfour, Arthur James 154

Baraka, Amiri 89
   see Leroi Jones
Barthes, Roland 18
   A Lover's Discourse 18–19
Baxter, Richard 138
   The Saints' Everlasting Rest 139
Bazin, Victoria 28, 110–11, 126
Beinecke Library, Yale 209, 213
Belafonte, Harry 73, 84
Benét, William Rose 235
Bernhardt, Sarah 39
Berry, Sarah 53, 110–11
Beyoncé 104–5
Bikila, Adebe 84
Bishop, Elizabeth 18, 25, 43, 74
   "Efforts of Affection" 25–26
blackness 83, 89, 96–97, 99–102
Blake, William 133
   "Ghost of a Flea" 143
Borges, Jorge Luis 153
Bourne, Randolph 117
Braddock, Jeremy 47
Bridges, Robert 143–44
Brier, Stephen 7
Brinkman 3, 27–41, 49
Browning, Elizabeth Barrett 20
Browning, Robert 21, 158

289

Bryher 17–19, 74, 107, 218
Bunyan, John 129
Burke, Kenneth 21, 64, 123
Burns, Robert 131
Bushnell, Sally 2
Byers, Mark 6

Carroll, Diahann 69, 73
Carson, Luke 6, 12, 131–51, 171
Carter, Rodney G. S. 112
category 6, 46, 64, 111, 124, 132, 134, 154–57, 166–69, 171, 179
Césaire, Aimé 176
   Cahier d'un retour au pays natal 176
Chamberlain, Marcia 18, 74
Chapman, Mary 7
Chauncey, George 64
   Gay New York 64
Chesterton, G. K. 144
Clavier, Aurore 3, 11–26
Clercq, Tanaquil le 69
collecting 46–48, 57, 111–12, 233–34
Conrad, Joseph 41
Costello, Bonnie 96
Cournos, John 18
Craft, William and Ellen 90
Crane, Louise 18, 22, 74
Culler, Jonathan 160

dance 5, 67, 68–70, 73, 75–76
Dance Theatre of Harlem 73, 75
Dante 133
   Divine Comedy 139
definition 39, 54, 124, 148, 157, 159, 163, 167–68
Demtu, Desta 86
The Depression 123, 126
Derrida, Jaques 7, 50–52
Dewey, John 117
The Dial 21, 210, 213, 225, 231–32
Dickinson, Emily 21–22
Diderot, Denis 21
digital humanities 1, 5, 7, 30
Douglass, Frederick 90
Driver, Clive 47, 214, 217–18

Du Bois, W. E. B. 96
   The World and Africa 96
Dunbar, Paul Laurence 90
   "Sympathy" 90
Duncan, Duncan 6, 189, 193
   "The Close" 191
   The H.D. Book 190, 193
   "Ideas of the Meaning of Form" 193
   "The Maiden" 191
   "Notes on the Poetics of Marianne Moore" 191
   "On Reading Marianne Moore" 6, 193–94
   The Opening of the Field 191
   "Poetry, a Natural Thing" 191

economics 5, 30, 107–9, 116–18, 122–23, 126, 165, 176
Eliot, T. S. 44, 131, 144–45, 214, 219, 233
   Ash Wednesday 132
   Introduction to Moore's *Selected Poems* 219
   Murder in the Cathedral 132
   "The Music of Poetry" 133
Eliot, William Greenleaf 63
Ellis, Jonathan 11, 15
Emerson, Ralph Waldo 171
Empson, William 134–35, 137
   Seven Types of Ambiguity 137
Engel, Laura 108, 112–13, 123
Equiano, Olaudah 81
Ethiopia 54, 79, 80–87, 92, 94–99, 104

figuration 4, 18, 24, 54, 81, 137–39, 146, 148–51, 164, 185, 191, 193–94
Findlay, Robert Alexander 82
Flynn, Gertrude 74
Foucault, Michel 56, 153
   The Archeology of Knowledge 56
   The Order of Things 153
Franklin, Benjamin 161
Fraser, Alison 2–3, 6
Freud, Sigmund 51

fugitivity 89–91, 96
Funk & Wagnalls 29

Galentine, Wheaton 74
Gallup, Donald 213
Gangnes, Madeline B. 7
Garafola, Lynn 62, 68
Gavaler, Chris 27
gay 62, 64–65, 73–74, 76–77, 162, 235
    see also homosexual; lesbian; LGBTQ; queer
Gelpi, Albert 73
gender 37, 62, 64–66, 74–75, 113, 116
Gilbert, Roger 6, 175–87
Graves, Percival 32–33, 35
Green, Fiona 17–18, 86
Gregory, Elizabeth 5, 24, 61–78
Gudding, Gabriel 177
    Rhode Island Notebook 177
Guest, Barbara 235

Hadas, Pamela White 160
Hammer, Langdon 226
Hannibal 121–22
Hardy, Thomas 41
Harrison, Frederic 154
Harter, Odile 108–9
H.D. (Hilda Doolittle) 18–19, 74, 190, 235
Herbert, George 133
Hetepheres, Queen 118
Hewlett, Maurice 33, 35
Hill, Robert A. 81
Hindrichs, Cheryl 153
Hinkson, Mary 68
Holder, Geoffrey 68–69
Hölderlin, Friederich 6, 133, 144–51
Holleran, Andrew 235
Holley, Margaret 162
homosexual 64, 76
Horace 169
Howarth, Peter 2, 6
Howe, Susan 113, 184
Hughes, Langston 81–82
    "Broadcast on Ethiopia" 81
    "Emperor Haile Selassie" 81

irony 13, 20, 78, 158–59, 182

Jacobs, Harriet 90
James, Henry 41
Jim Crow 82, 99, 122, 124
Jones, Kathrine 18, 74
Jones, Leroi 71
Joyce, James 48

Kallman, Chester 74
Kant, Immanuel 144
Karinska, Barbara 72
Keats, John 21
Kellog, E. H. 144
Kent, Victoria 74
King, Martin Luther 75
Kinnahan, Linda 5, 107–26
Kirstein, Fidelma 74
Kirstein, Lincoln 68–69, 71, 74–75, 78
Koch, Kenneth 71

La Fontaine, Jean de 133, 144–45
Lavallade, Carmen de 68
Lawrence, D. H. 21
learning 64, 154, 158, 167–68, 205, 216, 227, 235–36
Leavell, Linda 23, 28, 52, 97, 100, 107–8, 219
Leeds, Harold 74
Leishman, J. B. 131, 135
lesbian 63, 65
Levertov, Denise 190
LGBTQ 5, 61
Liu, Alan 5
Liu, Wei 1
Literary Digest 4, 27–29, 35, 38, 41
Lloyd, Loren 74
Loeb, Harold 116
    "The Mysticism of Money" 116
Lowell, Robert 71, 176
    For Lizzie and Harriet 176
    History 176
    Notebook 1967–68 176
Loy, Mina 116
Lynes, George Platt 74

Mackey, Nathaniel 89
magazine 4, 22, 27–32, 34, 36, 64–65, 85, 117, 145, 178, 210, 213, 233
  see also mass print; periodicals
Mallarmé, Stéphane 131
Maloney, Dan 74
Mann, Thomas 170–71
  The Magic Mountain 171
Mantle, Mickey 44
Marianne Moore Digital Archive (MMDA) 98, 197–205
Masefield, John 31
  "The Wanderer" 31
mass print 4, 27–29, 41
material xi, 1–8, 12, 14–16, 27–28, 33–34, 36, 41, 46–49, 52–58, 84–85, 108–16, 118, 120, 122–23, 177–78, 190, 201, 204, 211, 217, 226–27
Matthiessen, F. O. 132
  American Renaissance 132
Maynard, James 6, 189–94
McGrath, Campbell 177
  Seven Notebooks 177
McKay, Claud 82–83
  Amiable with Big Teeth 82–83
meaning 6, 46, 50, 58, 61, 78, 83, 90, 93, 100, 104, 120–21, 131–42, 144–45, 147, 157–60, 162–64, 167–68, 170–71, 179, 191, 193
Merrill, James 71
metaphor 15, 54, 80, 90, 94, 123, 126, 132, 140–41, 158, 169–71
  see also figuration; trope
Mexal, Stephen J. 3–4
migration 5, 61, 66, 73, 75, 77–78, 94
Miller, Cristanne 3, 53, 175, 181
Miller, James 210, 220
Miller, Margaret 74
Milton, John 133, 139
  Paradise Lost 139
Mitchell, Arthur 5, 62, 66–78
Monroe, Harriet 210, 218
Moore, David M. xi
Moore, John Milton 62

Moore, Marianne 22, 27, 62, 79, 131, 175, 209–10, 217, 233
books
  Collected Poems 65
  Complete Poems 138
  Complete Prose 209, 228, 230
  Like a Bulwark 166
  A Marianne Moore Reader 23
  Observations 19–20, 137, 157, 166, 177–79, 181, 191
  Poems 19–20, 237n3
  Selected Poems 16, 114, 118, 219
  Tell Me, Tell Me 138
essays
  "Humility, Concentration, and Gusto" 135, 145
  "If I Were Sixteen Today" 192
  "Impact, Moral and Technical; Independence versus Exhibitionism; and Concerning Contagion" 139
letters 11–12, 14–26, 46, 54, 62–63, 69, 73–75, 77–78, 107, 122–24, 157, 190–93, 210, 219
  Selected Letters of Marianne Moore 11
notebooks 1, 3, 6, 18, 28, 49, 56, 62, 80, 86, 98–102, 111, 122, 131–32, 150, 154–56, 158, 160, 162–63, 165, 167–67, 169–71, 175–87, 197–205, 216, 219
  Notebook 07.01.04 (MMDA) 198
  Notebook 07.02.02 (MMDA) x, 154–56, 160, 162–63, 165, 167, 169–71, 288
  Notebook 07.03.11 (MMDA 203–4
  Notebook 07.04.04 (MMDA) 98, 102, 158, 176, 181
  Notebook 07.04.07 (MMDA) x, 98–102, 176, 182–84
  Notebook RML VII:01:02 168
  Notebook RML VII:02:02 243n28
  Notebook RML VII:02:03 131–32, 150
  Notebook RML VII:08:03 272n47

poems
    "Apparition of Splendor" 166
    Armor's Undermining Modesty" 148
    "Arthur Mitchell" 71-72
    "Black Earth" 53-54, 99, 120-21
    "Blue Bug" 73
    "Bowls" 21, 178-79
    "The Buffalo" 99-100, 155, 183
    "Bulwarked against Fate" 159
    "Camellia Sabina" 183
    "Charity Overcoming Envy" 171
    "The Cobbler Sings at His Workbench" (La Fontaine) 140
    "Conseil to a Bacheler" 160
    "The Dairymaid and Her Milk-Pot" (La Fontaine) 139
    "Elephants" 157
    "England" 186
    "Ennui" 91, 98, 105
    "Fear is Hope" 137
    "The Fly and the Ant" (La Fontaine) 140-43
    "A Fool, A Foul Thing, A Distressful Lunatic" 158-59
    "The Frigate Pelican" 155, 157, 160-62, 183
    "A Glass-Ribbed Nest" 23
    "Half Deity" 148, 155, 184, 186
    "He 'Digesteth Harde Yron'" 103, 155-56
    "The Hero" 98, 103, 157
    "His Shield" 79-80, 85, 89, 91-96, 98, 101-3
    "In Distrust of Merits" 79, 83-84
    "Injudicious Gardening" 20, 157-58
    "The Jerboa" 5, 98, 108-29, 149, 155, 159-60, 162, 179, 183
    "The Labors of Hercules" 179
    Leaves of a Magazine" 29
    "Leonardo Da Vinci's" 79, 84, 95, 101-2
    "Marriage" 18, 64, 98, 109, 120, 160, 171, 179-80, 183
    "My Crow Pluto" 226
    "New York" 61
    "An Octopus" 98, 109, 176, 179-80, 183, 227-28
    "O to Be a Dragon" 102
    "The Pangolin" 111, 149, 151
    "The Paper Nautilus" 103, 171
    "People's Surroundings" 55, 179
    "Peter" 155
    "Pigeons" 155
    "The Plumet Basilisk" 91, 98, 155, 179
    "Poetry" 148-49
    "Saint Valentine" 24-25
    "Sea Unicorns and Land Unicorns" 98, 179
    "Silence" 179
    "Smooth Gnarled Crape Myrtle" 149, 155, 157, 160, 163-65
    "Sojourn in the Whale" 32
    "Spenser's Ireland" 32
    "The Steeple-Jack" 65, 98, 179
    "The Student" 198, 154, 157, 166-68, 186
    "Sun" 138
    "Then the Ermine" 157, 160, 165-66
    "To a Chameleon" 191
    "To Browning" 20-21
    "To See It Is to Know That Mendelssohn Would Never Do" 29
    "Virginia Britannia" 99, 109, 120, 139, 157, 162-63
    "Walking-Sticks and Paperweights and Watermarks" 12-18, 24, 157, 166, 168-71
    "What are Years" 183
    "When I Buy Pictures" 52
    "You, Your Horse" 155
scrapbooks 27-28, 31-32, 34, 36, 38, 40-41
translations
    Fables by Jean de La Fontaine 139-43

Moore, Mary Warner (MWM) 62–63
Moore, Warner 86
Moten, Fred 5, 89
museum 1, 5–6, 27, 43–52, 56, 62, 74–75, 84, 88, 111, 112, 124, 168, 175, 191–92, 197, 199, 201, 232, 234
Mussolini, Benito 80

Nashar, Claire 6, 197–205
Navasky, Victor S. 36
Nietzsche, Friedrich 155
　"Truth and Lying in a Nonmoral Sense" 155
Norcross, George 63
Norman, J.R. 156
　A History of Fishes 156
Nugent, Bruce 82
　"Pope Pious the Only" 82
Nurhussein, Nadia 81

Oberländer, Gerhard 36
Olson, Elder 220, 222

Page, Chester 74
Parkinson, Isabelle 30–31
Paul, Catherine 111–12
periodicals 28–29, 31, 34, 36, 49, 171
Pinsky, Robert 157
Pompey 115
Pope, Alexander 136
　The Rape of the Lock 136
Pound, Ezra 18, 54, 82, 86, 99, 157, 184, 186, 190–91, 210, 214, 233, 235
Prester John 5, 93–101
Prokosch, Frederic 133, 145–47
　translations of Hölderlin 140, 145–47
Pycraft, W. P. 156

queer 62, 64–65, 74

race 5, 62, 64, 70, 75, 77, 83, 89, 112, 121–24, 159, 182
racism 84, 124, 176
Ras Tafari (Haile Selassie) 80

Richards, I. A. 132, 144
　Philosophy of Rhetoric 132
　Practical Criticism 133
Rilke, Rainer Maria 131, 133
　Duino Elegies 135
　Later Poems 150
　"To Hölderlin" 150
Rodin, Auguste 38–39
Roffman, Karen 7, 209–36
Rogers, Carl 213
Roosevelt, Franklin D. 5, 123
Rosenbach Museum and Library 5, 43–44, 47, 49, 57–58, 62, 84, 88, 122, 175–76, 191, 197, 209, 214–19, 224–27, 230–34, 274n2, 281n1
Ruefle, Mary 11
Ruskin, John 133
Ryan, Hugh 65
　When Brooklyn Was Queer: A History 65

Salomon, Abbe 220
Schulze, Robin 20, 157
Schuyler, George 82
　Ethiopian Stories 82
Scipio 121–22
Sekula, Allan 108
Selassie, Haile 79–89, 91–99
　Ras Tafari 84
　"Three Priorities" 88
Sexton, Ann 177
　The Death Notebooks 177
Shaw, George Bernard 34, 38–39, 41
Shelley, Percy Bysshe 21
Shook, Karel 68, 73, 75
Silko, Leslie Marmon 235
Sitwell, Edith 190
Spender, Stephen 135
Spicer, Jack 192
　After Lorca 192
　Postscript for Marianne Moore 192
　"Radar" 192
Stead, Lisa 5
Stein, Gertrude 30, 67, 184, 190
Stevens, Wallace 177, 190, 222

Stonewall 65
Stowe, Harriet Beecher 90
Stravinsky, Igor 69
   Agon 69–71

teaching 3–4, 7, 27, 64, 66–68, 73, 190, 197–99, 201, 205, 211–14, 219, 222, 224
Thayer, Scofield 232
Thomas, Norman 123
Thomson, Virgil 67
Todd, Mabel Todd 21
Tolson, Melvin 82
   "The Bard of Addis Ababa" 82
Tracy, Ryan 5, 79–105
trope 6, 15, 19, 104, 181, 187
Trousdale, Rachel 36
Tyson, Cicely 73

Valéry, Paul 21
Varley, John 143
Veblen, Thorstein 116–17, 126
Verstehen 133, 137, 144, 147–48
Vogel, Shane 57
Volpicelli, Robert 5, 43–58

Warner, Ahren 6
Warner, John Riddle 62
Washington, George 65, 74
Watson, Hildegarde 18, 69, 157
Watson, James Sibley 18
Watson, Nicola J. 44
Weber, Max 142
Welch, James 235

Wescott, Glenway 74, 234–35
Westover 6, 153
Wheeler, Lesley 27
Wheeler, Monroe 74–75, 125, 234–36
   Museum of Modern Art 74–75
White, Edmund 235
White, Heather Cass 12, 171, 184
Whitman, Walt 65
   Leaves of Grass 65
Williams, William Carlos 13, 190, 193, 210, 214, 222, 226, 233
Willis, Bob 213
Willis, Patricia 7, 209–36
   author
      "A Modernist Epithalamium: Marianne Moore's 'Marriage'" 209
      "The Road to Paradise: First Notes on Marianne Moore's 'An Octopus'" 209
   editor
      Complete Prose of Marianne Moore 209
      Marianne Moore Newsletter 209
      Marianne Moore: Vision into Verse 209, 230
Wilson, Elizabeth 24
Wilson, Jennifer 81
Wilson, Woodrow 30, 37, 39–40

Yilma, Asfa 96–97

Zukofsky, Louis 185, 190

Printed in the USA
CPSIA information can be obtained
at www.ICGtesting.com
CBHW022219070624
9761CB00001B/3

9 781638 040972